American Big Gan

By Various

Edited by George Bird Grinnell

Contents

Preface

Although the Boone and Crockett Club has not appeared largely in the public eye during recent years, its activities have not ceased. The discovery of gold in Alaska, and the extraordinary rush of population to that northern territory had the usual effect on the wild life there, and proved very destructive to the natives and to the large mammals. A few years ago it became evident that the Kadiak bear and certain newly discovered forms of wild sheep and caribou were being destroyed by wholesale, and were actually threatened with extermination, and through the efforts of the Club, strongly backed by the Biological Survey of the Department of Agriculture, a bill was passed regulating the taking of Alaska large game, and especially the exportation of heads, horns, and hides. The bill promises to afford sufficient protection to some of these rare boreal forms, though for others it perhaps comes too late. The enforcement of the law is in charge of the Treasury Department, and permits for shooting and the export of trophies are issued by the Chief of the Biological Survey.

Although a local affair, yet of interest to the whole country, is the remarkable success of the New York Zoological Park, controlled and managed by the New York Zoological Society, brought into existence largely through the efforts of Madison Grant, the present secretary of the Club. The Society has also recently taken over the care of the New York Aquarium. The Society is in a most flourishing condition, and through its extensive collections exerts an important educational influence in a field in which popular interest is constantly growing.

Under the administration of President Roosevelt, the good work of national forest preservation continues, and the time appears not far distant when vast areas of the hitherto uncultivated West will prove added sources of wealth to our country.

The Club has for some time given much thoughtful attention to the subject of game refuges--that is to say, areas where game shall be absolutely free from interference or molestation, as it is to-day in the Yellowstone Park--to be situated within the forest reserves; and as is elsewhere shown, it has investigated a number of the forest reserves in order to learn something of their suitability for game refuges. It appears certain that only by means of such refuges can some forms of our large mammals be preserved from extinction. The first step to be taken to bring about the establishment of these safe breeding grounds is to secure legislation transferring the Bureau of Forestry from the Land Office to the Department of Agriculture. After this shall have been accomplished, the question of establishing such game refuges may properly come before the officials of the Government for action.

Among the notable articles in the present volume, one of the most important is Mr. Roosevelt's account of his visit to the Yellowstone National Park in April, 1903. The Park is an object lesson, showing very clearly what complete game protection will do to perpetuate species, and Mr. Roosevelt's account of what may be seen there is so convincing that all who read it, and appreciate the importance of preserving our large mammals, must become advocates of the forest reserve game refuge system.

Quite as interesting, in a different way, is Mr. Brown's contribution to the definition and the history of our larger North American mammals. To characterize these creatures in language "understanded of the people" is not easy, but Mr. Brown has made clear the zoological affinities of the species, and has pointed out their probable origin.

This is the fourth of the Boone and Crockett Club's books, and the first to be signed by a single member of the editorial committee, one name which usually appears on the title page having been omitted for obvious reasons. The preceding volume--Trail and Camp Fire--was published in 1897.

GEORGE BIRD GRINNELL.

NEW YORK, April 2, 1904.

FOUNDER OF THE BOONE AND CROCKETT CLUB.

It was at a dinner given to a few friends, who were also big-game hunters, at his New York house, in December, 1887, that Theodore Roosevelt first suggested the formation of the Boone and Crockett Club. The association was to be made up of men using the rifle in big-game hunting, who should meet from time to time to discuss subjects of interest to hunters. The idea was received with enthusiasm, and the purposes and plans of the club were outlined at this dinner.

Mr. Roosevelt was then eight years out of college, and had already made a local name for himself. Soon after graduation he had begun to display that energy which is now so well known; he had entered the political field, and been elected member of the New York Legislature, where he served from 1882 to 1884. His honesty and courage made his term of service one long battle, in which he fought with equal zeal the unworthy measures championed by his own and the opposing political party. In 1886 he had been an unsuccessful candidate for Mayor of New York, being defeated by Abram S. Hewitt.

Up to the time of the formation of the Boone and Crockett Club, the political affairs with which Mr. Roosevelt had concerned himself had been of local importance, but none the less in the line of training for more important work; but his activities were soon to have a wider range.

In 1889 the President of the United States appointed him member of the Civil Service Commission, where he served until 1895. In 1895 he was appointed one of the Board of Police Commissioners of New York City, and became President of the Board, serving here until 1897. In 1897 he was appointed Assistant Secretary of the Navy, and served for about a year, resigning in 1898 to raise the First United States Volunteer Cavalry. The service done by the regiment--popularly called Roosevelt's Rough Riders--is sufficiently well known, and Mr. Roosevelt was promoted to a Colonelcy for conspicuous gallantry at the battle of Las Guasimas. At the close of the war with Spain, Mr. Roosevelt became candidate for Governor of New York. He was elected, and served until December 31, 1900. In that year he was elected Vice-President of the United States on the ticket with Mr. McKinley, and on the death of Mr. McKinley, succeeded to the Presidential chair.

Of the Presidents of the United States not a few have been sportsmen, and sportsmen of the best type. The love of Washington for gun and dog, his interest in fisheries, and especially his fondness for horse and hound, in the chase of the red fox, have furnished the theme for many a writer; and recently Mr. Cleveland and Mr. Harrison have been more or less celebrated in the newspapers, Mr. Harrison as a gunner, and Mr. Cleveland for his angling, as well as his duck shooting proclivities.

It is not too much to say, however, that the chair of the chief magistrate has never been occupied by a sportsman whose range of interests was so wide, and so actively manifested, as in the case of Mr. Roosevelt. It is true that Mr. Harrison, Mr. Cleveland, and Mr. McKinley did much in the way of setting aside forest reservations, but chiefly from economic motives; because they believed that the forests should be preserved, both for the timber that they might yield, if wisely exploited, and for their value as storage reservoirs for the waters of our rivers.

The view taken by Mr. Roosevelt is quite different. To him the economics of the case appeal with the same force that they might have for any hard-headed, common sense business American; but beyond this, and perhaps, if the secrets of his heart were known, more than this, Mr. Roosevelt is influenced by a love of nature, which, though considered sentimental by some, is, in fact, nothing more than a far-sightedness, which looks toward the health, happiness, and general well-being of the American race for the future.

As a boy Mr. Roosevelt was fortunate in having a strong love for nature and for outdoor life, and, as in the case of so many boys, this love took the form of an interest in birds, which found its outlet in studying and collecting them. He published, in 1877, a list of the summer birds of the Adirondacks, in Franklin county, New York, and also did more or less collecting of birds on Long Island. The result of all this was the acquiring of some knowledge of the birds of eastern North America, and, what was far more important, a knowledge of how to observe, and an appreciation of the fact that observations, to be of any scientific value, must be definite and precise.

In the many hunting tales that we have had from his pen in recent years, it is seen that these two pieces of most important instruction acquired by the boy have always been remembered, and for this reason his books of hunting and adventure have a real value--a worth not shared by many of those published on similar subjects. His hunting adventures have not been mere pleasure excursions. They have been of service to science. On one of his hunts, perhaps his earliest trip after white goats, he secured a second specimen of a certain tiny shrew, of which, up to that time, only the type was known. Much more recently, during a declared hunting trip in Colorado, he collected the best series of skins of the American panther, with the measurements taken in the flesh, that has ever been gathered from one locality by a single individual.

Mr. Roosevelt's hunting experiences have been so wide as to have covered almost every species of North American big game found within the temperate zone. Except such Arctic forms as the white and the Alaska bears, and the muskox, there is, perhaps, no species of North American game that he has not killed; and his chapter on the mountain sheep, in his book, "Ranch Life and the Hunting Trail," is confessedly the best published account of that species.

During the years that Mr. Roosevelt was actually engaged in the cattle business in North Dakota, his everyday life led him constantly to the haunts of big game, and, almost in spite of himself, gave him constant hunting opportunities. Besides that, during dull seasons of the year, he made trips to more or less distant localities in search of the species of big game not found immediately about his ranch. His mode of hunting and of traveling was quite different from that now in vogue among big-game hunters. His knowledge of the West was early enough to touch upon the time when each man was as good as his neighbor, and the mere fact that a man was paid wages to perform certain acts for you did not in any degree lower his position in the world, nor elevate yours. In those days, if one started out with a companion, hired or otherwise, to go to a certain place, or to do a certain piece of work, each man was expected to perform his share of the labor.

This fact Mr. Roosevelt recognized as soon as he went West, and, acting upon it, he made for himself a position as a man, and not as a master, which he has never lost; and it is precisely this democratic spirit which to-day makes him perhaps the most popular man in the United States at large.

Starting off, then, on some trip of several hundred miles, with a companion who might be guide, helper, cook, packer, or what not--sometimes efficient, and the best companion that could be desired, at others, perhaps, hopelessly lazy and worthless, and even with a stock of liquor cached somewhere in the packs--Mr. Roosevelt helped to pack the horses, to bring the wood, to carry the water, to cook the food, to wrangle the stock, and generally to do the work of the camp, or of the trail, so long as any of it remained undone. His energy was indefatigable, and usually he infected his companion with his own enthusiasm and industry, though at times he might have with him a man whom nothing could move. It is largely to this energy and this determination that he owes the good fortune that has usually attended his hunting trips.

As the years have gone on, fortunes have changed; and as duties of one kind and another have more and more pressed upon him, Mr. Roosevelt has done less and less hunting; yet his love for outdoor life is as keen as ever, and as Vice-President of the United States, he made his well-remembered trip to Colorado after mountain lions, while more recently he hunted black bears in the Mississippi Valley, and still more lately killed a wild boar in the Austin Corbin park in New Hampshire.

Mr. Roosevelt's accession to the Presidential chair has been a great thing for good sportsmanship in this country. Measures pertaining to game and forest protection, and matters of sport generally, always have had, and always will have, his cordial approval and co-operation. He is heartily in favor of the forest reserves, and of the project for establishing, within these reserves, game refuges, where no hunting whatever shall be permitted. Aside from his love for nature, and his wish to have certain limited areas remain in their natural condition, absolutely untouched by the ax of the lumberman, and unimproved by the work of the forester, is that broader sentiment in behalf of humanity in the United States, which has led him to declare that such refuges should be established for the benefit of the man of moderate means and the poor man, whose opportunities to hunt and to see game are few and far between. In a public speech he has said, in substance, that the rich and the well-to-do could take care of themselves, buying land, fencing it, and establishing parks and preserves of their own, where they might look upon and take pleasure in their own game, but that such a course was not within the power of the poor man, and that therefore the Government might fitly intervene and establish refuges, such as indicated, for the benefit and the pleasure of the whole people.

In April, 1903, the President made a trip to the Yellowstone Park, and there had an opportunity to see wild game in such a forest refuge, living free and without fear of molestation. Long before this Mr. Roosevelt had expressed his approval of the plan, but his own eyes had never before seen precisely the results accomplished by such a refuge. In 1903 he was able to contrast conditions in the Yellowstone Park with those of former years when he had passed through it and had hunted on its borders, and what he saw then more than ever confirmed his previous conclusions.

Although politics have taken up a large share of Mr. Roosevelt's life, they represent only one of his many sides. He has won fame as a historical writer by such books as "The Winning of the West," "Life of Gouverneur Morris," "Life of Thomas Hart Benton," "The Naval War of 1812," "History of New York," "American Ideals and Other Essays," and "Life of Cromwell." Besides these, he has written "The Strenuous Life," and in somewhat lighter vein, his "Wilderness Hunter," "Hunting Trips of a Ranchman," "Ranch Life and the Hunting Trail," and "The Rough Riders" deal with sport, phases of nature and life in the wild country. For many years he was on the editorial committee of the Boone and Crockett Club, and edited its publications, "American Big Game Hunting," "Hunting in Many Lands," and "Trail and Camp Fire."

Mr. Roosevelt was the first president of the Boone and Crockett Club, and continues actively interested in its work. He was succeeded in the presidency of the Club by the late Gen. B.H. Bristow.

Wilderness Reserves

The practical common sense of the American people has been in no way made more evident during the last few years than by the creation and use of a series of large land reserves--situated for the most part on the great plains and among the mountains of the West--intended to keep the forests from destruction, and therefore to conserve the water supply. These reserves are created purely for economic purposes. The semi-arid regions can only support a reasonable population under conditions of the strictest economy and wisdom in the use of the water supply, and in addition to their other economic uses the forests are indispensably necessary for the preservation of the water supply and for rendering possible its useful distribution throughout the proper seasons.

In addition, however, to the economic use of the wilderness by preserving it for such purposes where it is unsuited for agricultural uses, it is wise here and there to keep selected portions of it--of course only those portions unfit for settlement--in a state of nature, not merely for the sake of preserving the forests and the water, but for the sake of preserving all its beauties and wonders unspoiled by greedy and shortsighted vandalism. These beauties and wonders include animate as well as inanimate objects. The wild creatures of the wilderness add to it by their presence a charm which it can acquire in no other way. On every ground it is well for our nation to preserve, not only for the sake of this generation, but above all for the sake of those who come after us, representatives of the stately and beautiful haunters of the wilds which were once found throughout our great forests, over the vast lonely plains, and on the high mountain ranges, but which are now on the point of vanishing save where they are protected in natural breeding grounds and nurseries. The work of preservation must be carried on in such a way as to make it evident that we are working in the interest of the people as a whole, not in the interest of any particular class; and that the people benefited beyond all others are those who dwell nearest to the regions in which the reserves are placed. The movement for the preservation by the nation of sections of the wilderness as national playgrounds is essentially a democratic movement in the interest of all our people.

On April 8, 1903, John Burroughs and I reached the Yellowstone Park and were met by Major John Pitcher of the Regular Army, the Superintendent of the Park. The Major and I forthwith took horses; he telling me that he could show me a good deal of game while riding up to his house at the Mammoth Hot Springs. Hardly had we left the little town of Gardiner and gotten within the limits of the Park before we saw prong-buck. There was a band of at least a hundred feeding some distance from the road. We rode leisurely toward them. They were tame compared to their kindred in unprotected places; that is, it was easy to ride within fair rifle range of them; but they were not familiar in the sense that we afterwords found the bighorn and the deer to be familiar. During the two hours following my entry into the Park we rode around the plains and lower slopes of the foothills in the neighborhood of the mouth of the Gardiner and we saw several hundred--probably a thousand all told--of these antelope. Major Pitcher informed me that all the prong-horns in the Park wintered in this neighborhood. Toward the end of April or the first of May they migrate back to their summering homes in the open valleys along the Yellowstone and in the plains south of the Golden Gate. While migrating they go over the mountains and through forests if occasion demands. Although there are plenty of coyotes in the Park there are no big wolves, and save for very infrequent poachers the only enemy of the antelope, as indeed the only enemy of all the game, is the cougar.

Cougars, known in the Park as elsewhere through the West as "mountain lions," are plentiful, having increased in numbers of recent years. Except in the neighborhood of the Gardiner River, that is within a few miles of Mammoth Hot Springs, I found them feeding on elk, which in the Park far outnumber all other game put together, being so numerous that the ravages of the cougars are of no real damage to the herds. But in the neighborhood of the Mammoth Hot Springs the cougars are noxious because of the antelope, mountain sheep and deer which they kill; and the Superintendent has imported some hounds with which to hunt them. These hounds are managed by Buffalo Jones, a famous old plainsman, who is now in the Park taking care of the buffalo. On this first day of my visit to the Park I came across the carcasses of a deer and of an antelope which the cougars had killed. On the great plains cougars rarely get antelope, but here the country is broken so that the big cats can make their stalks under favorable circumstances. To deer and mountain sheep the cougar is a most dangerous enemy--much more so than the wolf.

The antelope we saw were usually in bands of from twenty to one hundred and fifty, and they traveled strung out almost in single file, though those in the rear would sometimes bunch up. I did not try to stalk them, but got as near them as I could on horseback. The closest approach I was able to make was to within about eighty yards on two which were by themselves--I think a doe and a last year's fawn. As I was riding up to them, although they looked suspiciously at me, one actually lay down. When I was passing them at about eighty yards distance the big one became nervous, gave a sudden jump, and away the two went at full speed.

Why the prone bucks were so comparatively shy I do not know, for right on the ground with them we came upon deer, and, in the immediate neighborhood, mountain sheep, which were absurdly tame. The mountain sheep were nineteen in number, for the most part does and yearlings with a couple of three-year-old rams, but not a single big fellow--for the big fellows at this season are off by themselves, singly or in little bunches, high up in the mountains. The band I saw was tame to a degree matched by but few domestic animals.

They were feeding on the brink of a steep washout at the upper edge of one of the benches on the mountain side just below where the abrupt slope began. They were alongside a little gully with sheer walls. I rode my horse to within forty yards of them, one of them occasionally looking up and at once continuing to feed. Then they moved slowly off and leisurely crossed the gully to the other side. I dismounted, walked around the head of the gully, and moving cautiously, but in plain sight, came closer and closer until I was within twenty yards, where I sat down on a stone and spent certainly twenty minutes looking at them. They paid hardly any attention whatever to my presence-- certainly no more than well-treated domestic creatures would pay. One of the rams rose on his hind legs, leaning his fore-hoofs against a little pine tree, and browsed the ends of the budding branches. The others grazed on the short grass and herbage or lay down and rested--two of the yearlings several times playfully butting at one another. Now and then one would glance in my direction without the slightest sign of fear--barely even of curiosity. I have no question whatever but that with a little patience this particular band could be made to feed out of a man's hand. Major Pitcher intends during the coming winter to feed them alfalfa--for game animals of several kinds have become so plentiful in the neighborhood of the Hot Springs, and the Major has grown so interested in them, that he wishes to do something toward feeding them during the severe winter. After I had looked at the sheep to my heart's content, I walked back to my horse, my departure arousing as little interest as my advent.

Soon after leaving them we began to come across black-tail deer, singly, in twos and threes, and in small bunches of a dozen or so. They were almost as tame as the mountain sheep, but not quite. That is, they always looked alertly at me, and though if I stayed still they would graze, they kept a watch over my movements and usually moved slowly off when I got within less than forty yards of them. Up to that distance, whether on foot or on horseback, they paid but little heed to me, and on several occasions they allowed me to come much closer. Like the bighorn, the black-tails at this time were grazing, not browsing; but I occasionally saw them nibble some willow buds. During the winter they had been browsing. As we got close to the Hot Springs we came across several white-tail in an open, marshy meadow.

They were not quite as tame as the black-tail, although without any difficulty I walked up to within fifty yards of them. Handsome though the black-tail is, the white-tail is the most beautiful of all deer when in motion, because of the springy, bounding grace of its trot and canter, and the way it carries its head and white flag aloft.

Before reaching the Mammoth Hot Springs we also saw a number of ducks in the little pools and on the Gardiner. Some of them were rather shy. Others-- probably those which, as Major Pitcher informed me, had spent the winter there--were as tame as barnyard fowls.

Just before reaching the post the Major took me into the big field where Buffalo Jones had some Texas and Flat Head Lake buffalo--bulls and cows-- which he was tending with solicitous care. The original stock of buffalo in the Park have now been reduced to fifteen or twenty individuals, and the intention is to try to mix them with the score of buffalo which have been purchased out of the Flat Head Lake and Texas Panhandle herds. The buffalo were put within a wire fence, which, when it was built, was found to have included both black- tail and white-tail deer. A bull elk was also put in with them at one time--he having met with some accident which made the Major and Buffalo Jones bring him in to doctor him. When he recovered his health he became very cross. Not only would he attack men, but also buffalo, even the old and surly master bull, thumping them savagely with his antlers if they did anything to which he objected. When I reached the post and dismounted at the Major's house, I supposed my experiences with wild beasts for the day were ended; but this was an error. The quarters of the officers and men and the various hotel buildings, stables, residences of the civilian officials, etc., almost completely surround the big parade ground at the post, near the middle of which stands the flag-pole, while the gun used for morning and evening salutes is well off to one side. There are large gaps between some of the buildings, and Major Pitcher informed me that throughout the winter he had been leaving alfalfa on the parade grounds, and that numbers of black-tail deer had been in the habit of visiting it every day, sometimes as many as seventy being on the parade ground at once. As springtime came on the numbers diminished. However, in mid-afternoon, while I was writing in my room in Major Pitcher's house, on looking out of the window I saw five deer on the parade ground. They were as tame as so many Alderney cows, and when I walked out I got up to within twenty yards of them without any difficulty. It was most amusing to see them as the time approached for the sunset gun to be fired. The notes of the trumpeter attracted their attention at once. They all looked at him eagerly. One then resumed feeding, and paid no attention whatever either to the bugle, the gun or the flag. The other four, however, watched the preparations for firing the gun with an intent gaze, and at the sound of the report gave two or three jumps; then instantly wheeling, looked up at the flag as it came down. This they seemed to regard as something rather more suspicious than the gun, and they remained very much on the alert until the ceremony was over. Once it was finished, they resumed feeding as if nothing had happened. Before it was dark they trotted away from the parade ground back to the mountains.

The next day we rode off to the Yellowstone River, camping some miles below Cottonwood Creek. It was a very pleasant camp. Major Pitcher, an old friend, had a first-class pack train, so that we were as comfortable as possible, and on such a trip there could be no pleasanter or more interesting companion than John Burroughs--"Oom John," as we soon grew to call him. Where our tents were pitched the bottom of the valley was narrow, the mountains rising steep and cliff-broken on either side. There were quite a number of black-tail in the valley, which were tame and unsuspicious, although not nearly as much so as those in the immediate neighborhood of the Mammoth Hot Springs. One mid-afternoon three of them swam across the river a hundred yards above our camp. But the characteristic animals of the region were the elk--the wapiti. They were certainly more numerous than when I was last through the Park twelve years before.

In the summer the elk spread all over the interior of the Park. As winter approaches they divide, some going north and others south. The southern bands, which, at a guess, may possibly include ten thousand individuals, winter out of the Park, for the most part in Jackson's Hole--though of course here and there within the limits of the Park a few elk may spend both winter and summer in an unusually favorable location. It was the members of the northern band that I met. During the winter time they are very stationary, each band staying within a very few miles of the same place, and from their size and the open nature of their habitat it is almost as easy to count them as if they were cattle. From a spur of Bison Peak one day, Major Pitcher, the guide Elwood Hofer, John Burroughs and I spent about four hours with the glasses counting and estimating the different herds within sight. After most careful work and cautious reduction of estimates in each case to the minimum the truth would permit, we reckoned three thousand head of elk, all lying or feeding and all in sight at the same time. An estimate of some fifteen thousand for the number of elk in these northern bands cannot be far wrong. These bands do not go out of the Park at all, but winter just within its northern boundary. At the time when we saw them, the snow had vanished from the bottom of the valleys and the lower slopes of the mountains, but grew into continuous sheets further up their sides. The elk were for the most part found up on the snow slopes, occasionally singly or in small gangs--more often in bands of from fifty to a couple of hundred. The larger bulls were highest up the mountains and generally in small troops by themselves, although occasionally one or two would be found associating with a big herd of cows, yearlings, and two-year-olds. Many of the bulls had shed their antlers; many had not. During the winter the elk had evidently done much browsing, but at this time they were grazing almost exclusively, and seemed by preference to seek out the patches of old grass which were last left bare by the retreating snow. The bands moved about very little, and if one were seen one day it was generally possible to find it within a few hundred yards of the same spot the next day, and certainly not more than a mile or two off. There were severe frosts at night, and occasionally light flurries of snow; but the hardy beasts evidently cared nothing for any but heavy storms, and seemed to prefer to lie in the snow rather than upon the open ground. They fed at irregular hours throughout the day, just like cattle; one band might be lying down while another was feeding. While traveling they usually went almost in single file. Evidently the winter had weakened them, and they were not in condition for running; for on the one or two occasions when I wanted to see them close up I ran right into them on horseback, both on level plains and going up hill along the sides of rather steep mountains. One band in particular I practically rounded up for John Burroughs--finally getting them to stand in a huddle while he and I sat on our horses less than fifty yards off. After they had run a little distance they opened their mouths wide and showed evident signs of distress.

We came across a good many carcasses. Two, a bull and a cow, had died from scab. Over half the remainder had evidently perished from cold or starvation. The others, including a bull, three cows and a score of yearlings, had been killed by cougars. In the Park the cougar is at present their only animal foe. The cougars were preying on nothing but elk in the Yellowstone Valley, and kept hanging about the neighborhood of the big bands. Evidently they usually selected some outlying yearling, stalked it as it lay or as it fed, and seized it by the head and throat. The bull which they killed was in a little open valley by himself, many miles from any other elk. The cougar which killed it, judging from its tracks, was a very large male. As the elk were evidently rather too numerous for the feed, I do not think the cougars were doing any damage.

Coyotes are plentiful, but the elk evidently have no dread of them. One day I crawled up to within fifty yards of a band of elk lying down. A coyote was walking about among them, and beyond an occasional look they paid no heed to him. He did not venture to go within fifteen or twenty paces of any one of them. In fact, except the cougar, I saw but one living thing attempt to molest the elk. This was a golden eagle. We saw several of these great birds. On one occasion we had ridden out to the foot of a great sloping mountain side, dotted over with bands and strings of elk amounting in the aggregate probably to a thousand head. Most of the bands were above the snow line--some appearing away back toward the ridge crests, and looking as small as mice. There was one band well below the snow line, and toward this we rode. While the elk were not shy or wary, in the sense that a hunter would use the words, they were by no means as familiar as the deer; and this particular band of elk, some twenty or thirty in all, watched us with interest as we approached. When we were still half a mile off they suddenly started to run toward us, evidently frightened by something. They ran quartering, and when about four hundred yards away we saw that an eagle was after them. Soon it swooped, and a yearling in the rear, weakly, and probably frightened by the swoop, turned a complete somersault, and when it recovered its feet, stood still. The great bird followed the rest of the band across a little ridge, beyond which they disappeared. Then it returned, soaring high in the heavens, and after two or three wide circles, swooped down at the solitary yearling, its legs hanging down. We halted at two hundred yards to see the end. But the eagle could not quite make up its mind to attack. Twice it hovered within a foot or two of the yearling's head--again flew off and again returned. Finally the yearling trotted off after the rest of the band, and the eagle returned to the upper air. Later we found the carcass of a yearling, with two eagles, not to mention ravens and magpies, feeding on it; but I could not tell whether they had themselves killed the yearling or not.

Here and there in the region where the elk were abundant we came upon horses which for some reason had been left out through the winter. They were much wilder than the elk. Evidently the Yellowstone Park is a natural nursery and breeding ground of the elk, which here, as said above, far outnumber all the other game put together. In the winter, if they cannot get to open water, they eat snow; but in several places where there had been springs which kept open all winter, we could see by the tracks they had been regularly used by bands of elk. The men working at the new road along the face of the cliffs beside the Yellowstone River near Tower Falls informed me that in October enormous droves of elk coming from the interior of the Park and traveling northward to the lower lands had crossed the Yellowstone just above Tower Falls. Judging by their description the elk had crossed by thousands in an uninterrupted stream, the passage taking many hours. In fact nowadays these Yellowstone elk are, with the exception of the Arctic caribou, the only American game which at times travel in immense droves like the buffalo of the old days.

A couple of days after leaving Cottonwood Creek--where we had spent several days--we camped at the Yellowstone Canon below Tower Falls. Here we saw a second band of mountain sheep, numbering only eight--none of them old rams. We were camped on the west side of the canon; the sheep had their abode on the opposite side, where they had spent the winter. It has recently been customary among some authorities, especially the English hunters and naturalists who have written of the Asiatic sheep, to speak as if sheep were naturally creatures of the plains rather than mountain climbers. I know nothing of old world sheep, but the Rocky Mountain bighorn is to the full as characteristic a mountain animal, in every sense of the word, as the chamois, and, I think, as the ibex. These sheep were well known to the road builders, who had spent the winter in the locality. They told me they never went back on the plains, but throughout the winter had spent their days and nights on the top of the cliff and along its face. This cliff was an alternation of sheer precipices and very steep inclines. When coated with ice it would be difficult to imagine an uglier bit of climbing; but throughout the winter, and even in the wildest storms, the sheep had habitually gone down it to drink at the water below. When we first saw them they were lying sunning themselves on the edge of the canyon, where the rolling grassy country behind it broke off into the sheer descent. It was mid-afternoon and they were under some pines. After a while they got up and began to graze, and soon hopped unconcernedly down the side of the cliff until they were half way to the bottom. They then grazed along the sides, and spent some time licking at a place where there was evidently a mineral deposit. Before dark they all lay down again on a steeply inclined jutting spur midway between the top and bottom of the canyon.

Next morning I thought I would like to see them close up, so I walked down three or four miles below where the canyon ended, crossed the stream, and came up the other side until I got on what was literally the stamping ground of the sheep. Their tracks showed that they had spent their time for many weeks, and probably for all the winter, within a very narrow radius. For perhaps a mile and a half, or two miles at the very outside, they had wandered to and fro on the summit of the canyon, making what was almost a well-beaten path; always very near and usually on the edge of the cliff, and hardly ever going more than a few yards back into the grassy plain-and-hill country. Their tracks and dung covered the ground. They had also evidently descended into the depths of the canon wherever there was the slightest break or even lowering in the upper line of basalt cliffs. Although mountain sheep often browse in winter, I saw but few traces of browsing here; probably on the sheer cliff side they always got some grazing. When I spied the band they were lying not far from the spot in which they had lain the day before, and in the same position on the brink of the canon. They saw me and watched me with interest when I was two hundred yards off, but they let me get up within forty yards and sit down on a large stone to look at them, without running off. Most of them were lying down, but a couple were feeding steadily throughout the time I watched them. Suddenly one took the alarm and dashed straight over the cliff, the others all following at once. I ran after them to the edge in time to see the last yearling drop off the edge of the basalt cliff and stop short on the sheer slope below, while the stones dislodged by his hoofs rattled down the canon. They all looked up at me with great interest and then strolled off to the edge of a jutting spur and lay down almost directly underneath me and some fifty yards off. That evening on my return to camp we watched the band make its way right down to the river bed, going over places where it did not seem possible a four-footed creature could pass. They halted to graze here and there, and down the worst places they went very fast with great bounds. It was a marvelous exhibition of climbing.

After we had finished this horseback trip we went on sleds and skis to the upper Geyser Basin and the Falls of the Yellowstone. Although it was the third week in April, the snow was still several feet deep, and only thoroughly trained snow horses could have taken the sleighs along, while around the

Yellowstone Falls it was possible to move only on snowshoes. There was very little life in those woods. We saw an occasional squirrel, rabbit or marten; and in the open meadows around the hot waters there were geese and ducks, and now and then a coyote. Around camp Clark's crows and Stellar's jays, and occasionally magpies came to pick at the refuse; and of course they were accompanied by the whiskey acks with their usual astounding familiarity. At Norris Geyser Basin there was a perfect chorus of bird music from robins, purple finches, uncos and mountain bluebirds. In the woods there were mountain chickadees and nuthatches of various kinds, together with an occasional woodpecker. In the northern country we had come across a very few blue grouse and ruffed grouse, both as tame as possible. We had seen a pigmy owl no larger than a robin sitting on top of a pine in broad daylight, and uttering at short intervals a queer un-owllike cry.

The birds that interested us most were the solitaires, and especially the dippers or water-ousels. We were fortunate enough to hear the solitaires sing not only when perched on trees, but on the wing, soaring over a great canon. The dippers are to my mind well-nigh the most attractive of all our birds. They stay through the winter in the Yellowstone because the waters are in many places open. We heard them singing cheerfully, their ringing melody having a certain suggestion of the winter wren's. Usually they sang while perched on some rock on the edge or in the middle of the stream; but sometimes on the wing. In the open places the western meadow larks were also uttering their singular beautiful songs. No bird escaped John Burroughs' eye; no bird note escaped his ear.

On the last day of my stay it was arranged that I should ride down from Mammoth Hot Springs to the town of Gardiner, just outside the Park limits, and there make an address at the laying of the corner stone of the arch by which the main road is to enter the Park. Some three thousand people had gathered to attend the ceremonies. A little over a mile from Gardiner we came down out of the hills to the flat plain; from the hills we could see the crowd gathered around the arch waiting for me to come. We put spurs to our horses and cantered rapidly toward the appointed place, and on the way we passed within forty yards of a score of black-tails, which merely moved to one side and looked at us, and within a hundred yards of half a dozen antelope. To any lover of nature it could not help being a delightful thing to see the wild and timid creatures of the wilderness rendered so tame; and their tameness in the immediate neighborhood of Gardiner, on the very edge of the Park, spoke volumes for the patriotic good sense of the citizens of Montana. Major Pitcher informed me that both the Montana and Wyoming people were co-operating with him in zealous fashion to preserve the game and put a stop to poaching. For their attitude in this regard they deserve the cordial thanks of all Americans interested in these great popular playgrounds, where bits of the old wilderness scenery and the old wilderness life are to be kept unspoiled for the benefit of our children's children. Eastern people, and especially eastern sportsmen, need to keep steadily in mind the fact that the westerners who live in the neighborhood of the forest preserves are the men who in the last resort will determine whether or not these preserves are to be permanent. They cannot in the long run be kept as forest and game reservations unless the settlers roundabout believe in them and heartily support them; and the rights of these settlers must be carefully safeguarded, and they must be shown that the movement is really in their interest. The eastern sportsman who fails to recognize these facts can do little but harm by advocacy of forest reserves.

It was in the interior of the Park, at the hotels beside the lake, the falls, and the various geyser basins, that we would have seen the bears had the season been late enough; but unfortunately the bears were still for the most part hibernating. We saw two or three tracks, and found one place where a bear had been feeding on a dead elk, but the animals themselves had not yet begun to come about the hotels. Nor were the hotels open. No visitors had previously entered the Park in the winter or early spring--the scouts and other employees being the only ones who occasionally traverse it. I was sorry not to see the bears, for the effect of protection upon bear life in the Yellowstone has been one of the phenomena of natural history. Not only have they grown to realize that they are safe, but, being natural scavengers and foul feeders, they have come to recognize the garbage heaps of the hotels as their special sources of food supply. Throughout the summer months they come to all the hotels in numbers, usually appearing in the late afternoon or evening, and they have become as indifferent to the presence of men as the deer themselves--some of them very much more indifferent. They have now taken their place among the recognized sights of the Park, and the tourists are nearly as much interested in them as in the geysers.

It was amusing to read the proclamations addressed to the tourists by the Park management, in which they were solemnly warned that the bears were really wild animals, and that they must on no account be either fed or teased. It is curious to think that the descendants of the great grizzlies which were the dread of the early explorers and hunters should now be semi-domesticated creatures, boldly hanging around crowded hotels for the sake of what they can pick up, and quite harmless so long as any reasonable precaution is exercised. They are much safer, for instance, than any ordinary bull or stallion, or even ram, and, in fact, there is no danger from them at all unless they are encouraged to grow too familiar or are in some way molested. Of course among the thousands of tourists there is a percentage of thoughtless and foolish people; and when such people go out in the afternoon to look at the bears feeding they occasionally bring themselves into jeopardy by some senseless act. The black bears and the cubs of the bigger bears can readily be driven up trees, and some of the tourists occasionally do this. Most of the animals never think of resenting it; but now and then one is run across which has its feelings ruffled by the performance. In the summer of 1902 the result proved disastrous to a too inquisitive tourist. He was traveling with his wife, and at one of the hotels they went out toward the garbage pile to see the bears feeding. The only bear in sight was a large she, which, as it turned out, was in a bad temper because another party of tourists a few minutes before had been chasing her cubs up a tree. The man left his wife and walked toward the bear to see how close he could get. When he was some distance off she charged him, whereupon he bolted back toward his wife. The bear overtook him, knocked him down and bit him severely. But the man's wife, without hesitation, attacked the bear with that thoroughly feminine weapon, an umbrella, and frightened her off. The man spent several weeks in the Park hospital before he recovered. Perhaps the following telegram sent by the manager of the Lake Hotel to Major Pitcher illustrates with sufficient clearness the mutual relations of the bears, the tourists, and the guardians of the public weal in the Park. The original was sent me by Major Pitcher. It runs:

"Lake. 7-27-'03. Major Pitcher, Yellowstone: As many as seventeen bears in an evening appear on my garbage dump. To-night eight or ten. Campers and people not of my hotel throw things at them to make them run away. I cannot, unless there personally, control this. Do you think you could detail a trooper to be there every evening from say six o'clock until dark and make people remain behind danger line laid out by Warden Jones? Otherwise I fear some accident. The arrest of one or two of these campers might help. My own guests do pretty well as they are told. James Barton Key. 9 A.M."

Major Pitcher issued the order as requested.

At times the bears get so bold that they take to making inroads on the kitchen. One completely terrorized a Chinese cook. It would drive him off and then feast upon whatever was left behind. When a bear begins to act in this way or to show surliness it is sometimes necessary to shoot it. Other bears are tamed until they will feed out of the hand, and will come at once if called. Not only have some of the soldiers and scouts tamed bears in this fashion, but occasionally a chambermaid or waiter girl at one of the hotels has thus developed a bear as a pet.

The accompanying photographs not only show bears very close up, with men standing by within a few yards of them, but they also show one bear being fed from the piazza by a cook, and another standing beside a particular friend, a chambermaid in one of the hotels. In these photographs it will be seen that some are grizzlies and some black bears.

This whole episode of bear life in the Yellowstone is so extraordinary that it will be well worth while for any man who has the right powers and enough time, to make a complete study of the life and history of the Yellowstone bears. Indeed, nothing better could be done by some one of our outdoor fauna naturalists than to spend at least a year in the Yellowstone, and to study the life habits of all the wild creatures therein. A man able to do this, and to write down accurately and interestingly what he had seen, would make a contribution of permanent value to our nature literature.

In May, after leaving the Yellowstone, I visited the Grand Canyon of the Colorado, and spent three days camping in the Yosemite Park with John Muir. It is hard to make comparisons among different kinds of scenery, all of them very grand and very beautiful; yet personally to me the Grand Canyon of the Colorado, strange and desolate, terrible and awful in its sublimity, stands alone and unequaled. I very earnestly wish that Congress would make it a national park, and I am sure that such course would meet the approbation of the people of Arizona. As to the Yosemite Valley, if the people of California desire it, as many of them certainly do, it also should be taken by the National Government to be kept as a national park, just as the surrounding country, including some of the groves of giant trees, is now kept.

John Muir and I, with two packers and three pack mules, spent a delightful three days in the Yosemite. The first night was clear, and we lay in the open on beds of soft fir boughs among the giant sequoias. It was like lying in a great and solemn cathedral, far vaster and more beautiful than any built by hand of man. Just at nightfall I heard, among other birds, thrushes which I think were Rocky Mountain hermits--the appropriate choir for such a place of worship. Next day we went by trail through the woods, seeing some deer--which were not wild--as well as mountain quail and blue grouse. In the afternoon we struck snow, and had considerable difficulty in breaking our own trails. A snow storm came on toward evening, but we kept warm and comfortable in a grove of the splendid silver firs--rightly named magnificent, near the brink of the wonderful Yosemite Valley. Next day we clambered down into it and at nightfall camped in its bottom, facing the giant cliffs over which the waterfalls thundered.

Surely our people do not understand even yet the rich heritage that is theirs. There can be nothing in the world more beautiful than the Yosemite, its groves of giant sequoias and redwoods, the Canyon of the Colorado, the Canyon of the Yellowstone, the three Tetons; and the representatives of the people should see to it that they are preserved for the people forever, with their majestic beauty all unmarred.

Theodore Roosevelt.

The Zoology of North American Big Game

Among the many questions asked of the naturalist by an inquiring public, few come up more persistently than "What is the difference between a bison and a buffalo; and which is the American animal?"

The interest which so many people find in questions such as this must serve as a justification for the present paper, which proposes no more than to put into concise form what is known of the zoological relations of the animals which come within the special interest of the Boone and Crockett Club. In doing this, conclusions must, as a rule, be stated with few of the facts upon which they rest, for to give more than the plainest of these would be to far outrun the possible limits of space, and would furthermore lead into technical details which to most readers are obscure and wearisome.

Anyone who consults Dr. Johnson's famous dictionary will be illuminated by the definition of camelopard: "An Abyssinian animal taller than an elephant, but not so thick," and even but a few years back all that was considered necessary to answer the question, "what is a bison?" was to state that it is a wild ox with a shaggy mane and a hump on its shoulders, and the thing was done; but in our own time a satisfactory answer must take account of its relationship to other beasts, for we have come to believe that the differences between animals are simply the blank spaces upon the chart of universal life, against which are traced the resemblances, which, as we follow them back into remote periods of geologic time, reveal to us definite lines of succession with structural change, and these, correctly interpreted, are nothing less than actual lines of blood relationship. To know what an animal is, therefore, we must know something of its family tree.

It is perhaps well to emphasize the need of correct interpretation, for there are no bridges on the paths of palaeontology, and as we go back, more than one great gap occurs between series of strata, marking periods of intervening time which there is no means of measuring, but during which we know that the progress of change in the animals then living never ceased. When such a break is reached, the course of phylogeny is like picking up an interrupted trail, with the additional complication that the one we find is never quite like the one we left, and it is in such conditions that the systematist must apply his knowledge of the general progressive tendencies through the ages of change, to the determination of the particular changes he should expect to find in the special case before him, and so be enabled to recognize the footprints he is in search of. The genius to do this has been given to few, but in their hands the results have often been brilliant.

Back in the very earliest Tertiary deposits, and in all certainty even earlier, a group of comparatively small mammals was extensively spread through America, and apparently less widely in Europe, characterized by a primitive form of foot structure, each of which had five complete digits, the whole sole being placed upon the ground, as in the animals we call plantigrade. The grinding surfaces of their molar teeth were also primitive, bearing none of the complicated, curved crests and ridges possessed by present ruminants, but instead they had conical cusps, usually not more than three to a tooth; this tritubercular style of molar crown being about the earliest known in true mammals.

In the opinion of many palaeontologists, the ancestors of the present hoofed beasts, or ungulates, were contained among these _Condylarthra_, as they were named by Prof. Cope.

Of course, these early mammals are known to us only by their fossil and mostly fragmentary skeletons, but it may be said that at least in the ungulate line, the successive geological periods show steady structural progression in certain directions. Of great importance are a decrease in the number of functional digits; a gradual elevation of the heel, so that their modern descendants walk on the tips of their toes, instead of on the whole sole; a constant tendency to the development of deeply grooved and interlocked joints in place of shallow bearing surfaces; and to a complex pattern of the molar crowns instead of the simple type mentioned. To this may be added as the most important factor of all in survival, that these changes have progressed together with an increase in the size of the brain and in the convolutions of its outer layer.

The Condylarthra seem to have gone out of existence before the time of the middle Eocene, but before this they had become separated into the two great divisions of odd-toed and even-toed ungulates, into which all truly hoofed beasts now living fall.

The first group (_Perissodactyla_) has always one or three toes functionally developed, either the third, or third, second and fourth, the two others having entirely disappeared, except for a remnant of the fifth in the forefoot of tapirs. They have retained some at least of the upper incisor teeth, and, except in some rhinoceroses, the canines are also left; the molars and premolars are practically alike in all recent species, and in all of which we know the soft parts, the stomach has but one compartment, and there is an enormous caecum. It is probable that they took rise earlier than their split-footed relations, and their Tertiary remains are far more numerous, but their tendency is toward disappearance, and among existing mammals they are represented only by horses, asses, rhinoceroses, and tapirs.

Contrasted with these, Artiodactyla have always an even number of functional digits, the third and fourth reaching the ground symmetrically, bearing the weight and forming the "split hoof;" the second and fifth remain, in most cases, as mere vestiges, showing externally as the accessory hoofs or dewclaws; in the hippopotamus alone they are fully developed and the animal has a four-toed foot. In deer and bovine animals the incisors and frequently the canines have disappeared from the upper jaw, and the molars are unlike the premolars in having two lobes instead of one. The stomach is always more or less complex; at its extreme reaching the ruminant type with four compartments, in association with which is a caecum reduced in size and simple in form. Nearly all have horns or antlers, at least in one sex.

Most split-hoofed animals are ruminants, but there is a small remnant, probably of early types, which are not. The present ungulates may be summed up in this way:

Odd-toed: _(Perissodactyla)_ -- Horse, Ass, Rhinoceros, Tapir.

Even-toed: _(Artiodactyla)_ --

Non-ruminants-- Hippopotamus, Swine, Peccaries.

Ruminants-- Camels, Llamas, Chevrotains, Giraffe, Antelopes, Sheep, Goats, Musk-ox, Oxen, Deer.

The non-ruminant artiodactyls need not detain us long. Hippopotamuses are little more than large pigs with four toes; they were never American, though many species, some very small, are found in the European Tertiary. The two existing species are African.

In the western hemisphere swine are represented by the peccaries, differing from them chiefly in having six less teeth, one less accessory toe on the hind foot, and in a stomach of more complex character. Peccaries also have the metapodial bones supporting the two functional digits fused together at their upper ends, forming an imperfect "cannon bone," which is a characteristic of practically all the ruminants, but of no other hoofed beasts. One species only enters the United States along the Mexican border.

All non-ruminant ungulates have from four to six incisors in the upper jaw;

the canines are present, and sometimes, as in the wart hogs, reach an extraordinary size.

Coming now to the ruminants, all digits except the third and fourth have disappeared from camels and llamas, and the nails on these are limited to their upper surface without forming a hoof, the under side being a broad pad, upon which they tread. No camel-like beasts have inhabited North America since the Pliocene age. Chevrotains, or muis deer (_Tragulidae_), are not deer in any true sense, as they have but three compartments to the stomach; antlers are absent and in their place large and protruding canine teeth are developed in the upper jaw, and the lateral metacarpal bones are complete throughout their length, instead of being represented by a mere remnant. They are the smallest of ungulates, and inhabit only portions of the Indo-Malayan region. Camels also have upper canines, and the outer, upper incisors as well.

The giraffe is separated from all living ungulates by the primitive character of its so-called "horns," which are not horns in the usual sense, but simply bony prominences of the skull covered with hair. Some of the earliest deer-like animals seem to have had simple or slightly branched antlers which were not shed, and which there is reason to believe were also hairy, and in these, as well as in other characters, giraffes and the early deer may not have been far apart. The "okapi," Sir Harry Johnston's late discovery in the Uganda forests, seems to have come from the same ancestral stock, but the giraffe has no other existing relatives.

The true deer, to which we shall return, are readily enough distinguished from the ox tribe and its allies by their solid and more or less branched antlers, usually confined to males, and periodically shed.

So, through this rapid survey, we have dropped out of the hoofed beasts all but the bovines and their near allies, and are thus far advanced toward our definition of a bison, but from this point we shall not find it easy to draw sharp distinctions, for while the _Bovidae_, as a whole, are well enough distinguished from all other animals, their characteristics are so much mixed among themselves that it is hardly possible to find any one or more striking features peculiar to one group, and for most of them recourse must be had to associations of a number of lesser characters.

Oxen, antelopes, sheep and goats agree in having hollow horns of material similar to that of which hair and nails are formed, permanently fixed upon the skull in all but one species; none of them have more than the two middle digits functionally developed, one on each side of the axis of the leg; none have the lower ends remaining of the meta-podial bones belonging to the two accessory digits; and none have either incisor or canine teeth in the upper jaw.

From animals so constructed we may first take out goats and sheep, in which the female horns are much smaller than those of males, and in some species are even absent. In nearly all of them the horns are noticeably compressed in section, either triangular or sub-triangular near the base, and are directed sometimes outwardly from the head with a circular sweep; at others with a backward curve, often spirally. The muzzle is always hairy; there is no small accessory column on the inner side of the upper molars, found always in oxen and in some antelopes; the tail is short, and scent glands are present between the digits of some or all the feet.

Now, as to the perplexing animals popularly known as antelopes. No definition could be framed which would include them all in one group, for every subordinate character seems to be present in some and absent in others, so that the most that can be done with this vast assemblage is to arrange its contents in series of genera, which may or may not be called sub-families, but which probably correspond in some degree to their real affinities. We can only say of any one of them that it is an antelope because it is not a sheep, nor a goat, nor an ox. They concern us here only to be eliminated, for they are not American, our prong-buck having a sub-family all to itself, as we shall see later, and the so-called "white goat" being usually regarded as neither goat nor truly antelope.

Within the limits of the real bovine animals, four quite distinct types may be made out, chiefly by the position of the horns upon the skull and by the shape of the horns themselves. There are also differences in the relations of the nasal and premaxillary bones, the development of the neural spines of the vertebrae, and the hairy covering of the body.

In the genus Bos the horns are placed high up on the vertex of the skull, which forms a marked transverse ridge from which the hinder portion falls sharply away. The horns are nearly circular in section and almost smooth;

usually they curve outward, then upward and often inward at the tip; the premaxillaries are long and generally reach to the nasals, and the anterior dorsal vertebrae are without sharply elongated spines, so that the line of the back is nearly straight. These, the true oxen, as they are sometimes termed, now exist only in domesticated breeds of cattle.

In the gaur oxen (_Bibos_) the horns are situated as in _Bos_, high up on the vertex, but are more elliptical in section; the premaxillaries are short; the dorsal vertebrae, from the third to the eleventh, bear elongated spines which produce a hump reaching nearly to the middle of the back; the tail is shorter, and the hair is short all over the body. The three species--gaur, gayal and banteng--inhabit Indo-Malayan countries, and all of them are dark brown with white stockings.

The buffaloes (_Bubalus_) are large and clumsy animals with horns more or less compressed or flattened at their bases, set low down on the vertex, which does not show the high transverse ridge of true oxen and gaurs. In old bulls of the African species the horns meet at their base and completely cover the forehead. In the arni of India they are enormously long. The dorsal spines are not much elongated, and there is no distinct hump; the premaxillae are long enough to reach the nasals. Hair is scanty all over the body, and old animals are almost wholly bare. The small and interesting anoa of Celebes, and the tamarao of Mindoro, are nearly related in all important respects to the Indian buffalo, and the carabao, used for draught and burden in the Philippines, belongs to a long domesticated race of the same animal.

Finally, in the genus Bison the horns are below the vertex as in buffaloes, but are set far apart at the base, which is cylindrical; they are short and their curve is forward, upward and inward; the anterior dorsal and the last cervical vertebrae have long spines which bear a distinct hump on the shoulders; the premaxillae are short and never reach the nasals; there are fourteen, or occasionally fifteen, pairs of ribs, all other oxen having but thirteen, and there is a heavy mane about the neck and shoulders. The yak of central Asia is very bison-like in some respects, but in others departs in the direction of oxen.

So at last, group by group, we have gone through the ungulates, and the bisons alone are left, and as the American animal has short, incurved horns, set low down on the skull and far apart at the base; premaxillaries falling short of the nasals; the last cervical and the anterior dorsal vertebrae with spines; fourteen pairs of ribs, and a mane covering the shoulders, we conclude that it is a bison, and as the same characteristics with minor variations are shown by the European species, often, but wrongly, called "aurochs," we say that these two alone of existing Bovidae are bisons, with the yak as a somewhat questionable relative.

In all essential respects the two bisons are very similar, but minute comparison shows that the European species, _Bison bonasus_, has a wider and flatter forehead, bearing longer and more slender horns, and all the other distinctive features are less pronounced. In the American species, _Bison bison_, the pelvis is less elevated, producing the characteristic slope of the hindquarters. It is a coincidence that the two regions originally inhabited by the bisons are those in which the white races of men have to the greatest extent thrown their restless energies into the struggle for existence, with the result that extinction to nearly the same degree has overtaken these two near cousins among oxen. A few wild members of the European species still exist in the Caucasus, as a few of the American are left in British America, but elsewhere both exist only under protection.

The carefully kept statistics of the Bielowitza herd in Grodno, western Russia, which includes nearly all but the few wild ones, shows that between 1833 and 1857 they increased in number from 768 to 1,898, but from this maximum the decrease has been constant, with trifling halts, until in 1892 less than five hundred were left; so that even if the Peace River bison are counted with the remnant of the American species, it is probable that the survivors of each race are about equal in number.

It is true that the number of our own species has lately been placed as high as a thousand, but even if these figures are correct, the seeds of decay from internal causes, such as inbreeding and the degeneration of restraint, are already sown, and the inevitable end of the race is not far off.

The Peace River, or woodland, bison has lately been separated as a sub-species _(B. bison athabascae)_, distinguished from the southern and better known form by superior size, a wider forehead, longer, more slender and incurved horns, and by a thicker and softer coat, which is also darker in color. Now, it is an interesting fact that a fossil bison skull from the lower Pliocene of India resembles the present European species, and in later geological times very similar bisons closely allied to each other, if not identical, inhabited all northern regions, including America. These were large animals with wide skulls, and there is little doubt that from this circumpolar form came both of the bisons now inhabiting Europe and America. Out of some half dozen fossil bison which have been described from America, none earlier than the latest Tertiary, Bison latifrons from the Pleistocene seems likely to have been the immediate ancestor of recent American species, and as the one skull of the woodland bison which has been examined resembles both latifrons and the European species more than the plains species does, it seems probable that these two more nearly represent the primitive bison, of which the former inhabitant of the prairies is a more modified descendant.

The process of elimination has at last led to this outline definition of a bison, but among the ungulates we have passed over, there are certain others which concern us because they are American.

Sheep and goats agree together and differ from oxen in being usually of smaller size; the tail is shorter, the horns of females are much smaller than those of males, they lack the accessory column on the inner side of the upper molars, and the cannon bone is longer and more slender; but when it comes to a comparison of the one with the other, it is by no means always easy to tell the difference. It is true that the early Greeks seem to have had a rough and ready rule under which mistakes were not easy, for Aristotle tells us "Alcmaeon is mistaken when he says that goats breathe through their ears," but the severely practical methods of our own day leave us little but some very minute points of difference. One of the best of these lies in the shape of the basi-occipital bone, but naturally this can be observed only in the prepared skull. The terms often employed to denote difference in the horns can have only a general application, for they break down in certain species in which the two groups approach each other. The following table expresses some fairly definite points of separation:

SHEEP (_Ovis_). GOAT (_Capra_).

1. Muzzle hairy except between 1. Muzzle entirely hairy. and just above the nostrils.

2. Interdigital glands on all 2. Interdigital glands, when the feet. present, only on fore feet.

3. Suborbital gland and pit 3. Suborbital gland and pit usually present. never present.

4. No beard nor caprine 4. Male with a beard and smell in male. caprine smell.

5. Horns with coarse transverse 5. Horns with fine transverse wrinkles; yellowish striations, or bold knobs or brown; sub-triangular in front; blackish; in male in male, spreading outward more compressed or angular, and forward with a sweeping backward circular sweep, points with a scythe-like curve or turned outward and forward spirally, points turned upward and backward.

These features are distinctive as between most sheep and most goats, but the Barbary wild sheep (_Ovis tragelaphus_) has no suborbital gland or pit, a goat-like peculiarity which it shares with the Himalayan bharal (_Ovis nahura_), in which the horns resemble closely those of a goat from the eastern Caucasus called tur (_Capra cylindricornis_), which for its part has the horns somewhat sheep-like and a very small beard. This same bharal has the goat-like habit of raising itself upon its hind legs before butting.

Both groups are a comparatively late development of the bovine stock, as they do not certainly appear before the upper Pliocene of Europe and Asia, and even at a later date their remains are not plentiful. Goats appear to have been rather the earlier, but are entirely absent from America.

The number of distinct species of sheep in our fauna is a matter of too much uncertainty to be treated with any sort of authority at this time. Most of us grew up in the belief that there was but one, the well-known mountain sheep (_Ovis canadensis_), but seven new species and sub-species have been produced from the systematic mill within recent years, six of them since 1897. It is no part of the purpose of the present paper to dwell upon much vexed questions of specific distinctness, and it will only be pointed out here that the ultimate validity of most of these supposed forms will depend chiefly upon the exactness of the conception of species which will replace among zoologists the vague ideas of the present time. Whatever the conclusion may be, it seems probable that some degree of distinction will be accorded to, at least, one or two Alaskan forms.

As sheep probably came into America from Asia during the Pleistocene, at a time when Bering's Strait was closed by land, it might be expected that those now found here would show relationship to the Kamtschatkan species (_Ovis nivicola_); and such is indeed the case, while furthermore, in the small size of the suborbital gland and pit, and in comparative smoothness of the horns, both species approach the bharal of Thibet and India, which in these respects is goat-like.

When one considers the poverty of the new world in bovine ruminants, it seems strange that three such anomalous forms should have fallen to its share as the prong-horn, the white goat and the musk-ox, of none of which have we the complete history; two of the number being entirely isolated species, sometimes regarded as the types of separate families.

The prong-horn is a curious compound. It resembles sheep in the minute structure of its hair, in its hairy muzzle, and in having interdigital glands on all its feet. Like goats, it has no sub-orbital gland nor distinct pit. Like the chamois, it has a gland below and behind the ear, the secretion of which has a caprine odor. It has also glands on the rump. It is like the giraffe in total absence of the accessory hoofs, even to the metapodials which support them. It differs from all hollow horned ungulates in having deciduous horns with a fork or anterior branch. There is not the least similarity, however, between these horns and the bony deciduous antlers of deer, for, like those of all bovines, they are composed of agglutinated hairs, set on a bony core projecting from the frontal region of the skull.

It is well known that these horn sheaths are at times shed and reproduced, but the exact regularity with which the process takes place is by no means certain, although such direct evidence as there is goes to prove that it occurs annually in the autumn. Prong-bucks have shed on eight occasions in the Zoological Gardens at Philadelphia, five times by the same animal, which reached the gardens in October, 1899, and has shed each year early in November, the last time on October 22, 1903,[1] and the writer has seen one fine head killed about November 5 in a wild state, on which the horn-sheaths were loose and ready to drop off.

[Footnote 1: It is interesting to note that the first pair shed measured 7-1/4 inches, on the anterior curve; the second pair 9-1/2, and the last three 11 inches each. The largest horns ever measured by the writer were those of a buck killed late in November, 1892, near Marathon, Texas, and were 15-3/4 inches in vertical height and 21 along the curve.]

But few of these delicate animals have lived long enough in captivity to permit study of the same individual through a course of years, and the scarcity of observations made upon them in a wild state is remarkable. That irregularity in the process would not be without analogy, is shown by the case of the Indian sambur deer, of which there is evidence from such authority as that king of sportsmen, Sir Samuel Baker, and others, that the shedding does not always occur at the same season, nor is it always annual in the same buck; and by Pore David's deer, which has been known to shed twice in one year.

When resemblances such as those of the prong-horn are so promiscuously distributed, the task of fixing their values in estimating affinities is not a light one, and in fact the most rational conclusion which we may draw from them is that they point back to a distant and generalized ancestor, who possessed them all, but that in the distribution of his physical estate, so to speak, these heirlooms have not come down alike to all descendants. There is again a complicating possibility that some may be no more than adaptive or analogous characters, similarly produced under like conditions of life, but quite independent of a common origin, and it is seldom that we know enough of the history of development of any species to conclude with certainty whether or not this has been the case. At all events, the prong-buck is quite alone in the world at present, and we know no fossils which unmistakably point to it, although it has been supposed that some of the later Miocene species of _Cosoryx_--small deer-like animals with non-deciduous horns, probably covered with hair, and molars of somewhat bovine type--may have been ancestral to it, but this is little more than a speculation. What is certain is that Antilocapra is now a completely isolated form, fully entitled to rank as a family all by itself.

In the musk-ox (_Ovibos moschatus_), or "sheep-ox," as the generic name given by Blainville has it, we meet with another strange and lonely form which has contributed its full share to the problems of systematic zoology. Its remote and inaccessible range has greatly retarded knowledge of its structure, and it is only within the last three years that acquaintance has been made with its soft anatomy, and at the same time with a maze of resemblances and differences toward other ruminants, that perhaps more than equals the irregularities of the prong-buck. But unlike that species, there is in the musk-ox no extreme modification, such as a deciduous horn, to separate it distinctly from the rest of the family. A recapitulation of these differences would be too minutely technical for insertion here, and it must be enough to say that while it cannot be assigned to either group, yet in the distribution of hair on the muzzle, in the presence of a small suborbital gland, in shortness of tail and the light color of its horns, it is sheep-like; in the absence of interdigital glands, the shortness and stoutness of its cannon bones, and in the presence of a small accessory inner column on the upper molars, it is bovine. But in the coarse longitudinal striation of the bases of its horns it differs from both. The shape of the horns is also peculiar. Curving outward, downward and then sharply upward, with broad, flattened bases meeting in the middle line, their outlines are not unlike those of old bulls of the African buffalo.

At the present time the musk-ox inhabits only arctic America, from Greenland westward nearly to the Mackenzie River, but its range was formerly circumpolar, and in Pleistocene times it inhabited Europe as far south as Germany and France. The musk-ox of Greenland has lately been set aside as a distinct species. The most we can say is that Ovibos is a unique form, standing perhaps somewhere between oxen and sheep, and descended from an ancient ruminant type through an ancestry of which we know nothing, for the only fossil remains which are at all distinguishable from the existing genus, are yet closely similar to it, and are no older than the Pleistocene of the central United States; in earlier periods its history is a blank about which it is useless to speculate.

The last of our three anomalies, the white, or mountain goat (_Oreamnos montanus_), is not as completely orphaned as the other two, for it seems quite surely to be connected with a small and peculiar series consisting of the European chamois and several species of Nemorhaedus inhabiting eastern Asia and Sumatra. These are often called mountain antelopes, or goat antelopes. So little is yet known of the soft anatomy of the white goat that we are much in the dark as to its minute resemblances, but its glandular system is certainly suggestive of the chamois, and many of its attitudes are strikingly similar. In all the points in which it approaches goats it is like some, at least, among antelopes, while in the elongated spines of the anterior dorsal vertebrae, which support the hump, and in extreme shortness of the cannon bone, it is far from goat-like. The goat idea, indeed, has little more foundation than the suggestive resemblance of the profile with its caprine beard. It is truly no goat at all, and should more properly be regarded as an aberrant antelope, if anything could be justly termed "aberrant" in an aggregation of animals, hardly any two of which agree in all respects of structure. No American fossils seem to point to _Oreamnos_, and as Nemorhaedus extends to Japan and eastern Siberia, it is probable that it was an Asiatic immigrant, not earlier than the Pleistocene.

From this intricate genealogical tangle one turns with relief to the deer family, where the course of development lies reasonably plain. If the rank of animals in the aristocracy of nature were to be fixed by the remoteness of the period to which we know their ancestors, the deer would out-rank their bovine cousins by a full half of the Miocene period, and the study of fossils onward from this early beginning presents few clearer lines of evidence supporting modern theories respecting the development of species, than is shown in the increasing size and complexity of the antlers in succeeding geological ages, from the simple fork of the middle Miocene to those with three prongs of the late Miocene, the four-pronged of the Pliocene, and finally to the many-branched shapes of the Pleistocene and the present age. Now it is further true that each one of these types is represented today in the mature antlers of existing deer, from the small South American species with a simple spike, up to the wapiti and red deer carrying six or eight points, and still more significant is it that the whole story is recapitulated in the growth of each individual of the higher races. The earliest cervine animals known seem to have had no antlers at all, a stage to which the fawn of the year corresponds; the subsequent normal addition in the life-history, of a tine for each year of growth until the mature antler is reached, answering with exactness to the stages of advance shown in the development-history of the race. A year of individual life is the symbol of a geological period of progression. This is a marvelous record, of which we may say--paraphrasing with Huxley the well-known saying of Voltaire--"if it had not already existed, evolution must have been invented to explain."

The least technical, and for the present purpose the most useful of the characters distinguishing existing deer from all of the bovine stock, lies in the antlers, which are solid, of bony substance, and are annually shed. They are present in the males of all species except the Chinese water deer, and the very divergent musk-deer, which probably should not be regarded as a deer at all. They are normally absent from all females except those of the genus Rangifer. Most deer have canine teeth in the upper jaw, though they are absent in the moose, in the distinctively American type and a few others. The cleaned skull always shows a large vacuity in the outer wall in front of the orbit, which prevents the lachrymal bone from reaching the nasals. No deer has a gall bladder. There are many other distinctions, but as all have exceptions they are of value only in combinations.

The earliest known deer, belonging to the genus _Dremotherium_, or _Amphitragulus_, from the middle Tertiary of France, were of small size and had four toes, canine teeth and no antlers. Their successors seem to have borne simple forked antlers or horns, probably covered with hair, and permanently fixed on the skull. Very similar animals existed in contemporaneous and later deposits in North America. From this point the course of progress is tolerably clear as to deer in general, although we are not sure of all the intermediate details--for it must not be forgotten that a series of types exhibiting progressive modifications in each succeeding geological period is quite as conclusive in pointing out the genealogy of an existing group as if we knew each individual term in the ancestral series of each of its members. Thus we do not yet know whether the peculiar antler of the distinctively American deer, of the genus _Mazama_, is derived from an American source or took its origin in the old world, for the fossil antlers known as _Anoglochis_, from the Pliocene of Europe, are quite suggestive of the Mazama style, but as nothing is known of the other skeletal details of _Anoglochis_, any such connection must at present be purely speculative, but the element of doubt in this special case in no way disturbs the certainty of the general conclusion that all our present _C 開 vidae_ have come through distinct stages in the successive periods, from the simple types of the middle Tertiary.

The family is undoubtedly of old world origin, and for the most part belongs to the northern hemisphere, South America being the only continental area in which they are found south of the equator.

The analytical habit of mind which finds vent in the subdivision of species, is also exhibited in a tendency to break up large genera into a number of small ones, but in the present group this practice has the disadvantage of obscuring a broad distinction between the dominant types inhabiting respectively the old world and the new. The former, represented by the genus _Cervus_, has a brow-tine to the antlers; has the posterior portion of the nasal chamber undivided by the vertical plate of the vomer; and the upper ends only of the lateral metacarpals remain, whereas in all these particulars the typical American deer are exactly opposite. As there are objections to considering these characters as of family value, arising from the intermediate position of the circumpolar genera Alces and _Rangifer_, as well as the water deer and the roe, a broader meaning is given to classification by retaining the comprehensive genera Cervus and _Mazama_, and recognizing the subordinate divisions only as sub-genera.

The one representative of Cervus inhabiting America is the wapiti, or "elk" (_C. canadensis_), which is without doubt an immigrant from Asia by way of Alaska, and it may be of interest to state the grounds upon which this conclusion rests, as they afford an excellent example of the way in which such results are reached. It is an accepted truth in geographical distribution, that the portion of the earth in which the greatest number of forms differentiated from one type are to be found, is almost always the region in which that type had its origin. Now, out of about a dozen species and sub-species of wapiti and red deer to which names have been given, not less than eight are Asiatic, so that Asia, and probably its central portion, is indicated as the region in which the elaphine deer arose; in confirmation of which is the further fact that the antler characteristic of these deer seems to have originated from the same ancestral form as that which produced the sikine and rusine types, which are also Asiatic. From this centre the elaphines spread westward and eastward, resulting in Europe in the red deer, which penetrated southward into north Africa at a time when there was a land connection across the Mediterranean. In the opposite direction, the nearer we get to Bering's Straits the closer is the resemblance to the American wapiti, until the splendid species from the Altai Mountains (_C. canadensis asiaticus_), and Luehdorf's deer (_C. c. luehdorfi_) from Manchuria, are regarded only as sub-species of the eastern American form, which they approach through _C. c. occidentalis_ of Oregon and the northwestern Pacific Coast.

This evidence is conclusive in itself, and is further confirmed by the geological record, from which we know that the land connection between Alaska and Kamtschatka was of Pliocene age, while we have no knowledge of the wapiti in America until the succeeding period.

While there is not the least doubt that the smaller American deer had an origin identical with those of the old world, the exact point of their separation is not so clear. Two possibilities are open to choice: Mazama may be supposed to have descended from the group to which Blastomeryx belonged, this being a late Miocene genus from Nebraska, with cervine molars, but otherwise much like _Cosoryx,_ which we have seen to be a possible ancestor of the pronghorn; or we may prefer to believe that the differentiation took place earlier in Europe or Asia, from ancestors common to both. But there is a serious dilemma. If we choose the former view, we must conclude that the deciduous antler was independently developed in each of the two continents, and while it is quite probable that approximately similar structures have at times arisen independently, it is not easy to believe that an arrangement so minutely identical in form and function can have been twice evolved. On the second supposition, we have to face the fact that there is very little evidence from palaeontology of the former presence of the American type in Eurasia. But, on the whole, the latter hypothesis presents fewer difficulties and is probably the correct one; in which case two migrations must have taken place, an earlier one of the generalized type to which Blastomeryx and Cosoryx belonged, and a later one of the direct ancestor of Mazama. There is little difficulty in the assumption of these repeated migrations, for evidence exists that during a great part of the last half of the Tertiary this continent was connected by land to the northwest with Asia, and to the northeast, through Greenland and Iceland, with western Europe.

The distinction between the two groups is well marked. All the Mazama type are without a true brow-tine to the antlers; the lower ends of the lateral metacarpals only remain; the vertical plate of the vomer extends downward and completely separates the hind part of the nasal chamber into two compartments; and with hardly an exception they have a large gland on the inside of the tarsus, or heel. The complete development of these characters is exhibited in northern species, and it has been beautifully shown that as we go southward there is a strong tendency to diminished size; toward smaller antlers and reduction in the number of tines; to smaller size, and finally complete loss of the metatarsal gland on the outside of the hind leg; and to the assumption of a uniform color throughout the year, instead of a seasonal change.

The two styles of antler which we recognize in the North American deer are too well known to require description. That characterizing the mule deer (_Mazama hemionus_) and the Columbia black-tailed deer (_M. columbiana_), seems never to have occurred in the east, nor south much beyond the Mexican border, and these deer have varied little except in size, although three subspecies have lately been set off from the mule deer in the extreme southwest.

The section represented by _M. virginiana,_ with antlers curving forward and tines projecting from its hinder border, takes practically the whole of America in its range, and under the law of variation which has been stated, has proved a veritable gold mine to the makers of names. At present it is utterly useless to attempt to determine which of the forms described will stand the scrutiny of the future, and no more will be attempted here than to state the present gross contents of cervine literature. The sub-genus Dorcelaphus contains all the forms of the United States; of these, the deer belonging east of the Missouri River, those from the great plains to the Pacific, those along the Rio Grande in Texas and Mexico, those of Florida, and those again of Sonora, are each rated as sub-species of _virginiana_; to which we must add six more, ranging from Mexico to Bolivia. One full species, _M. truei,_ has been described from Central America, and another rather anomalous creature (_M. crookii_), resembling both white-tail and mule deer, from New Mexico.

The other sub-genera are _Blastoceros,_ with branched antlers and no metatarsal gland; _Xenelaphus,_ smaller in size, with small, simply forked antlers and no metatarsal gland; _Mazama_, containing the so-called brockets, very small, with minute spike antlers, lacking the metatarsal and sometimes the tarsal gland as well. The last three sub-genera are South American and do not enter the United States. Another genus, _Pudua_, from Chili, is much like the brockets, but has exceedingly short cannon bones, and some of the tarsal bones are united in a manner unlike other deer. In all, thirty specific and sub-specific names are now carried on the roll of Mazama and its allies.

Attention has already been directed to the parallelism between the course of progress from simple to complex antlers in the development of the deer tribe, and the like progress in the growth of each individual, and to the further fact that all the stages are represented in the mature antlers of existing species. But a curious result follows from a study of the past distribution of deer in

America. At a time when the branched stage had been already reached in North America, the isthmus of Panama was under water; deer were then absent from South America and the earliest forms found fossil there had antlers of the type of _M. virginiana_. The small species with simple antlers only made their appearance in later periods, and it follows that they are descended from those of complex type. This third parallel series, therefore, instead of being direct as are the other two, is reversed, and the degeneration of the antler, which we have seen taking place in the southern deer, has followed backward on the line of previous advance, or, in biological language, appears to be a true case of retrogressive evolution--representing the fossil series, as it were, in a mirror.

The reindeer-caribou type, of the genus _Rangifer,_ agrees with American deer in having the vertical plate of the vomer complete, and in having the lower ends of the lateral metacarpals remaining, but, like _Cervus,_ it has a brow-tine to the antlers. Of its early history we know nothing, for the only related forms which have yet come to light are of no great antiquity, being confined to the Pleistocene of Europe as far south as France, and are not distinguishable from existing species. Until recently it has been supposed that one species was found in northern Europe and Asia, and two others, a northern and a southern, in North America, but lately the last two have been subdivided, and the present practice is to regard the Scandinavian reindeer (_Rangifer tarandus_) as the type, with eight or nine other species or sub-species, consisting of the two longest known American forms, the northern, or barren-ground caribou (_R. arcticus_); the southern, or woodland (_R. caribou_); the three inhabiting respectively Spitzbergen, Greenland and Newfoundland, and still more lately four more from British Columbia and Alaska. The differences between these are not very profound, but they seem on the whole to represent two types: the barren-ground, small of size, with long, slender antlers but little palmated; and the woodland, larger, with shorter and more massive antlers, usually with broad palms. There is some reason to believe that both these types lived in Europe during the interglacial period, the first-named being probably the earlier and confined to western Europe, while the other extended into Asia. The present reindeer of Greenland and Spitzbergen seem to agree most closely with the barren-ground, while the southern forms are nearest to the woodland, and these are said to also resemble the reindeer of Siberia. It is, therefore, not an improbable conjecture that there were two migrations into America, one of the barren-ground type from western Europe, by way of the Spitzbergen land connection, and the other of the woodland, from Siberia, by way of Alaska.

Little more can be said, perhaps even less, of the other circumpolar genus, _Alces_, known in America as "moose," and across the Atlantic as "elk." It also is of mixed character in relation to the two great divisions we have had in mind, but in a different way from reindeer.

Like American deer it has the lower ends of the lateral metacarpals remaining, and the antlers are without a brow-tine, but like Cervus it has an incomplete vomer, and unlike deer in general, the antlers are set laterally on the frontal bone, instead of more or less vertically, and the nasal bones are excessively short. The animal of northern Europe and Asia is usually considered to be distinct from the American, and lately the Alaskan moose has been christened _Alces gigas_, marked by greater size, relatively more massive skull, and huge antlers. Of the antecedents of _Alces_, as in the case of the reindeer, we are ignorant. The earlier Pleistocene of Europe has yielded nearly related fossils,[2] and a peculiar and probably rather later form comes from New Jersey and Kentucky. This last in some respects suggests a resemblance to the wapiti, but it is unlikely that the similarity is more than superficial, and as moose not distinguishable from the existing species are found in the same formation, it is improbable that Cervalces bore to Alces anything more than a collateral relationship.

[Footnote 2: The huge fossil known as "Irish elk" is really a fallow deer and in no way nearly related to the moose.]

Even to an uncritical eye, the differences between ungulates and carnivores of to-day are many and obvious, but as we trace them back into the past we follow on converging lines, and in our search for the prototypes of the carnivora we are led to the _Creodonta_, contemporary with _Condylarthra_, which we have seen giving origin to hoofed beasts, but outlasting them into the succeeding age. These two groups of generalized mammals approached each other so nearly in structure, that it is even doubtful to which of them certain outlying fossils should be referred, and the assumption is quite justified that they had a common ancestor in the preceding period, of which no record is yet known.

The most evident points in which Carnivora differ from Ungulata are their possession of at least four and frequently five digits, which always bear claws and never hoofs; all but the sea otter have six small incisor teeth in each jaw; the canines are large; the molars never show flattened, curved crests after the ruminant pattern, but are more or less tubercular, and one tooth in the hinder part of each jaw becomes blade-like, for shearing off lumps of flesh. This tooth is called the sectorial, or carnassial.

Existing carnivores are conveniently divided into three sections: _Arctoidea_ --bears, raccoons, otters, skunks, weasels, etc.; _Canoidea_ --dogs, wolves and foxes; _Aeluroidea_ --cats, civets, ichneumons and hyaenas.

It is highly probable that these three chief types have descended in as many distinct lines from the _Creodonta_, and that they were differentiated as early as the middle Eocene, but their exact degree of affinity is uncertain; bears and dogs are certainly closer together than either of them are to cats, and it is questionable if otters and weasels--the _Mustelidae_, as they are termed--and raccoons are really near of kin to bears.

Seals are often regarded as belonging to this order, but their relation to the rest of the carnivores is very doubtful. Many of their characters are suggestive of _Arctoidea_, but it is an open question if their ancestors were bear or otter-like animals which took to an aquatic life, or whether they may not have had a long and independent descent. At all events, doubt is cast upon the proposition that they are descended from anything nearly like present land forms by the fact that seals of already high development are known as early as the later Miocene.

The difficulty so constantly met with in attempting to state concisely the details of classification, is well shown in this order, for its subdivisions rest less upon a few well defined characters than upon complex associations of a number of lesser and more obscure ones, a recapitulation of which would be tedious beyond the endurance of all but practiced anatomists. For the present purposes it must be enough to say that bears and dogs have forty-two teeth in the complete set, of which four on each side above and below are premolars, and two above, with three below, are molars, but these teeth in bears have flatter crowns and more rounded tubercles than those of dogs, and the sectorial teeth are much less blade-like, this style of tooth being better adapted to their omnivorous food habits. Bears, furthermore, have five digits on each foot and are plantigrade, while dogs have but four toes behind and are digitigrade.

These differences are less marked in some of the smaller arctoids, which may have as few as thirty-two teeth, and come very near to dogs in the extent of the digital surface which rests upon the ground in walking.

In distinction from these, Aeluroidea never have more than two true molars below, and the cusps of their teeth are much more sharply edged, reaching in the sectorials the extreme of scissor-like specialization. In all of them the claws are more or less retractile, and they walk on the ends of their fingers and toes.

Cats are distinguished from the remainder of this section by the shortness of the skull, and reduction of the teeth to thirty, there being but one true molar on each side, that of the upper jaw being so minute that it is probably getting ready to disappear.

Civets, genets, and ichneumons are small as compared with most cats; they are fairly well distinguished by skull and tooth characters; their claws are never fully retractile, and many have scent glands, as in the civets. No member of this family is American.

Hyaenas have the same dental formula as cats, but their teeth are enormously strong and massive, in relation to their function of crushing bone.

No carnivore has teeth so admirably adapted to a diet of flesh as the cat, and, in fact, it may be doubted if among all mammals, it has a superior in structural fitness to its life habits in general.

The Felidae are an exceedingly uniform group, although they do present minor differences; thus, some species have the orbits completely encircled by bone, while in most of them these are more or less widely open behind; in some the first upper premolar is absent, and some have a round pupil, while in others it is elliptical or vertical, but if there is a key to the apparently promiscuous distribution of these variations, it has not yet been found, and no satisfactory sub-division of the genus has been made, beyond setting aside the hunting-leopard or cheetah as _Cynaelurus_, upon peculiarities of skull and teeth.

True cats of the genus Felis were in existence before the close of the Miocene, and yet earlier related forms are known. Throughout the greater part of the Tertiary the remarkable type known as sabre-toothed cats were numerous and widely spread, and in South America they even lasted so far into the Pleistocene that it is probably true that they existed side by side with man. Some of them were as large as any existing cat and had upper canines six inches or more in length. Cats have no near relations upon the American continent, nor do they appear to have ever had many except the sabre-tooths. Of present species some fifty are known, inhabiting all of the greater geographical areas except Australia. They are tropical and heat loving, but the short-tailed lynxes are northern, while both the tiger and leopard in Asia, and puma in America, range into sub-arctic temperatures, and it is a curious anomaly that while Siberian tigers have gained the protection of a long, warm coat of hair, pumas from British America differ very little in this respect from those of warm regions.

No other cat has so extensive a range as Felis concolor and its close allies, variously known as puma, cougar and mountain lion, which extends from the Atlantic to the Pacific, and from latitude fifty-five or sixty north, to the extreme southern end of the continent. As far as is known, it is a recent development, for no very similar remains appear previous to post-tertiary deposits.

Bears of the genus Ursus are of no great antiquity in a geological sense, for we have no knowledge of them earlier than the Pliocene of Europe, and even later in America, but fossils becoming gradually less bear-like and approximating toward the early type from which dogs also probably sprung, go back to the early Tertiary creodonts.

Cats, as we have seen, are chiefly tropical, while bears, with two exceptions, are northern, one species inhabiting the Chilian Andes, while the brown bear of Europe extends into North Africa as far as the Atlas Mountains.

The family Procyonidae contains the existing species which appear to be nearest of kin to bears. These are all small and consist of the well-known raccoon, the coatis, the ring-tailed bassaris and the kinkajou, all differing from bears in varying details of tooth and other structures. The curious little panda (_Aelurus fulgens_) from the Himalayas, is very suggestive of raccoons, and as forms belonging to this genus inhabited England in Pliocene times, it is possible that we have pointed out to us here the origin of this, at present, strictly American family; but, on the other hand, evidence is not wanting that they have always been native to the soil and came from a dog-like stock.

As we have already seen, bears have the same dental formula as dogs, but as they are less carnivorous, their grinders have flatter surfaces and the sectorials are less sharp; in fact they have very little of the true sectorial character. It is unusual to find a full set of teeth in adult bears, as some of the premolars invariably drop out.

It is fully as true of bears as of any other group of large mammals, that our views as to specific distinction are based upon data at present utterly inadequate, for all the zoological museums of the world do not contain sufficient material for exhaustive study and comparison. The present writer has examined many of these collections and has no hesitation in admitting that his ideas upon the subject are much less definite than they were ten years ago. It does appear, though, that in North America four quite distinct types can be made out. First of these is the circumpolar species, _Ursus maritimus_, the white or polar bear, which most of us grew up to regard as the very incarnation of tenacious ferocity, but which, as it appears from the recitals of late Arctic explorers, dies easily to a single shot, and does not seem to afford much better sport than so much rabbit shooting. The others are the great Kadiak bear (_U. middendorfi_); the grizzly (_U. horribilis_), and the black or true American bear (_U. americanus_). The extent to which the last three may be subdivided remains uncertain, but the barren-ground bear (_U. richardsoni_) is surely a valid species of the grizzly type. The grizzlies and the big Alaska bears approach more nearly than americanus to the widespread brown bear (_U. arctos_) of Europe and Asia, and the hypothesis is reasonable that they originated from that form or its immediate ancestors, in which case we have the interesting series of parallel modifications exhibited in the two continents, for the large bear of Kamtschatka approaches very nearly to those of Alaska, while further to the south in America, where the conditions of life more nearly resemble those surrounding _arctos_, these bears have in the grizzlies retained more of their original form. Whether or not the large Pleistocene cave bear (_U. spelaeus_) was a lineal ancestor is questionable, for in its later period, at least, it was contemporary with the existing European species. The black bear, with its litter-brother of brown color, seems to be a genuine product of the new world.

Many differential characters have been pointed out in the skulls and teeth of bears, and to a less extent, in the claws; but while these undoubtedly exist, the conclusions to be drawn from them are uncertain, for the skulls of bears change greatly with age, and the constancy of these variations, with the values which they should hold in classification, we do not yet know.

* * * * *

It is not improbable that the reader may leave this brief survey with the feeling that its admissions of ignorance exceed its affirmations of certainty, and such is indeed the case, for the law of scientific validity forbids the statement as fact, of that concerning which the least element of doubt remains. But the real advance of zoological knowledge must not thereby be discredited, for it is due to those who have contributed to it to remember that little more than a generation ago these problems of life seemed wrapped in hopeless obscurity, and the methods of investigation which have led to practically all our present gains, were then but new born, and with every passing year doubts are dispelled, and theories turned into truths. There was no break in physical evolution when mental processes began, nor will there be in the evolution of knowledge as long as they continue to exist.

Arthur Erwin Brown.

Big Game Shooting in Alaska

I.

BEAR HUNTING ON KADIAK ISLAND

Early in April, 1900, I made my first journey to Alaska for the purpose of searching out for myself the best big-game shooting grounds which were to be found in that territory. Few people who have not traveled in that country have any idea of its vastness. Away from the beaten paths, much of its 700,000 square miles is practically unknown, except to the wandering prospector and the Indian hunter. Therefore, since I could obtain but little definite information as to just where to go for the best shooting, I determined to make the primary object of my journey to locate the big-game districts of southern and western

Alaska.

My first two months were spent in the country adjacent to Fort Wrangell. Here one may expect to find black bear, brown bear, goats, and on almost all of the islands along the coast great numbers of the small Sitka deer, while grizzlies may these are the black, the grizzly, and the glacier or blue bear.[3] It is claimed that this last species has never fallen to a white man's rifle. It is found on the glaciers from the Lynn Canal to the northern range of the St. Elias Alps, and, as its name implies, is of a bluish color. I should judge from the skins I have seen that in size it is rather smaller than the black bear. What it lives upon in its range of eternal ice and snow is entirely a subject of surmise.

[Footnote 3: The Polar bear is only found on the coast, and never below 61? It is only found at this latitude when carried down on the ice in Bering Sea.]

Of all the varieties of brown bears, the one which has probably attracted most attention is the large bear of the Kadiak Islands. Before starting upon my journey I had communicated with Dr. Merriam, Chief of the Biological Survey, at Washington, and had learned from him all that he could tell me of this great bear. Mr. Harriman, while on his expedition to the Alaskan coast in 1899, had by great luck shot a specimen, and in the second volume of "Big Game Shooting" in "The Badminton Library," Mr. Clive Phillipps-Wolley writes of the largest "grizzly" of which he has any trustworthy information as being shot on Kadiak island by a Mr. J.C. Tolman. These were the only authentic records I could find of bears of this species which had fallen to the rifle of an amateur sportsman.

After spending two months in southern Alaska, I determined to visit the Kadiak Islands in pursuit of this bear. I reached my destination the latter part of June, and three days later had started on my shooting expedition with native hunters. Unfortunately I had come too late in the season. The grass had shot up until it was shoulder high, making it most difficult to see at any distance the game I was after.

The result of this, my first hunt, was that I actually saw but three bear, and got but one shot, which, I am ashamed to record, was a miss. Tracks there were in plenty along the salmon streams, and some of these were so large I concluded that as a sporting trophy a good example of the Kadiak bear should equal, if not surpass, in value any other kind of big game to be found on the North American continent. This opinion received confirmation later when I saw the size of the skins brought in by the natives to the two trading companies.

* * * * *

As I sailed away from Kadiak that fall morning I determined that my hunt was not really over, but only interrupted by the long northern winter, and that the next spring would find me once more in pursuit of this great bear.

It was not only with the hope of shooting a Kadiak bear that I decided to make this second expedition, but I had become greatly interested in the big brute, and although no naturalist myself, it was now to be my aim to bring back to the scientists at Washington as much definite material about him as possible. Therefore the objects of my second trip were:

Firstly, to obtain a specimen of bear from the Island of Kadiak; secondly, to obtain specimens of the bears found on the Alaska Peninsula; and, lastly, to obtain, if possible, a specimen of bear from one of the other islands of the Kadiak group. With such material I hoped that it could at least be decided definitely if all the bears of the Kadiak Islands are of one species; if all the bears on the Alaska Peninsula are of one species; and also if the Kadiak bear is found on the mainland, for there are unquestionably many points of similarity between the bears of the Kadiak Islands and those of the Alaska Peninsula. It was also my plan, if I was successful in all these objects, to spend the fall on the Kenai Peninsula in pursuit of the white sheep and the moose.

Generally I have made it a point to go alone on all big-game shooting trips, but on this journey I was fortunate in having as companion an old college friend, Robert P. Blake.

My experience of the year before was of value in getting our outfit together. At almost all points in Alaska most of the necessary provisions can be bought, but I should rather advise one to take all but the commonest necessities with him, for frequently the stocks at the various trading posts run low. For this reason we took with us from Seattle sufficient provisions to last us six months, and from time to time, as necessity demanded, added to our stores. As the rain falls almost daily in much of the coast country, we made it a point to supply ourselves liberally with rubber boots and rain-proof clothing.

On the 6th of March, 1901, we sailed from Seattle on one of the monthly steamers, and arrived at Kadiak eleven days later. I shall not attempt to describe this beautiful island, but shall merely say that Kadiak is justly termed the "garden spot of Alaska." It has numerous deep bays which cut into the land many miles. These bays in turn have arms which branch out in all directions, and the country adjacent to these latter is the natives' favorite hunting ground for bear.

In skin canoes (baidarkas) the Aleuts, paddling along the shore, keep a sharp lookout on the nearby hillsides, where the bears feed upon the young and tender grass. It was our plan to choose the most likely one of these big bays as our shooting grounds, and hunt from a baidarka, according to local custom.

It may be well to explain here that the different localities of Alaska are distinctly marked by the difference in the canoes which the natives use. In the southern part, where large trees are readily obtained, you find large dugouts capable of holding from five to twenty persons. At Yakutat, where the timber is much smaller, the canoes, although still dugouts, have decreased proportionately in size, but from Yakutat westward the timber line becomes lower and lower, until the western half of the island of Kadiak is reached, where the trees disappear altogether, and the dugout gives place to the skin canoe or baidarka. I have never seen them east of Prince William Sound, but from this point on to the west they are in universal use among the Aleuts--a most interesting race of people, and a most wonderful boat.

The natives of Kadiak are locally called Aleuts, but the true Aleuts are not found east of the Aleutian Islands. The cross between the Aleut and white--principally Russian--is known as the "Creole."

The natives whom I met on the Kadiak Islands seemed to show traces of Japanese descent, for they resembled these people both in size and features. I found them of docile disposition, remarkable hunters and weather prophets, and most expert in handling their wonderful canoes, with which I always associate them.

The baidarka is made with a light frame of some strong elastic wood, covered with seal or sea lion skin; not a nail is used in making the frame, but all the various parts are tied firmly together with sinew or stout twine. This allows a slight give, for the baidarka is expected to yield to every wave, and in this lies its strength. There may be one, two, or three round hatches, according to the size of the boat. In these the occupants kneel, and, sitting on their heels, ply their sharp-pointed paddles; all paddling at the same time on the same side, and then all changing in unison to the other side at the will of the bowman, who sets a rapid stroke. In rough water, kamlaykas--large shirts made principally of stretched and dried bear gut--are worn, and these are securely fastened around the hatches. In this way the Aleuts and the interior of the baidarka remain perfectly dry, no matter how much the sea breaks and passes over the skin deck.

I had used the baidarka the year before, having made a trip with my hunters almost around the island of Afognak, and believed it to be an ideal boat to hunt from. It is very speedy, easily paddled, floats low in the water, will hold much camp gear, and, when well handled, is most seaworthy. So it was my purpose this year to again use one in skirting the shores of the deep bays, and in looking for bears, which show themselves in the early spring upon the mountain sides, or roam the beach in search of kelp.

The Kadiak bear finds no trouble in getting all the food he wants during the berry season and during the run of the various kinds of salmon, which lasts from June until October. At this period he fattens up, and upon this fat he lives through his long winter sleep. When he wakes in the spring he is weak and hardly able to move, so his first aim is to recover the use of his legs. This he does by taking short walks when the weather is pleasant, returning to his den every night. This light exercise lasts for a week or so, when he sets out to feed upon the beach kelp, which acts as a purge. He now lives upon roots, principally of the salmon-berry bush, and later nibbles the young grass.

These carry him along until the salmon arrive, when he becomes exclusively a fish eater until the berries are ripe. I have been told by the natives that just before he goes into his den he eats berries only, and his stomach is now so filled with fat that he really eats but little.

The time when the bears go into their winter quarters depends upon the severity of the season. Generally it is in early November, shortly after the cold weather has set in. Most bears sleep uninterruptedly until spring, but they are occasionally found wandering about in mid-winter. My natives seemed to think that only those bears are restless which have found uncomfortable quarters, and that they leave their dens at this time of year solely for the purpose of finding better ones. They generally choose for their dens caves high up on the mountain sides among the rocks and in remote places where they are not likely to be discovered. The same winter quarters are believed to be used year after year.

The male, or bull bear, is the first to come out in the spring. As soon as he recovers the use of his muscles he leaves his den for good and wanders aimlessly about until he comes upon the track of some female. He now persistently follows her, and it is at this time that the rutting season of the Kadiak bear begins, the period lasting generally from the middle of April until July.

In Eagle Harbor, on Kadiak Island, a native, three years ago, during the month of January, saw a female bear which he killed near her den. He then went into the cave and found two very small cubs whose eyes were not yet open. This would lead to the belief that this species of bear brings forth its young about the beginning of the new year. At birth the cubs are very small, weighing but little more than a pound and a half, and there are from one to four in a litter. Two, however, is the usual number. The mother, although in a state of semi-torpor, suckles these cubs in the den, and they remain with her all that year, hole up with her the following winter, and continue to follow her until the second fall, when they leave her and shift for themselves.

For many years these bears have been so persistently hunted by the natives, who are constantly patrolling the shores in their skin canoes, that their knowledge of man and their senses of smell and hearing are developed to an extreme degree. They have, however, like most bears, but indifferent sight. They range in color from a light tawny lion to a very dark brown; in fact, I have seen some bears that were almost black. Many people have asked me about their size, and how they compare in this respect with other bears. The Kadiak bear is naturally extremely large. His head is very massive, and he stands high at the shoulders. This latter characteristic is emphasized by a thick tuft of hair which stands erect on the dorsal ridge just over the shoulders. The largest bear of this kind which I shot measured 8 feet in a straight line from his nose to the end of the vertebrae, and stood 51-1/2 inches in a straight line at the shoulders, not including between 6 and 7 inches of hair.

Most people have an exaggerated idea of the number of bears on the Kadiak Islands. Personally I believe that they are too few ever to make shooting them popular. In fact, it was only by the hardest kind of careful and constant work that I was finally successful in bagging my first bear on Kadiak. When the salmon come it is not so difficult to get a shot, but this lying in wait at night by a salmon stream cannot compare with seeking out the game on the hills in the spring, and stalking it in a sportsmanlike manner.

It was more than a week after our landing at Kadiak before the weather permitted me to go to Afognak, where my old hunters lived, to make our final preparations. One winter storm after another came in quick succession, but we did not mind the delay, for we had come early and did not expect the bears would leave their dens before April.

I decided to take with me on my hunt the same two natives whom I had had the year before. My head man's name was Fedor Deerinhoff. He was about forty years of age, and had been a noted sea otter and bear hunter. In size he was rather larger than the average of his race, and absolutely fearless. Many stories are told of his hand-to-hand encounters with these big bears. I think the best one is of a time when he crawled into a den on his hands and knees, and in the dark, and at close quarters, shot three. He was unable to see, and the bears' heavy breathing was his only guide in taking aim.

Nikolai Pycoon, my other native, was younger and shorter in stature, and had also a great reputation as a hunter, which later I found was fully justified, and furthermore was considered the best baidarka man of Afognak. He was a nice little fellow, always good natured, always keen, always willing, and the only native whom I have ever met with a true sense of gratitude.

The year before I had made all arrangements to hire for this season a small schooner, which was to take us to our various shooting grounds. I was now much disappointed to find that the owner of this schooner had decided not to charter her. We were, therefore, obliged to engage a very indifferent sloop, but she was fortunately an excellent sea boat. Her owner, Charles Payjaman, a

Russian, went with us as my friend's hunter. He was a fisherman and a trapper by profession, and had the reputation of knowing these dangerous island waters well. His knowledge of Russian we expected to be of great use to us in dealing with the natives; Alaska was under Russian control for so many years that that language is the natural local tongue.

It was the first of April before we got our entire outfit together, and it was not until four days later that the weather permitted us to hoist our sail and start for the shooting grounds, of which it was of the utmost importance that we should make good choice. All the natives seemed to agree that Kiliuda Bay, some seventy-five miles below the town of Kadiak, was the most likely place to find bear, and so we now headed our boat in that direction. It was a most beautiful day for a start, with the first faint traces of spring in the air. As we skirted the shore that afternoon I sighted, through the glasses, on some low hills in the distance, bear tracks in the snow. My Aleuts seemed to think that the bears were probably near, having come down to the shore in search of kelp. It promised a pretty fair chance for a shot, but there was exceedingly bad water about, and no harbor for the sloop to lie, so Payjaman and my natives advised me not to make the attempt. As one should take no chances with Alaskan waters, I felt that this was wise, and we reluctantly passed on.

The next forenoon we put into a large bay, Eagle Harbor, to pick up a local hunter who was to accompany us to Kiliuda Bay, for both my Aleuts and the Russian were unacquainted with this locality. Ignati Chowischpack, the native whose services we secured, was quite a character, a man of much importance among the Aleuts of this district, and one who had a thorough knowledge of the country chosen as a hunting ground.

We expected to remain at Eagle Harbor only part of the day, but unfortunately were storm-bound here for a week. Several times we attempted to leave, but each time had to put back, fearing that the heavy seas we encountered outside would crush in the baidarka, which was carried lashed to the sloop's deck. It was not until early on the morning of April 12, just as the sun was topping the mountains, that we finally reached Kiliuda Bay.

Our hunting grounds now stretched before us as far as the eye could see. We had by this time passed the tree area, and it was only here and there in isolated spots that stunted cottonwoods bordered the salmon streams and scattered patches of alders dotted the mountain sides. In many places the land rolled gradually back from the shore until the mountain bases were reached, while in other parts giant cliffs rose directly from the water's edge, but with the glasses one could generally command a grand view of this great irregular bay, with its long arms cutting into the island in all directions.

We made our permanent camp in a large barabara, a form of house so often seen in western Alaska that it deserves a brief description. It is a small, dome-shaped hut, with a frame generally made of driftwood, and thatched with sods and the rank grass of the country. It has no windows, but a large hole in the roof permits light to enter and serves also as an outlet for the smoke from the fire, which is built on a rough hearth in the middle of the barabara. These huts, their doors never locked, offer shelter to anyone, and are frequently found in the most remote places. The one which we now occupied was quite large, with ample space to stow away our various belongings, and we made ourselves most comfortable, while our Aleuts occupied the small banya, or Russian bathhouse, which is also generally found by the side of the barabara. This was to be the base of supplies from which my friend and I were to hunt in different directions.

The morning after reaching our shooting grounds I started with one of my natives and the local hunter in the baidarka to get the lay of the land. Blake and I agreed that it was wise to divide up the country, both because we could thus cover a much greater territory, and our modes of hunting differed materially. Although at the time I believed from what I had heard that Payjaman was an excellent man, I preferred to hunt in a more careful manner, as is the native custom, in which I had had some experience the year before. I firmly believe that had Payjaman hunted as carefully as my Aleuts did, my friend would have been more successful.

We spent our first day skirting the shores of the entire bay, paddling up to its very head. Ignati pointed out to Fedor all the most likely places, and explained the local eccentricities of the various winds--a knowledge of these being of the first importance in bear hunting. I was much pleased with the looks of the country, but at the same time was disappointed to find that in the inner bays there was no trace of spring, and that the snow lay deep even on the shores down to the high water mark. Not a bear's track was to be seen, and it was evident that we were on the grounds ahead of time.

We stopped for tea and lunch about noon at the head of the bay. Near by a long and narrow arm of water extended inland some three miles, and it was the country lying adjacent to this and to the head of the bay that I decided to choose as my hunting grounds.

We had a hard time to reach camp that night, for a severe storm suddenly burst upon us, and a fierce wind soon swept down from the hills, kicking up a heavy sea which continually swept over the baidarka's deck, and without kamlaykas on we surely should have swamped. It grew bitterly cold, and a blinding snow storm made it impossible to see any distance ahead, but Ignati knew these waters well, and safely, but half frozen, we reached the main camp just at dark.

Next day the storm continued, and it was impossible to venture out. My friend and I passed the time playing piquet, and listening to our natives, who talked earnestly together, going over many of their strange and thrilling hunting experiences. We understood but little Russian and Aleut, yet their expressive gestures made it quite possible to catch the drift of what was being said. It seemed that Ignati had had a brother killed a few years ago, while bear hunting in the small bay which lies between Eagle Harbor and Kiliuda Bay. The man came upon a bear, which he shot and badly wounded. Accompanied by a friend he followed up the blood trail, which led into a thick patch of alders. Suddenly he came upon a large unwounded male bear which charged him unprovoked, and at such close quarters that he was unable to defend himself. Before his companion, who was but a short distance away, could reach him, he was killed. The bear frightfully mangled the body, holding it down with his feet and using his teeth to tear it apart.

Ignati at once started out to avenge his brother, and killed in quick succession six bears, allowing their bodies to remain as a warning to the other bears, not even removing their skins.

During the past few years three men while hunting have been killed by bears in the same vicinity as Ignati's brother, two instantly, and one living but a short time. I think it is from these accidents that the natives in this region have a superstitious dread of a "long-tailed bear" which they declare roams the hills between Eagle Harbor and Kiliuda Bay.

The storm which began on the 13th continued until the 17th, and this was but one of a series. Winter seemed to come back in all its fury, and I believe that whatever bears had left their winter dens went back to them for another sleep. It was not until the middle of May that the snow began to disappear, and spring with its green grass came.

All this time I was camped with my natives at the head of the bay, some fifteen miles from our base of supplies. On the 23d of April we first sighted tracks, but it was not until May 15 that I finally succeeded in bagging my first bear.

The tracks in the snow indicated that the bears began again to come out of their winter dens the last week in April; and should one wish to make a spring hunt on the Kadiak Islands, the first of May would, I should judge, be a good time to arrive at the shooting grounds.

When the wind was favorable, our mode of hunting was to leave camp before daylight, and paddle in our baidarka up to the head of one of these long bays, and, leaving our canoe here, trudge over the snow to some commanding elevation, where we constantly used the glasses upon the surrounding hillsides, hoping to see bear. We generally returned to camp a little before noon, but in the afternoon returned to the lookout, where we remained until it was too dark to see.

When the wind was blowing into these valleys we did not hunt, for we feared that whatever bears might be around would get our scent and quickly leave. New bears might come, but none which had once scented us would remain. For days at a time we were storm-bound, and unable to hunt, or even leave our little tent, where frequently we were obliged to remain under blankets both day and night to keep warm.

On May 15, by 4 o'clock, I had finished a hurried breakfast, and with my two Aleuts had left in the baidarka for our daily watching place. This was a large mound lying in the center of a valley, some three miles from where we were camped. On the right of the mound rose a gently sloping hill with its sides sparsely covered with alders, and at right angles and before it, extended a rugged mountain ridge with rocky sides stretching all across our front, while to the left rose another towering mountain ridge with steep and broken sides. All the surrounding hills and much of the low country were covered with deep snow. The mountains on three sides completely hemmed in the valley, and their snowy slopes gave us an excellent chance to distinguish all tracks. Such were the grounds which I had been watching for over a month whenever the wind was favorable.

The sun was just topping the long hill to our right as we reached our elevated watching place. The glasses were at once in use, and soon an exclamation from one of my natives told me that new tracks were seen. There they were-- two long unbroken lines leading down from the mountain on our right, across the valley, and up and out of sight over the ridge to our left. It seemed as if two bears had simply wandered across our front, and crossed over the range of mountains into the bay beyond.

As soon as my hunters saw these tracks they turned to me, and, with every confidence, said: "I guess catch." Now, it must be remembered that these tracks led completely over the mountains to our left, and it was the most beautiful bit of hunting on the part of my natives to know that these bears would turn and swing back into the valley ahead. To follow the tracks, which were well up in the heart of our shooting grounds, would give our wind to all the bears that might be lurking there, and this my hunters knew perfectly well, yet they never hesitated for one moment, but started ahead with every confidence.

We threaded our way through a mass of thick alders to the head of the valley, and then climbing a steep mountain took our stand on a rocky ridge which commanded a wide view ahead and to our left in the direction in which the tracks led. We had only been in our new position half an hour when Nikolai, my head hunter, gripped my arm and pointed high up on the mountain in the direction in which we had been watching. There I made out a small black speck, which to the naked eye appeared but a bit of dark rock protruding through the snow. Taking the glasses I made out a large bear slowly floundering ahead, and evidently coming downward. His coat seemed very dark against the white background, and he was unquestionably a bull of great size. Shortly after I had the satisfaction of seeing a second bear, which the first was evidently following. This was, without doubt, a female, by no means so large as the first, and much lighter in color. The smaller bear was apparently hungry, and it was interesting to watch her dig through the snow in search of food. Soon she headed down the mountain side, paying absolutely no attention to the big male, which slowly followed some distance in the rear. Shortly she reached a rocky cliff which it seemed impossible that such a clumsy animal could descend, and I almost despaired of her making the attempt, but without a pause she wound in and out, seemingly traversing the steepest and most difficult places in the easiest manner, and headed for the valley below. When the bull reached this cliff we lost sight of him; nor could we locate him again with even the most careful use of the glasses. He had evidently chosen this secure retreat to lie up in for the rest of the day. If I could have killed the female without alarming him, and then waited on her trail, I should undoubtedly have got another shot, as he followed her after his rest.

It was 8 o'clock when we first located the bears, and for nearly three hours I had a chance to watch one or both of them through powerful glasses. The sun had come up clear and strong, melting the crust upon the snow, so that as soon as the female bear reached the steep mountain side her downward path was not an easy one. At each step she would sink up to her belly, and at times would slip and fall, turning somersault after somersault; now and again she would be buried in the snow so deep that it seemed impossible for her to go either ahead or backward. Then she would roll over on her back, and, loosening her hold on the steep hillside, would come tumbling and slipping down, turning over and over, sideways and endways, until she caught herself by spreading out all four legs. In this way she came with each step and turn nearer and nearer. Finally she reached an open patch on the hillside, where she began to feed, digging up the roots of the salmon-berry bushes at the edge of the snow. If now I lost sight of her for a short time, it was very difficult to pick her up again even with the glasses, so perfectly did the light tawny yellows and browns of her coat blend in with the dead grass of the place on which she was feeding.

The wind had been blowing in our favor all the morning, and for once continued true and steady. But how closely we watched the clouds, to see that no change in its direction threatened us.

We waited until the bear had left the snow and was quietly feeding before we made a move, and then we slowly worked ahead and downward, taking up a new position on a small ridge which was well to leeward, but still on the opposite side of the valley from the bear. She seemed in an excellent position for a stalk, and had I been alone I should have tried it. But the Aleut mode of hunting is to study the direction in which your game is working, and then take up a position which it will naturally approach.

Taking our stand, we waited, watching with much interest the great ungainly creature as she kept nibbling the young grass and digging up roots. At times she would seem to be heading in our direction, and then again would turn and slowly feed away. Suddenly something seemed to alarm her, for she made a dash of some fifty yards down the valley, and then, seeming to recover her composure, began to feed again, all the while working nearer and nearer. The bear was now well down in the bottom of the valley, which was at this point covered with alders and intersected by a small stream. There were open patches in the underbrush, and it was my intention to shoot when she passed through one of these, for the ground was covered with over a foot of snow, which would offer a very tempting background.

While all this was passing quickly through my mind, she suddenly made another bolt down the valley, and, when directly opposite our position, turned at right angles, crossed the brook, and came straight through the alders into the open, not eighty yards away from us. As she made her appearance I could not help being greatly impressed by the massive head and high shoulders on which stood the pronounced tuft of hair. I had most carefully seen to my sights long before, for I knew how much would probably depend on my first shot. It surely seemed as if fortune was with me that day, as at last I had a fair chance at the game I had come so far to seek. Aiming with the greatest care for the lungs and heart, I slowly pressed the trigger. The bear gave a deep, angry growl, and bit for the wound,[4] which told me my bullet was well placed; but she kept her feet and made a dash for the thicket. I was well above, and so commanded a fairly clear view as she crashed through the leafless alders. Twice more I fired, and each time with the most careful aim. At the last shot she dropped with an angry moan. My hunters shook my hand, and their faces told me how glad they were at my final success after so many long weeks of persistent work. Including the time spent last year and this year, this bear represented eighty-seven days of actual hunting.

[Footnote 4: When a bullet strikes a Kadiak bear, he will always bite for the wound and utter a deep and angry growl; whereas of the eleven bears which my friend and I shot on the Alaska peninsula, although they, too, bit for the wound, not one uttered a sound.]

I at once started down to look at the bear, when out upon the mountain opposite the bull was seen. He had heard the shots and was now once more but a moving black speck on the snow, but it will always be a mystery to me how he could have heard the three reports of my small-bore rifle so far away and against a strong wind. My natives suggested that the shots must have echoed, and in this I think they were right; but even then it shows how abnormally the sense of hearing has been developed in these bears.

I was sorry to find that the small-bore rifle did not give as great a shock as I had expected, for my first two bullets had gone through the bear's lungs and heart without knocking her off her feet.

The bear was a female, as we had supposed, but judging from what my natives said, only of medium size. She measured 6 feet 4 inches in a straight line between the nose and the end of the vertebrae, and 44-5/8 inches at the shoulders. The fur was in prime condition, and of an average length of 4-1/2 inches, but over the shoulders the mane was two inches longer. Unfortunately, as in many of the spring skins, there was a large patch over the rump apparently much rubbed. The general belief is that these worn patches are made by the bears sliding down hill on their haunches on the snow; but my natives have a theory that this is caused by the bears' pelt freezing to their dens and being torn off when they wake from their winter's sleep.

Although this female was not large for a Kadiak bear, as was proved by one I shot later in the season, I was much pleased with my final success, and our camp that night was quite a merry one.

Shortly after killing this bear, Blake and I returned to the trading post at Wood Island to prepare for a new hunt, this time to the Alaska Peninsula.

II.

BEAR HUNTING ON THE ALASKA PENINSULA

The year before I had chanced to meet an old pilot who had the reputation of knowing every nook and corner of the Alaskan coast. He told me several times of the great numbers of bears that he had often seen in a certain bay on the Alaska Peninsula, and advised me most strongly to try this place. We now determined to visit this bay in a good sized schooner we had chartered from the North American Commercial Company.

There were numerous delays in getting started, but finally, on May 31, we set sail, and in two days were landed at our new shooting grounds. Rarely in modern days does it fall to the lot of amateurs to meet with better sport than we had for the next month.

The schooner landed us with our natives, two baidarkas, and all our provisions, near the mouth of the harbor. Here we made our base of supplies, and the next morning in our two canoes started with our hunters to explore this wonderful bay. At high tide Chinitna Bay extends inland some fifteen miles, but at low water is one vast bog of glacial deposit. Rugged mountains rise on all sides, and at the base of these mountains there are long meadows which extend out to the high water mark. In these meadows during the month of June the bears come to feed upon the young and tender salt grass.

There was a long swell breaking on the beach as we left our base of supplies, but we passed safely through the line of breakers to the smooth waters beyond, and now headed for the upper bay. The two baidarkas kept side by side, and Blake and I chatted together, but all the while kept the glasses constantly fixed upon the hillsides. We had hardly gone a mile before a small black bear was sighted; but the wind was unfavorable, and he got our scent before we could land. This looked decidedly encouraging, and we continued on in the best of spirits. About mid-day we went on shore, lunched, and then basked in the sun until the afternoon, when we again got into the baidarkas and paddled further up the bay to a place where a wide meadow extends out from the base of the mountains. Here Nikolai, my head hunter, went on shore with the glasses, and raising himself cautiously above the bank, took a long look at the country beyond. It was at once quite evident that he had seen something, and we all joined him, keeping well hidden from view. There, out upon the marsh, could be seen two large bears feeding upon the young grass. They seemed in an almost unapproachable position, and we lay and watched them, hoping that they would move into a more advantageous place. After an hour or so they fed back toward the trees, and soon passed out of sight.

We matched to see which part of the meadow each should watch, and it fell to my lot to go further up the marsh. I had been only a short time in this place when a new bear came into sight. We now made a most beautiful stalk right across the open to within a hundred yards. All this while a new dog, which I had bought at Kadiak and called Stereke, had crawled with us flat on his stomach, trembling all over with excitement as he watched the bear. I had plenty of time to take aim, and was in no way excited, but missed clean at one hundred yards. At the report of my rifle Stereke bit himself clear from Nikolai, who was holding him, and at once made for the bear, which he tackled in a most encouraging manner, nipping his heels, and then quickly getting out of the way as the bear charged. But I found that one dog was not enough to hold these bears, and this one got safely away.

It was a dreary camp that night, for I had missed an easy shot without a shadow of excuse. We pitched our small tent at the extreme edge of the marsh behind a large mass of rocks. I turned in thoroughly depressed, but awoke the next morning refreshed, and determined to retrieve my careless shooting of the day before. A bad surf breaking on the beach prevented our going further up the bay in our baidarkas, as we had planned to do. We loafed in the sun until evening, while our natives kept constant watch of the great meadow where we had seen the bears the day before. We had just turned in, although at ten o'clock it was still daylight, when one of the natives came running up to say that a bear was in sight, so Blake, with three natives and Stereke, made the stalk. I had a beautiful chance to watch it from the high rocks beside our camp. The men were able to approach to within some fifty yards, and Blake, with his first shot, hit, and with his third killed the bear before it could get into the brush. Stereke, when loosed, acted in a gallant manner, and tackled the bear savagely.

Unfortunately no measurements were taken, but the bear appeared to be somewhat smaller than the female I killed at Kiliuda Bay, and weighed, I should judge, some 450 pounds. It appeared higher on the legs and less massive than the Kadiak bear, and had a shorter mane, but was of much the same tawny color on the back, although darker on the legs and belly.

Two days later we set out from our camp behind the rocks and paddled a short distance up the bay.

Here we left the baidarkas and crossed a large meadow without sighting bear. We then followed some miles the banks of a small stream. Leaving my friend with his two men, I pushed ahead with my natives to investigate the country beyond. But the underbrush was so dense it was impossible to see more than a few yards ahead. We had gone some distance, and Fedor and I had just crossed a deep stream on a rickety fallen tree, while the other native was following, when I chanced to look back and saw a small black bear just opposite. He must have smelt us, and, wanting to see what sort of creature man was, had deliberately followed up our tracks. Nikolai had my rifle on the other side of the brook, so I snatched up Fedor's and twice tried to shoot; but the safety bolt would not work, and when I had it adjusted the bear showed only one shoulder beyond a tree. It was just drawing back when I pressed the trigger. The bullet grazed the tree, was deflected, and a patch of hair was all that I had for what promised the surest of shots.

In the afternoon we made for a place which our hunters declared was a sure find for bear; but unlike most "sure places," we sighted our game even before we reached the ground. There they were, two large grizzled brutes, feeding on the salt marsh grass like two cows. We made a most exciting approach in our baidarkas, winding in and out, across the open, up a small lagoon which cut into the meadow where the bears were feeding. We got to within two hundred yards when they became suspicious, but could not quite make us out. One now rose on his hind legs to get a better view, and offered a beautiful chance, but I waited for my friend, whose turn it was to have first shot, and he delayed, thinking that I was not ready. The result was that the bears at once made for the woods, and we both missed.

Stereke again did his part well, catching one of the bears and tackling him in a noble manner, turning him and doing his best to hold him, but this was more than one dog could do, and the bear broke away and soon reached cover.

I am glad to record that with this day's miss ended some of the most careless shooting I have ever done.

This evening we made our camp on the beach on the other side of the bay. I was up frequently during the night, for bears were constantly moving about on the mountain side just behind our sleeping place, but although I could distinctly hear them, the thick brush prevented my getting a shot.

In this latitude there is practically no night during the month of June, and I can recall no more enchanting spot than where we were now camped. Even my hard day's work would not bring sleep, and I lay with my faithful dog at my feet and gazed on the vast mountains about us, their summits capped with snow, while their sides were clothed in the dull velvet browns of last year's herbage, through which the vivid greens of a northern summer were rapidly forcing themselves.

It was after five next morning when we left in our two baidarkas for the extreme head of the bay, where there was another vast meadow. My friend chose to hunt the right side of this marsh, while I took the left.

On reaching our watching place I settled myself for the day in my fur rug, and soon dozed off to finish my night's rest, while my men took turns with the glasses. About ten o'clock a black bear was sighted a long way off, but he soon wandered into the thicket which surrounded the marsh on three sides. At twelve o'clock he appeared again, and we now circled well to leeward and waited where two trails met at the edge of the meadow, expecting the bear would work down one of them to us. It was a long tiresome wait, for we were perched upon some tussocks through which the water soon found its way. About five o'clock we returned to our original watching place, where my friend joined me.

The wind had been at a slant, and although we had worked safely around the bear, he must have got the scent of Blake's party, although a long way off, for my friend reported that the bear was coming in our direction, as we had counted upon, when he suddenly threw up his head, gave one whiff, and started for the woods.

On Friday morning, June 7, we made a three o'clock start from where we had passed the night on the beach. The sun was not over the mountains for another hour, and there was that great charm which comes in the early dawn of a summer's day. Blake in his baidarka, and I in mine, paddled along, side by side, and pushed up to the extreme head of the bay, where we came upon an old deserted Indian camp of the year before. Numerous stretchers told of their success with bear; but the remains of an old fire in the very heart of our shooting grounds warned us that in this section the bears might have been disturbed; for the Alaskan bear is very wary, and is quick to take alarm at any unusual scent. We came back to our camp on the beach by ten o'clock, and had our first substantial meal of the day; for we had now adopted the Aleutian habit of taking simply a cup of tea and a piece of bread in order to make the earliest of starts each morning.

After our mid-day breakfast, we usually took a nap until afternoon; but this day I was not sleepy, and so read for a while, then I loaded my rifle, which I always kept within arm's reach, and was just settling my rugs to turn in, when Stereke gave a sharp bark, and Blake shouted, "Bear." Seizing my rifle I looked up, and walking toward us on the beach, just 110 yards away, was a good sized bull bear. My dog at once made for him, while Blake jumped for his rifle. The bear was just turning when I fired. He bit for the wound, but uttered no sound, and was just disappearing in the brush when I fired a hasty second; Blake and I followed into the thick alders after the dog, which was savagely attacking the bear. His barking told us where the bear was, and I arrived just in time to see him make a determined charge at the dog, which quickly avoided him, and just as quickly renewed the attack.

I forced my way through the alders and got in two close shots, which rolled him over. It appeared that my first shot had broken his shoulder, as well as cut the lower portion of the heart; but this bear had gone some fifty yards, and was still on his feet, when I came up and finished him off. He was a fair sized bull, six feet two inches in a straight line along the vertebrae, and stood exactly three feet at the shoulders. He had evidently been fighting, for one ear was badly torn, and his skin was much scarred with old and recent wounds. After removing the pelt the carcass was thrown into the bay, so that there might be no stench, which my natives declared would be enough to spoil any future shooting in this locality. This same afternoon we moved our camp to a new marsh, but the wind was changeable, and we saw nothing.

The next morning we sighted a bear, which fed into the woods before we had time to come up with him. Shortly after five o'clock the brute made a second appearance, but as the wind had changed and now blew in the wrong direction, a stalk could not be made without our scent being carried into the woods, where many bears were apt to be. We made it a great point never to make a stalk unless the wind was right, for we were extremely anxious not to spoil the place by diffusing our scent, and driving away whatever bears might be lurking near. Therefore, many times we had a chance to watch bears at only a few hundred yards' distance.

It was most interesting to see how careful these big animals were, and how, from time to time, they would feel the wind with their noses, and again stop feeding and listen. No two bears seemed to be built on quite the same lines. Some were high at the shoulders and then sloped down toward the rump and nose; and again, others were saddle-backed; still others stood with their front feet directly under them, making a regular curve at the shoulders; while others had the front legs wide apart, and seemed to form a triangle, the apex of which was at the shoulders.

Their range of color seemed to be from very dark, silver-tipped, to a very light dirty yellow, but with dark legs and belly.

This evening, just as we were having our tea, another bear made his appearance. The first, which we had been watching, evidently heard him coming through the woods, and as the second came out into the open the former vanished. The new one was a dirty yellowish white, with very dark belly and legs, which gave him a most comical appearance.

The wind still continued unfavorable, and my friend and I passed an extremely interesting evening with the glasses, for this watching game, especially bear, gives me almost as much pleasure as making the actual stalk.

About ten o'clock the wind changed, and Blake went after the bear, but unfortunately missed at about one hundred yards.

The following day opened dull, and we spent the morning keeping a sharp watch on the marsh. About ten o'clock a large bear was seen to come out from the trees. The wind was wrong, and as the bear was in an unapproachable position I had to sit with folded arms and watch him. I used the glasses with much interest until shortly after four o'clock, when he slowly fed into the brush.

We had just finished supper when we saw another bear in a better position, and I proceeded to make the stalk, going part of the way in the baidarka, for the great meadow was intersected by a stream from which small lagoons made off in all directions. The wind was very baffling, and although we successfully reached a clump of brush in the middle of the marsh, the bear for some time continued to graze in an unapproachable spot. We had almost given up hope of getting a shot, when he turned and fed slowly some fifty yards in a new direction, which was up-wind. This was our chance. Quickly regaining the baidarka, we paddled as noiselessly and rapidly as possible up the main stream of the marsh to a small lagoon, which now at high tide had sufficient water to float us.

There was great charm in stalking game in this manner, although I was, in a sense, but a passenger in my natives' hands. But it was fascinating to watch their keenness and skill as they guided the frail craft round the sharp turns, the noiseless use of the paddles, the light in their eye as they constantly stood up in the canoe to keep a hidden gaze upon the game ahead, watching its every movement as well as the local eddies and currents in the light evening breeze. All was so in keeping with the sombre leaden clouds overhead, and the grizzled sides of the ungainly brute, blending in with the background of weather-beaten tree trunks and the dull gray rocks. And so, silently and swiftly, stopping many times when the bear's head was up, we approached nearer and nearer, until my head man whispered, Boudit (enough), and I knew that I was to have a fair shot. Stealthily raising my head above the bank I saw the bear feeding, only seventy-five yards away. Creeping cautiously out of the boat I lay flat upon my stomach, rifle cocked and ready, waiting for a good shot. Soon it came. The bear heard some sound in the forest, and raised his head. Now was my chance, and the next second he dropped without a sound; he struggled to rise, but I could see he was anchored with a broken shoulder. My men were unable to restrain themselves any longer, and as I shot for the second time, their rifles cracked just after mine. We now rushed up to close quarters. The bear, shot through the lungs, was breathing heavily and rapidly choking.

Suddenly I heard a yap, and then, out over the marsh, came Stereke at full speed. I had left him with my friend, as we thought we might have to do some delicate stalking across the open. He had sighted the bear, and watched our approach all a-tremble, and at the report of my rifle there was no holding him. Over the ground he came in great bounds, and arrived just in time to give the bear a couple of shakes before he breathed his last. We carried the entire carcass to the baidarka, and even the cartridge shells were taken away, to avoid tainting the place with an unusual scent.

The next day we returned to the main camp, for Fedor, who was ill, had become very weak, and was in no condition to stand any hardships. We left him at the main camp in care of Payjaman. He was greatly depressed, and seemed to give way completely, frequently saying that he never expected to see his home again. Knowing the Aleut's character so well, I much feared that his mental state might work fatal results. Our medicines were of the simplest, and there was but little we could do. Fortunately he did recover, but it was not until two weeks later, when our hunt was nearly over, that he began to get better.

Three days afterward we were back again at our camp behind the rocks. We had wanted rain for some time to wash out all scent. Then again bears are supposed to move about more freely in such weather. Therefore we were rather pleased when the wind changed, bringing a northwest storm which continued all the next day. The lofty mountains were rapidly losing the snow on their summits, and the night's rain had wrought marvels in their appearance, seeming to bring out every shade of green on their wooded slopes. One of our natives was kept constantly on the lookout, and a dozen times a day both Blake and I would leave our books and climb to the watching place for a view across the great meadow. By this time we knew the bear trails and the most tempting feeding grounds, and the surest approaches to the game when it had once come into the open. Therefore when I was told this evening that a bear had been sighted, I felt pretty sure of getting a shot. He had not come well out into the open, and was clearly keeping near cover and working parallel to the brush. If he continued in this direction he would soon be out of sight. Our only chance was to make a quick approach, and Nikolai and I were immediately under way, leaving my dog with my friend, who was to loose him in case I got a shot.

The wind was coming in great gusts across our front, and the corner where the bear was feeding offered a dangerous place for eddies and back-currents against the mountain side. In order to avoid these, we kept just inside the woods. Nikolai going first showed the greatest skill in knowing just how close to the wind we could go. We quickly reached the place where we expected to sight the bear, but he was hidden in the bed of the river, and it was some minutes before we could make out the top of his head moving above the grass. Then noiselessly we crawled up as the bear again fed slowly into view. He was now about 125 yards away, and offered an excellent shot as he paused and raised his head to scent the breeze; but Nikolai whispered, "No," and we worked nearer, crawling forward when the bear's head was down, and lying flat and close when his head was up.

It is curious to note that often when game is being stalked it becomes suspicious, although it cannot smell, hear, or see the stalker; instinct, perhaps-- call it what you will. And now this bear turned and began moving slowly toward cover. For some time he was hidden from view, and then, just before he would finally vanish from sight, he paused a moment, offering a quartering shot. The lower half of his body was concealed by the grass, but it was my last chance, and I took it, aiming for the lungs and rather high in order to get a clear shot. I saw as he bit for the wound that the bullet was well placed, and as he turned and lumbered across our front, I fired two more deliberate shots, one going through the fore leg and one breaking a hind leg.

Nikolai also fired, giving the bear a slight skin wound, and hitting the hind leg just above where one of my bullets had previously struck. As the bear entered the brush we both ran up, my hunter going to the left while I went a little below to head the bear off. We soon came upon him, and Nikolai, getting the first sight, gave him another bullet through the lungs with my heavy rifle, and in a few moments he rolled over dead.

It was my thought always to keep a wounded bear from getting into the brush, as the blood trail would have ruined future shooting.

I think it important to point out that when my bullet struck this bear he bit for the wound. As he did so he was turned from his original direction, which would have carried him in one bound out of sight among the trees, and instead turned and galloped across our front, thereby giving me an opportunity to fire two more shots. It frequently happened that bears were turned from their original direction to the sides upon which they received the first bullet, and we always gave this matter careful consideration when making an approach.

My Aleuts were not permitted to shoot unless we were following up a wounded bear in the thick brush; but I found it most difficult to keep them to this rule. The large hole of the bullet from my .50-caliber which Nikolai carried made it easy to distinguish his hits, and if a bear had received the mortal wound from his rifle, I should not have kept the skin.

The pelt of this bear which we had just killed was in excellent condition, and although he was not fat, he was of fair size, measuring 6 feet 3-1/8 inches along the vertebrae.

Great care was taken as usual to pick up the empty cartridge shells, and we pulled up the bloody bits of grass, throwing them into a brook, into which we put also the bear's carcass.

The storm continued for several days, and was accompanied by an unfavorable wind, which drew up into all our shooting grounds. We kept quietly in camp, which was so situated that although we were just opposite the great marsh, our scent was carried safely away. Then we were most careful to have only small fires for our cooking, and we were extremely particular to select dry wood, so that there would be as little smoke as possible.

All this while we kept a constant watch upon the meadow, but no bears made their appearance.

On the morning of the 19th, my friend and his hunter went up the shore to investigate a small marsh lying a mile or so from camp. Here they saw that the grass had been recently nibbled, and that there were fresh signs about. They returned to this spot again that evening and sighted a bear. The bear fed quickly up to within sixty-five yards, when Blake rolled him over. This bear was not a large one, and was of the usual tawny color.

The next morning a bear was seen by my natives in the big meadow by our camp, but he did not remain long enough for a stalk. At 9:30 he again came out into the open, and Nikolai and I made a quick approach, but the bear, although he was not alarmed, did not wait long enough for us to get within range. We had skirted the marsh, keeping just inside of the thicket, and now when the bear disappeared we settled ourselves for a long wait should he again come into the open. We were well hidden from view, and the wind blew slanting in our faces and across our front. I had just begun to think that we should not get a shot until the bear came out for his evening feed, when Nikolai caught my arm and pointed ahead. There, slowly leaving the dense edge of the woods, was a new bear, not so large as the first, but we could see at a glance that she had a beautiful coat of a dark silver-tip color.

Removing boots and stockings, and circling around, we came out about seventy-five yards from where we had last seen the bear; but she had moved a short distance ahead, and offered us a grand chance for a close approach. Keeping behind a small point which made out into the open, we were able to crawl up to within fifty yards, and then, waiting until the bear's head was up, I gave her a quartering shot behind the shoulders. She half fell, and bit for the wound, and as she slowly started for the woods I gave her another shot which rolled her over. This bear proved to be a female, the first we had shot upon the mainland, probably the mate of the bear we had originally attempted to stalk. The skin, although small, was the most beautiful I have ever killed.

Upon examining the internal effects of my shots, I was disappointed to find that my first bullet, on coming in contact with one of the ribs, had torn away from the metal jacket and had expanded to, such an extent that it lost greatly in penetration. I had of late been forced to the conclusion that the small-bore rifle I was using on such heavy game lacked the stopping force I had credited it with, and that the bullets were not of sufficient weight.

The next morning I sent our men to the main camp for provisions, for we now intended to give this marsh a rest, and go to the head of the bay. They returned that evening, and reported that they had seen a bear on the mountain side; they had stalked to within close range, and had made an easy kill. They had but one rifle with them, and had taken turns, Ivan having the first shot, while Nikolai finished the bear off. This skin was a beautiful one, of light yellowish color, and although our men wanted to present it to us, neither Blake nor I cared to bring it home with the trophies we had shot.

On June 23 we turned our baidarkas' bows to the upper bay, at the head of which we ascended a small river that wound through a vast meadow until the stream met the mountains. Here we unloaded our simple camp gear, and while the men prepared breakfast, Blake and I ascended an elevation which commanded an uninterrupted view of the grassy plain. No bears were in sight, so we had time and undisturbed opportunity to enjoy the beauty of the scene. We lay for some time basking in the sun, talking of books and people, and of many subjects of common interest. Now and then one would take the glasses and scan the outskirts of the vast meadow which stretched before us. All at once Blake gave a low exclamation and pointed to the west. I followed the direction of his gaze, and saw four bears slowly leaving the woods. They were at some distance, and we did not think we had time to reach them before they would probably return to the underbrush for their mid-day sleep, so for the present we let them go.

After breakfast, as they were still In the same place, we attempted the stalk, going most of the way in our baidarkas, winding in and out through the meadow in the small lagoons which intersected it in all directions. Every little while the men would ascend the banks with the glasses, thus keeping a watchful eye upon the bears' movements. Taking a time when they had fed into the underbrush, we made a quick circle to leeward over the open, then reaching the edge of the thicket, we approached cautiously to a selected watching place. We reached this spot shortly after one o'clock. The bears had entered the woods, so we settled ourselves for a long wait. It was Blake's turn to shoot, which meant that he was to have an undisturbed first shot at the largest bear, and after he had fired I could take what was left.

Just before three o'clock three bears again made their appearance. Two were yearlings which in the fall would leave their mother and shift for themselves, and one much larger, which lay just at the edge of the underbrush. Had these yearlings not been with the mother she would not have come out so early in the afternoon, and, as it was, she kept in the shadow of the alders, while the two smaller ones fed out some distance from the woods.

We now removed our boots, and, with Stereke well in hand, for he smelt the bears and was tugging hard on his collar, noiselessly skirted the woods, keeping some tall grass between the bears and ourselves. In this way we approached to within one hundred yards. Twice one of the smaller animals rose on his hind legs and looked in our direction; but the wind was favorable, and we were well concealed, so they did not take alarm.

My friend decided to shoot the mother, while I was to reserve my fire until after his shot. I expected that at the report of his rifle the bear I had chosen would pause a moment in surprise, and thus offer a good standing shot. As my friend's rifle cracked, the bear I had selected made a sudden dash for the woods, and I had to take him on the run. At my first shot he turned a complete somersault, and then, quickly springing up, again made a dash for cover. I fired a second time, and rolled him over for good and all. Stereke was instantly slipped, and made at once for my bear. By the time we had run up he was shaking and biting his hindquarters in a most approved style. We at once put him after the larger bear, which Blake had wounded, and his bark in the thick alders told us he had located her. We all followed in and found that the bear, although down, was still alive. Blake gave her a final shot through the lungs.

The third bear got away, but I believe it was wounded by Nikolai. The one that Blake had killed was the largest female we got on the Peninsula, measuring 6 feet 6 feet 6-1/2 inches along the vertebrae.

It is interesting to note that the two yearlings differed greatly in color. One was a grizzled brown, like the mother, while the other was very much lighter, of a light dirty yellowish color.

We had watched these bears for some hours in the morning, and I feel positive that the mother had no cubs of this spring with her; yet on examination milk was found in her breasts. My natives told me that frequently yearling cubs continue to suckle, and surely we had positive proof of this with the large female bear.

On our way back to camp that night we saw two more bears on the other side of the marsh, but they did not stay in the open sufficiently long to allow us to come up.

The mosquitoes had by this time become almost unbearable, and it was late before they permitted us to get to sleep. About 3 A.M. it began to rain, but I was so tired that I slept on, although my pillow and blankets were soon well soaked. As the rain continued, we finally put up our small tent; but everything had become thoroughly wet, and we passed a most uncomfortable day.

In the afternoon a black bear appeared not far from our camping place. My friend went after this with his hunter, who made a most wonderful stalk. The bear was in an almost unapproachable position, and the two men appeared to be going directly down wind; but Ivan insisted that there was a slight eddy in the breeze, and in this he must have been correct, for he brought Blake up to within sixty yards, when my friend killed the bear with a bullet through the brain.

I think it is interesting to note that our shooting grounds were the extreme western range of the black bear. A few years ago they were not found in this locality, but it is quite evident that they are each year working further and further to the westward.

The next day the heavy rain still continued. The meadow was now one vast bog, and the small lagoons were swollen into deep and rapid streams. Everything was wet, and we passed an uncomfortable day. Our two hunters were camped about fifty yards off under a big rock, and I think must have had a pretty hard time of it, but all the while they kept a sharp lookout.

About one o'clock the men reported that a large bear had been seen some distance off, but that it had remained in sight only a short time. We expected this bear would again make his appearance in the afternoon, and in this surmise we were correct, for he came out into the open three hours later, when Nikolai and I with Stereke made the stalk. We circled well to leeward, fording the many rapid streams with great difficulty. The rain had melted the snow on the hills, and we frequently had to wade almost up to our shoulders in this icy water.

In crossing one of the lagoons Stereke was carried under some fallen trees, and for a while I very much feared that my dog would be drowned. The same thing almost happened to myself, for the swift current twice carried me off my feet.

The bear had fed well into the open, and it was impossible, even by the most careful stalking, to get nearer than a small patch of tall grass about 175 yards away. I put up my rifle to shoot, but found that the front sight was most unsteady, for I was wet to the skin and shaking all over with cold. Half expecting to miss, I pressed the trigger, and was not greatly surprised to see my bullet splash in the marsh just over the bear's head. He saw the bullet strike on the other side, and now came in our direction, but Stereke, breaking loose from Nikolai, turned him. He now raced across our front at about 125 yards, with the dog in close pursuit. This gave me an excellent chance, and I fired three more shots. At my last, I saw the bear bite for his shoulder, showing that my bullet was well placed. He continued to dash ahead, when Nikolai fired, also hitting him in the shoulder with the heavy rifle. He dropped, but gamely tried to rise and face Stereke, who savagely attacked his quarters. Nikolai now fired again, his bullet going in at the chest, raking him the entire length, and lodging under the skin at the hind knee joint. Unfortunately this bear fell in so much water that it was impossible to take any other accurate measurement than the one along his back. This was the largest bear we shot on the mainland, and the one measurement that I was able to take was 6 feet 10 inches along the vertebrae.

[Illustration: THE HUNTER AND HIS HOME]

On examining the internal effects of his wounds, I found that my bullet had struck the shoulder blade and penetrated one lung, but had gone to pieces on coming in contact with the bone. Although it would have eventually proved a mortal wound, the shock at the time was not sufficient to knock the bear off his feet.

The next morning the storm broke, and we started back to our camp behind the rocks, for the skins we had recently shot needed to be cleaned and dried. We reached camp that afternoon, where I found my old hunter, Fedor, who was now better, and had come to join us. He had arrived the night before, and reported that he had seen three bears on the marsh. He said he had watched them all the evening, and that the next morning two more had made their appearance. He could no longer withstand this temptation, and just before we had arrived had shot a small black bear with an excellent skin.

Two days after, a bear was reported in the meadow, and as it was my friend's turn to shoot, he started with his hunter to make the stalk. It was raining at the time, and I was almost tempted to lie among my blankets; but my love of sport was too strong, and, armed with powerful glasses, I joined the men on the rocks to watch the hunters.

The bear had fed well out into the meadow not far from a small clump of trees. In order to reach this clump of trees, Blake and Ivan were obliged to wade quite a deep stream, and had removed their clothes. Unfortunately my friend carelessly left his coat, in the pocket of which were all the extra cartridges for his and Ivan's rifles.

I saw them reach the clump of trees, and then turned the glasses on the bear.

At the first shot he sprang back in surprise, while Blake's bullet went high. The bear now located the shot, and began a quick retreat to the woods, when one of my friend's bullets struck him, rolling him over. He instantly regained his feet, and continued making for cover, walking slowly and looking back over his shoulder all the while. Blake now fired another shot, and again the bear was apparently badly hit. He moved at such a slow pace that I thought he had surely received a mortal wound.

Entirely against orders, Ivan now shot three times in quick succession, hitting the bear with one shot in the hind leg, his other two shots being misses. Blake now rushed after the bear with his hunter following some fifty yards behind, and approached to within ten steps, when he fired his last cartridge, hitting the bear hard. The beast fell upon its head, but once more regaining its feet, continued toward the woods. At this point Ivan fired his last cartridge, but missed. The bear continued for several steps, while the two hunters stood with empty rifles watching. Suddenly, quick as a flash, he swung round upon his hind legs and gave one spring after Blake, who, not understanding his Aleut's shouts not to run, started across the marsh, with the bear in close pursuit. At every step the bear was gaining, and Ivan, appreciating that unless the bear's attention was distracted, my friend would soon be pulled down, began waving his arms and shouting at the top of his voice, in order to attract the bear's attention from Blake. The latter saw that his hunter was standing firm, and, taking in the situation, suddenly stopped. The bear charged to within a few feet of the two men; but, when he saw their determined stand, paused, and, swinging his head from side to side, watched them for some seconds, apparently undecided whether to charge home or leave them. Then he turned, and, looking back over his shoulder, made slowly for the woods.

This bear while charging had his head stretched forward, ears flat, and teeth clinched, with his lips drawn well back, and his eyes glaring. I am convinced that it was only Ivan's great presence of mind which prevented a most serious accident.

It is a strange fact that a well placed bullet will knock the fight out of such game; but if they are once thoroughly aroused it takes much more lead to kill them. When they had got more cartridges my friend with two natives proceeded to follow this bear up; but though they tracked him some miles, he was never recovered.

The Aleuts when they follow up a wounded bear in thick cover, strip to the skin, for they claim in this way they are able to move with greater freedom, and at the same time there are no clothes to catch in the brush and make noise. They go slowly and are most cautious, for frequently when a bear is wounded, if he thinks that he is being pursued, he will swing around on his own trail and spring out from the side upon the hunters.

The next day I started with my two natives to visit a meadow well up the bay.

As we had but a day or two left before the schooner would come to take us away, we headed in the only direction in which the wind was favorable. We left camp about three o'clock in the afternoon, following the shore with the wind quartering in our faces. We had gone but a mile from camp when I caught an indistinct outline of a bear feeding on the grass at the edge of the timber, about 125 yards away. I quickly fired, missing through sheer carelessness.

At the report the bear jumped sideways, unable to locate the sound, and my next bullet struck just above his tail and ranged forward into the lungs. Fedor now fired, missing, while I ran up with Nikolai, firing another shot as I ran, which knocked the bear over. Stereke savagely attacked the bear, biting and shaking him, and seeing that he was breathing his last, I refrained from firing again, as the skin was excellent.

This bear had had an encounter with a porcupine. One of his paws was filled with quills, and in skinning him we found that some quills had worked well up the leg and lodged by the ankle joint, making a most loathsome wound.

This bear was almost as large as the one I had last shot at the head of the bay, and his pelt made a grand trophy. I was much disgusted with myself that afternoon for missing my first shot. It is not enough simply to get your bear, but one should always endeavor to kill with the first shot, otherwise much game will be lost, for the first is almost always the easiest shot, hence one should kill or mortally wound at that chance.

This was the last bear that we shot on the Alaska Peninsula. I had been fortunate in killing seven brown bears, while Blake had killed three brown and one black, and our natives had killed one brown and one black bear, making a total of thirteen between the 7th and 28th of June.

The skulls of these brown bears we sent to Dr. Merriam, Chief of the Biological Survey, at Washington, and they proved to be most interesting from a scientific point of view, for from them the classification of the bears of the Alaska Peninsula has been entirely changed, and it seems that we were fortunate enough to bring out material enough to establish a new species as well as a new sub-species.

The teeth of these two kinds of bears show a marked and uniform difference, proving conclusively that there is no interbreeding between the species. I was told by Dr. Merriam that the idea which is so commonly believed, that different species of bears interbreed like dogs, is entirely wrong.

III.

MY BIG BEAR OF SHUYAK

As I had been fortunate in shooting bears upon the Island of Kadiak and the Alaska Peninsula, nothing remained but for me to obtain a specimen from one of the outlying islands of the Kadiak group, to render my trip in every way successful.

I therefore determined to take my two natives and hunt from a baidarka the deep bays of the Island of Afognak, while Blake, not yet having obtained his bear from Kadiak, went back to hunt there.

He had been extremely good to his men, and in settling with them on his return from the Alaska Peninsula had good-naturedly paid the excessive demands they made. The result was that his kindness was mistaken for weakness, and just as he was about to leave his hunters struck for an increase of pay. He sent them to the right-about, and fortunately succeeded in filling their places.

A sportsman in going into a new country owes it to those who follow to resist firmly exorbitant demands and at the same time to be fair and just in all his dealings.

I have already described bear hunting in the spring, when we stalked our game upon the snowy hillsides, and again on the Alaska Peninsula, where we hunted across the open on foot, and also in the baidarka. I will now speak of another form.

Toward the end of June the red salmon begin to run. These go up only the streams that have their sources in lakes. After the red salmon, come the humpbacks, and after the humpbacks, the dog salmon. Both of these latter in great numbers force their way up all the streams, and are the favorite food of the bears, which come down from the mountains by deep, well-defined trails to catch the fish in the shallow streams. When the salmon have begun to run, the only practical way of hunting these bears is by watching some likely spot on the bank of a stream.

Early in July Blake and I parted, intending to meet again two weeks later. My friend sailed away in a small schooner, while I left with my two natives in the baidarka. In Fedor's place I had engaged a native by the name of Lofka. We three paddled with a will, as we were anxious to reach a deep bay on the north side of the Island of Afognak as soon as possible.

This was all familiar country to me, for I had spent over a month in this locality the year before, and as we camped for the night I could hardly realize that twelve months had gone by since I left this beautiful spot. For the Island of Afognak, with its giant cliffs and deep bays, is to my mind one of the most picturesque regions I have ever seen.

The next morning the wind was unfavorable, but in the afternoon we were able to visit one of the salmon streams. The red salmon had come, but it would be another week or more before the humpbacks would begin their run. It was a bleak day, with the rain driving in our faces. We forced our way up the banks of a stream for some miles, following well-defined bear trails through the tall grass. Some large tracks were seen, but we sighted no game. We returned to camp after ten o'clock that night, wet to the skin and chilled through. The following day was a repetition of this, only under worse weather conditions, if that were possible.

I now decided to push on to a large bay on the northeast side of the island.

This is locally known as Seal Bay, and is supposed to be without question the best hunting ground on Afognak.

Unfortunately a heavy wind detained us in Paramonoff Bay for two days. The morning after the storm broke we made a four o'clock start. There was a strong favoring breeze, and we made a sail of one of the blankets. The baidarka fairly flew, but it was rather ticklish work, as the sea was quite rough. Early that afternoon we turned into the narrow straits which lie between the islands of Afognak and Shuyak. Shuyak is uninhabited, but some natives have hunting barabaras there. Formerly this island contained great numbers of silver gray foxes. A few years ago some white trappers visited it and put out poison. The result was the extermination of all the foxes upon the island, for not only the foxes that ate the poison died, but the others which ate the poisoned carcasses. The hunters obtained but one skin, as the foxes died in their holes or in the woods, and were not found until their pelts were spoiled. This is a fair example of the great need for Alaskan game laws.

At the present time Shuyak is rich in bear and in land otter, and I can imagine no better place for a national game preserve. It has lakes and salmon streams, and would be an ideal place to stock.

The straits between Shuyak and Afognak are extremely dangerous, for the great tides from Cook Inlet draw through this narrow passage. My nerve was tested a bit as the baidarka swept by the shore, for had it once got well started we should have been drawn into the rapids and then into a long line of angry breakers beyond. At one point it seemed as if we were heading right into these dangerous waters, and then abruptly turning at a sharp angle, we glided around a point into a shallow bay. Circling this shore we successfully passed inside the line of breakers and soon met the long ground swell of the Pacific, while Seal Bay stretched for many miles inland on the other side.

It had been a long day, but as the wind was favorable we stopped only for a cup of tea and then pushed on to the very head of the bay. Here, at the mouth of a salmon stream, we came upon many fresh bear tracks, and passed the night watching. As we had seen nothing by four o'clock in the morning, we cautiously withdrew, and, going some distance down the shore, camped in an old hunting barabara. It had been rather a long stretch, when one considers that we had breakfasted a little over twenty-four hours before. Watching a salmon stream by night is poor sport, but it is the only kind of hunting that one can do at this time of the year.

I slept until seven o'clock, when the men called me, and after a cup of tea we started for the salmon stream, which we followed up beyond where we had watched it the night previous. We were very careful to wade so as not to give our scent to any bears which might approach the stream from below. There were many tracks and deep, well-used trails leading in all directions, while every few yards we came upon places where the tall grass was trampled down, showing where bears had been fishing. These bear trails are quite a feature of the Alaskan country, and some of them are two feet wide and over a foot deep, showing that they have been in constant use for many years.

That night we heard a bear pass within ten yards of us, but could not see it. We returned to camp next morning at five o'clock, and I wrote up my journal, for this night work is extremely confusing, and one completely loses track of the days unless careful.

My men came to me after their mid-day sleep with very cheerful countenances, and assured me that there was no doubt but that I should surely soon meet with success, for the palm of Nikolai's hand had been itching, and he had dreamed of blood and a big dog fighting, while Lofka's eyelid trembled. My hunters told me in all seriousness that these signs never failed.

In the afternoon we decided to watch a new place. We carried the baidarka up a small stream and launched it in quite a large and picturesque lake. We slowly paddled along the shores and watched near the mouths of several salmon streams. By twelve o'clock we had not even seen a track, so I decided to return to camp and get some much needed sleep. The natives were to call me early the next morning, for I had decided to return to Paramonoff Bay.

I think this was the only time in my hunting life that I was deliberately lazy; but, although my natives called me several times, I slept right on until nine o'clock. I was strongly tempted when we got under way to start back by continuing around the Island of Afognak; but Nikolai was anxious to have me give Paramonoff Bay another trial. He thought the run of the humpback salmon might have begun since we left, and if this was so, we were likely to find some large bears near the streams we had watched the week before. I had great confidence in his judgment, and therefore decided to retrace our steps.

We made a start about ten o'clock, but after a couple of hours' paddling, when we had met a fair tide to help us on, I lit my pipe and allowed my men to do all the work, while I lay back among my rugs half dreaming in the charm of my surroundings. Myriads of gulls flew overhead, uttering their shrill cries, while now and then the black oyster-catchers with their long red bills would circle swiftly around the baidarka, filling the air with their sharp whistles, and seemingly much annoyed at our intrusion. Many different kinds of ducks rose before us, and the ever-present eagles watched us from the lofty rocks. We soon turned the rugged headland and were once more in the swift tide of Shuyak Straits, where the water boiled and eddied about us as we sped quickly on.

Nikolai now pointed out one of his favorite hunting grounds for seals, and asked if he might not try for one; so we turned into a big bay, and he soon had the glasses in use. He at once sighted several lying on some rocks, and we had just started in their direction when Nikolai suddenly stopped paddling, again seized the glasses, and looked excitedly across the straits to the Shuyak shore. Following the direction of his gaze I saw upon the beach a black speck which my native at once pronounced to be a bear. He was nosing around among some seaweed and turning over the rocks in search of food. Each one of us now put all his strength into every stroke in order to reach the other side before the bear could wander off. We cautiously landed behind some big rocks, and quickly removing our boots my hunter and I were soon on shore and noiselessly peering through the brush to the place where we had last seen the bear; but he had disappeared.

The wind was favorable, and we knew that he had not been alarmed. It took us some time to hit off his trail, for he had wandered in all directions before leaving this place; but after it was once found, his footprints in the thick moss made tracking easy, and we moved rapidly on. We had not expected a long stalk, and our feet were badly punished by the devil clubs which were here most abundant. We could see by the tracks that the bear had not been alarmed, and knew that we should soon come up with him. After a mile or so the trail led in the direction of a low marsh where the coast line makes a big bend inward, so apparently we had crossed a long point into a bay beyond.

I at once felt sure that the bear was near, having probably come to this beach to feed, and as Nikolai looked at me and smiled I knew he, too, felt that we were on a warm trail.

We had just begun to descend toward the shore when I thought I heard a slight noise ahead. Keeping my eyes fixed in that direction, I whispered to Nikolai, who was standing a few feet in front of me, intently peering to the right. Suddenly I caught just a glimpse of a tawny, brownish bit of color through the brush a short distance ahead. Quickly raising my rifle I had just a chance for a snap shot, and the next instant a large hear made a dash through some thick underbrush. It was but an indistinct glimpse which I had had, and before I could throw another cartridge into the barrel of my rifle the bear was out of sight. Keeping my eyes moving at about the rate of speed I judged he was going, I fired again through the trees, and at once a deep and angry growl told me that my bullet had gone home.

Then we raced ahead, my hunter going to the left while I entered the thick brush into which the bear had disappeared. I had gone but a short distance when I heard Nikolai shoot three times in rapid succession, and as quickly as I could break through I hurried in his direction. It seemed that as we separated, Nikolai had at once caught sight of the bear slowly making away. He immediately fired but missed; at the report of his rifle the bear turned and came toward him, but was too badly wounded by my first two shots to be dangerous. At close range Nikolai fired two more shots, and it was at this moment that I joined him. The bear was down, but trying hard to get upon his feet, and evidently in an angry mood, so I ran up close and gave him another shot, which again knocked him over.

Now for the first time I had a good view of the bear, which proved to be a very large one. As my men declared that this was one of the largest they had ever seen, I think we may safely place it as a fair example of the Kadiak species. Unfortunately I had no scales with me, and could not, therefore, take its weight; but the three of us were unable to budge either end from the ground, and after removing the pelt the carcass appeared to be as large as a fair sized ox. We had much difficulty in skinning him, for he fell on his face, and it took us some half hour even to turn him over; we were only able to do this by using his legs as levers. It required over two hours to remove the pelt. Then we had tea and shot the bear all over again many times, as we sat chatting before the fire.

It seemed that at the time when I had first caught sight of this bear, Nikolai had just located the bear which we had originally seen and were following, and it was a great piece of luck my taking this snap shot, for the other bear was much smaller.

We took the skin and skull with us, while I made arrangements with my natives to return some months later and collect all the bones, for I decided to present the entire skeleton to the National Museum.

It was six o'clock when we again made a start. I had a deep sense of satisfaction as I lay lazily back in the baidarka with the large skin at my feet, only occasionally taking the paddle, for it had been a hard trip, and I felt unlike exerting myself. We camped that night in a hunting barabara which belonged to Nikolai, and was most picturesquely situated on a small island.

My natives were extremely fond of bear meat, and they sat long into the night gorging themselves. Each one would dig into the kettle with his fork, and bringing out a big chunk would crowd as much as possible into his mouth, and holding it there with his teeth would cut off with his hunting knife a liberal portion, which he would swallow after a munch or two.

I had tried to eat Kadiak bear before, but it has rather a bitter taste, and this one was too tough to be appetizing. The flesh of the bears which we had killed on the Alaska Peninsula was excellent and without this strong gamy flavor.[5]

[Footnote 5: The true Kadiak bear is found only on the Kadiak Islands and not on the mainland.]

The next morning we made an early start, for to save this large skin I had decided to push on with all haste to the little settlement of Afognak, where I had arranged to meet my friend some days later. It was a beautiful morning, and once more we had a favoring breeze. Some forty miles across Shelikoff Straits was the Alaskan shore. The rugged, snow-clad mountains seemed to be softened when seen through the hazy blue atmosphere. One white-capped peak boldly pierced a line of clouds and stood forth against the pale blue of the sky beyond; while the great Douglas Glacier, ever present, wound its way down,

down to the very sea. It was all grandly beautiful, and seemed In keeping with the day.

We paddled steadily, stopping only once for tea, and at six o'clock that evening were back at the little fishing hamlet of Malina Place. Here I was asked to drink tea with a man whom my hunters told me had killed many bears on these islands.

This man said that at times there were no bears on Shuyak, and that again they were there in great numbers, showing that they freely swim from Afognak across the straits, which, at the narrowest point, are some three miles wide.

While I was having tea in one of the barabaras I heard much shooting outside, which announced the return of a sea otter party that had been hunting for two months at Cape Douglas. It was a beautiful sight, this fleet of twenty odd baidarkas, the paddles all rising and falling in perfect time, and changing sides without a break. There is nothing more graceful than one of these canoes when handled by expert Aleuts. These natives had already come forty miles that day, and were now going to stop only long enough for tea, and then push on to the little settlement of Afognak Place, some twenty-five miles away, where most of them lived. In one of the canoes I saw a small chap of thirteen years. He was the chief's son, and already an expert in hunting and in handling the baidarka. So is the Aleut hunter trained.

As it had been a very warm day I feared that the skin might spoil. Therefore I concluded to continue to Afognak Place without camping for the night, and so we paddled on and on. As darkness came, the mountains seemed to rise grander and more majestic from the water on either side of us. At midnight we again stopped for tea, and while we sat by the fire the host of baidarkas of the sea otter party silently glided by like shadows. We joined them, for my men had much to tell of their four months with the white hunter, and many questions were asked on both sides.

Some miles from Afognak the baidarkas drew up side by side in a long, even line, our baidarka joining in. Drasti and _Chemi_[6] came to me from all sides, for I had from time to time met most of the native hunters of this island, and they seemed to regard me as quite one of them.

[Footnote 6: Russian and Aleut for "How do you do?"]

When all the straggling baidarkas had caught up and taken their places in the line, the chief gave the word Kedar ("Come on"), and we all paddled forward, and just as the sun was rising above the hills we reached our journey's end.

Two days later my friend joined me. He also had been successful, and had killed a good sized male bear in Little Uganuk Bay on Kadiak Island.

Our bear hunt was now over, and we had been fortunate in accomplishing all we had hoped for.

IV.

THE WHITE SHEEP OF KENAI PENINSULA

The last of July Blake and I sailed from the Kadiak Islands, and one week later were landed at the little settlement of Kenai, on the Kenai Peninsula.

The mountains of this region are unquestionably the finest big-game shooting grounds in North America at the present day. Here one may expect to find four different kinds of bears--black, two species of brown, and the Alaska grizzly-- the largest of moose, and the Kenai form of the white sheep (_Ovis dalli_).

These hills lie back from the coast some thirty miles, and may be reached by one of several rivers. It takes a couple of days to ascend some of these streams, but we determined to select a country more difficult to enter, thinking it would be less often visited by the local native hunters. We therefore chose the mountains lying adjacent to the Kenai Lake--a district which it took from a week to ten days to reach.

On August 14, shortly after noon, we started up the river which was to lead us to our shooting grounds. One cannot oppose the great tides of Cook Inlet, and all plans are based on them. Therefore we did not leave until the flood, when we were carried up the stream some twelve miles--the tide limit--where we camped.

The next morning we were up at daylight, for at this point began the hard river work. There was much brush on the banks, but our natives proved themselves most expert in passing the line, for from now on until we reached the lake our boats had to be towed against a swift current.

That day we made about eight miles, and camped shortly after five o'clock. It rained hard during the night, and the next morning broke cloudy. The river for the first two days wound through the lowlands, but from this point on the banks seemed higher and the current perceptibly swifter, while breaking water showed the presence of rocks under the surface. The country back from the stream began to be more rolling, and as the river occasionally made some bold bend the Kenai Mountains could be seen in the distance.

Again it rained hard during the night and continued well on into the next morning, so we made a late start, breaking camp at eight o'clock. Spruce, alders, willows, and birch were the trees growing along the banks, and we now passed through the country where the moose range during the summer months. Already the days had become perceptibly shorter, and there was also a feeling of fall in the air, for summer is not long in this latitude.

At this point in the river we encountered bad water, and all hands were constantly wet, while the natives were in the glacial stream up to their waists for hours at a time. Therefore we made but little progress. That night there was a heavy frost, and the next morning dawned bright and clear. The day was a repetition of the day before, and the natives were again obliged to wade with the tow-line most of the way. But they were a good-natured lot, and seemed to take their wetting as a matter of course. About ten o'clock the next morning we reached the Kenai Rapids, where the stream narrows and the water is extremely bad, for the current is very swift and the channel full of rocks. We navigated this place safely and came out into the smooth water beyond. Here we had tea and a good rest, for we felt that the hardest part of this tiresome journey was over. Above the rapids there are a few short stretches of less troubled water where the oars can be used; but these are few and far between, and one must count upon warping the boat from tide water to within two miles of the lake--an estimated distance of between thirty-five and forty miles.

We had hardly got started the following day before it began to rain heavily. We were soon wet to the skin and thoroughly chilled, but we kept on until late in the afternoon, when we camped in a small Indian cabin some three miles from the lake.

It stormed hard during the night with such heavy wind that we much feared that we should be unable to cross the lake the next day. In the morning, however, the wind had gone down, and we made an early start. Just before reaching the mouth of the river we sighted game for the first time. A cow moose with her calf were seen on the bank. They stood idly watching our boats for a short time, and then slowly ambled off into the brush.

Occasionally as the river had made some big bend we had been able to sight the mountains which were to be our shooting grounds. Day by day they had grown nearer and nearer, and finally, after one week of this toilsome travel, we glided from the river to the crescent-shaped lake, and they now rose close before us.

This range of hills with their rough and broken sides compares favorably in grandeur with the finest of Alaskan scenery. Half way up their slopes was a well defined timber line, and then came the stunted vegetation which the autumn frosts had softened into velvet browns in deep contrast to the occasional berry patches now tinged a brilliant crimson; and beyond, the great bleak, open tablelands of thick moss sloped gently upward to the mountain bases; and above all, the lofty peaks of dull gray rock towered in graceful curves until lost in the mist. Great banks of snow lay in many of the highest passes, and over all the landscape the sun shone faintly through leaden and sombre storm clouds.

Such was my first near view of the Kenai Mountains, and, as I learned to know them better, they seemed to grow more awe-inspiring and beautiful.

When we reached Kenai Lake, Blake and I decided that it would probably be the wisest plan to divide things up into two separate shooting outfits. We could then push over the hills in different directions until we came upon the sheep. Each would then make his own shooting camp, and our natives would carry out the heads we might shoot to our united base of supplies on the lake, and pack back needed provisions.

At noon of August 22 Blake and outfit started for his shooting grounds at the eastern end of the sheep range, and shortly after my outfit was under way. My head man and the natives carried packs of some sixty pounds, while I carried about fifty pounds besides my rifle, glasses, and cartridges; even my dog Stereke had some thirty pounds of canned goods in a pack saddle.

Our first march led up the mountain over a fairly steep trail, a gale accompanied by rain meeting us as we came out from the timber on to the high mossy plateau. The wind swept down from the hills in great gusts, and our small tent tugged and pulled at its stakes until I greatly feared it would not stand the strain. It had moderated somewhat by the next morning, and we made an early start.

Our line of march, well above timber, led along the base of the summits for some miles, then swinging to the left we laboriously climbed over one range and dropped into the valley beyond. A strong wind made it hard going, and sometimes turned us completely around as it struck slanting upon the packs which we carried. During the day sheep were seen in the distance, but we did not stop, for we were anxious to reach before dark a place where Hunter--my head man--had usually made his hill camp. It must be remembered that at such an altitude there is very little fuel, and that good camping places are few and far between.

The next morning we were up early, intending to take our first hunt, but the small Killy River, on which we were now located, was much swollen by the heavy rains, and could not be crossed. We devoted the forenoon to bridging this stream, but during the afternoon a small bunch of sheep was sighted low down on the mountains, and I started with Hunter to see if it contained any good rams. We left camp about noon and reached the sheep in a little over an hour. There was one ram which I shot for meat, but unfortunately his head was smaller than I thought, and valueless as a trophy.

As sheep hunting in these hills is at best hard work, I decided to move the camp as high up as we could find wood and water. The next morning as we started on our first real hunt, we took the native with us, and after selecting a spot at the edge of the timber line, left him to bring up our camp to this place while my man and I continued over the mountains in search of rams. The day was dull and the wind was fortunately light.

After a stiff climb we came out upon a mossy tableland, intersected by several deep gulches, down which tumbled rapid glacial streams from many perpetual snow banks. Above this high plateau rose sharp and barren mountains which seemed but glacial heaps of jagged boulders and slide rock all covered with coarse black moss or lichen, which is the only food of sheep during the winter months.

It is generally supposed that when the heavy snows of winter set in the sheep seek a lower level, but my guide insisted that they work higher and higher up the mountain sides, where the winds have swept the snow away, and they are able to get this coarse but nourishing food.

The sky-line of these hills made a series of unbroken curves telling of the mighty power of the glaciers which once held this entire country in their crushing grasp.

We passed over the great plateau, which even at this latitude was sprinkled generously with beautiful small wild flowers. Crossing gulch after gulch we continually worked higher and higher by a gradual and easy ascent.

We had been gone from camp but little over an hour, when, on approaching a small knoll, I caught sight of the white coat of a sheep just beyond. At once dropping upon my hands and knees I crawled up and carefully peered over to the other side. We had unknowingly worked into the midst of a big band of ewes, lambs, and small rams. I counted twenty-seven on my left and twenty-five on my right, but among them all there was not a head worth shooting.

This was the first great band of white sheep I had seen, and I watched them at this close range with much interest. Soon a tell-tale eddy in the breeze gave them our scent, and they slowly moved away, not hurriedly nor in great alarm, but reminding me much of tame sheep, or deer in a park. Man was rather an unfamiliar animal to them, and his scent brought but little dread. From this time until darkness hid them, sheep were in plain view the entire day. In a short while I counted over one hundred ewes and lambs.

We worked over one range and around another with the great valley of the river lying at our feet, while beyond were chain upon chain of bleak and rugged mountains. Finally we came to a vast gulch supposed to be the home of the large rams. My men had hunted in this section two years before, and had never failed to find good heads here, but we now saw nothing worth stalking. By degrees we worked to the top of the gulch, and coming to the summit of the ridge paused, for at our feet was what at first appeared but a perpendicular precipice of jagged rock falling hundreds of feet. The clouds now lifted a bit and we could see below a vast circular valley with green grass and rapid glacial streams. On all sides it was hemmed in and guarded by mighty mountains with giant cliffs and vast slides of broken rocks reaching from the bottom to the very summits. Opposite was a great dull blue glacier from which the north fork of the Killy River belched forth, while other smaller glaciers and snow banks seemed kept in place only by granite barriers.

We seated ourselves on the brink of this great cliff and the glasses were at once in use. Soon Hunter saw rams, but they were so far below that even with my powerful binoculars it was impossible to tell more than that they carried larger heads than other sheep near them.

It was impossible to descend the cliff at the point where we then were, so we moved around, looking for a place where we might work down, and finally found one where it was possible to descend some fifty yards to a sort of shute. From where we were we could not see whether we should be able to make a still further descent, and if we did go down that far it would be an extremely difficult climb to get back, but we thought it probable that there would be slide rock at the other end of this shute, in which case the rest would be fairly easy.

Moving with the greatest caution, we finally reached the shute, and after a bit of bad climbing found the slide rock at the lower end as we had expected; but it took us a good two hours to get low enough to tell with the glasses how big were the horns the sheep carried.

There were eight rams in all. A bunch of three small ones about half a mile away, and just beyond them four with better heads, but still not good enough to shoot, and apart from these, a short distance up the mountain side, was a solitary ram which carried a really good head. The bunch of three was unfortunately between us and the big sheep, and it required careful stalking to get within distance of the one we sought. We knew very well that if we suddenly alarmed the three, and they rushed off, they, in turn, would alarm the four and also the big ram. When we were still at some distance we showed ourselves to the three, and they took the hint and wandered slowly up the mountain side. The others, although they had not seen us, became suspicious, so we remained crouched behind some rocks until they once more began to feed. The big ram now came down from his solitary position and passed from view behind a mass of boulders near the remaining sheep.

The head of the ram which I had shot the day before was much smaller than I had supposed at the time. In order to avoid this in future I had asked Hunter to advise me in selecting only really good heads. My man, who now had the glasses, declared that the big sheep had not joined the bunch of four, and I must confess that I was also deceived.

Although the four had become suspicious from seeing the three go slowly up the cliff, still they had not made us out, and the wind remained favorable. Lying close only long enough for them to get over their uneasiness, we cautiously stalked up to within some two hundred yards. Again we used the glasses most carefully, but could not see the big ram. Suddenly the sheep became alarmed and started up the mountain. I expected each second to see the large ram come out from behind the boulders, and therefore withheld from shooting. But when he did not appear I turned my attention to the four which had paused and were looking down upon us from a rocky ridge nearly four hundred yards above. As they stood in bold relief against the black crags, I saw that one carried horns much larger than the others, and that it was the big ram. My only chance was to take this long shot. We had been crossing a snow bank at the time, and I settled myself, dug my heels well in, and with elbows resting on my knees took a steady aim. I was fortunate in judging the correct distance, for at the report of the rifle the big ram dropped, gave a few spasmodic kicks, and the next minute came rolling down the mountain side, tumbling over and over, and bringing with him a great shower of broken rocks. I feared that his head and horns would be ruined, but fortunately found them not only uninjured, but a most beautiful trophy. The horns taped a good 34 inches along the curve and 13-1/2 inches around the butts.

That night the weather changed, and thenceforth the mountains were constantly enveloped in mist, while it rained almost daily. These were most difficult conditions under which to hunt, for sheep have wonderful vision and can see a hunter through the mist long before they can be seen.

I was anxious to bring out as trophies only the finest heads, and daily refused chances which some might have gladly taken. If we could not plainly see with the naked eye horns at 300 to 400 yards, we always let the sheep pass, knowing that the head was small, but if at any time we could make out that a sheep carried a full turn to his horns, we knew that the head was well matured. If we saw a sheep facing us we could always tell when the horns made a full turn, for then the tips curved outward.

A week after killing the big ram we again visited the great basin, but found nothing, and cautiously moved a little higher to a sheltered position. From here we carefully scanned the bottom of this large gulch, and soon spied a bunch of ewes and lambs, and shortly afterward three medium sized rams. When we first saw them one had become suspicious and was looking intently in our direction, so we crouched low against the rocks, keeping perfectly still until they once more began to feed. When they had gradually worked over a slight knoll we made a quick approach, cautiously stalking up to the ridge over which the sheep had gone. I had expected to get a fair shot at two hundred yards or under, but when I peered over nothing was in sight. I concluded they had not gone up the mountain side, for their white coats against the black rocks would have rendered them easily seen. I, therefore, started to walk boldly in the direction in which we had seen them go, thinking they had probably taken shelter from the gale behind some rocks.

I had only gone some paces when we located them standing on a snow patch which had made them indistinguishable. I sat down and tried to shoot from my knees, but the wind was coming in such fierce gusts that I could not hold my rifle steady, so I ran as hard as I could in their direction, looking hastily about for some rock which would offer shelter.

The sheep made up the mountain side for some three hundred yards, when they paused to look back. I had by this time found a sheltered position behind a large boulder, and soon had one of the rams wounded, but, although I fired several shots I seemed unable to knock him off his feet. Fearing that I might lose him after all, I aimed for the second ram, which was now on the move some distance further up the mountain, and at my second shot he stopped. Climbing up to within one hundred and fifty yards I found that both the sheep were badly wounded, and were unable to go further, so I finished them off. What was my surprise to find that the larger ram had seven bullets in him, while the smaller one had three.

These sheep would almost never flinch to the shot, and it was difficult to tell when you had hit, unless in an immediately vital spot.

The weather continued unfavorable for hill shooting until the third of September, but that day opened bright and clear, and fearing lest the good conditions might not last, we made an early start. Crossing the high plateau we followed the valley of the Killy River, keeping well up and skirting the bases of the mountain summits. As we trudged along, the shrill cries of alarm of the whistling marmots were heard, and the little fellows could be seen in all directions scampering for their holes. Ptarmigan were also frequently met with, but not in such great numbers as one would have supposed in a region where they had never been hunted. On several occasions we found these birds on the highest summits where there was nothing but rocks covered with black moss. It would have been interesting to have shot one of them and learned upon what they were then feeding, but it was just in the locality where we hoped to find rams, and this was out of the question. That morning we traveled some distance before we saw sheep, but having once reached their feeding ground I had the satisfaction of watching more wild game than on any previous day.

The Kussiloff hills were dotted with scattered bands, and I counted in one large flock forty-eight, while the long and narrow valley on both sides of the stream was sprinkled with smaller bunches containing from two or three to twenty. It was a beautiful sight, for every ewe had at least one, and many of them two, lambs frolicking at her side.

In addition to these sheep we saw three moose feeding in a small green valley at the base of the opposite hills. The river was impassable for some miles, and although they were hardly more than a mile away in a straight line, they were quite unapproachable, so we sat and watched them with much interest until they slowly fed into the timber.

Shortly after noon we located some large sheep on a rocky knoll across the Killy River just below where the stream gushes out from a mighty glacier. They were a long way off, but with the glasses we could see that one lying apart from the others was a ram, and we surmised that if we could see his horns at such a distance even through the glasses he probably carried a good head.

Working down to the stream we finally found a point shallow enough to wade. We now made a cautious and careful stalk to the place where we had last located the sheep, but a bunch of ewes and a small ram were all that we could see.

Hunter and I were both much disgusted, for we had expected surely to find a head that was up to our standard.

It was well on in the afternoon when we started back to camp. We had been going steadily over the broken hillsides since early morning, and had met sheep at almost every turn. At the sight of us some would bound up the steep mountain sides in great alarm, while several times at only a couple of hundred yards others merely turned their heads in our direction, and after observing us for a short time continued to graze. Somehow these ewes seemed to understand that I had no intention of molesting them.

It is strange how the hope of seeing game keeps one from feeling tired, but as we trudged homeward, a bit depressed that in all the great number of sheep seen, there had not been one good head, and that our hard day was all to no purpose, my man and I both began to feel pretty well fagged out.

Late in the afternoon we paused for a brief rest and a smoke, and here Hunter sighted two lone rams in a gulch at the top of the mountain above us. By this time we were both pretty well used up, but the glasses showed that they carried good heads, and I determined to stalk them, even if it meant passing the night on the hills. So we worked our way up to the top of a ridge which commanded a view of the gulch in which the sheep were grazing, but they had fed some distance away by the time we reached the place where I had expected to shoot, and were at too long a range to make my aim certain. If we had had plenty of time, we should have worked up the ridge nearer, and this Hunter was still anxious for me to do, but when I saw one of the sheep suddenly raise his head and look intently in our direction I knew my only chance was to take the long shot. T had seen what the .30-40 Winchester rifle would do in the hills, and the question was one of holding. However, I could count on several shots before they ran out of sight, and even at such a distance I hoped to get one and possibly the pair. Both sheep carried good heads, but I aimed at the one which stood broadside to me. Hunter, who had the glasses, told me afterward that the ram with the more massive horns got away, but I succeeded in wounding the other so that he was unable to move. Knowing he would shortly die, and that I could find him the next morning, we at once started at our best pace for camp.

We only reached our tent at nine o'clock that night, both completely fagged out. A cup of tea made us feel better, but it was late before I could get to sleep. Such days are a bit too much for steady practice, but if they end in success the trophy means all the more.

The following day we were literally wind-bound, and not until the day after could we set out for the wounded sheep, which we eventually found, not fifty yards from where we had last seen him. It was a long and hard climb to reach him, but he carried a very pretty head with massive horns of over a full turn. I found that two shots of the seven which I had fired had taken effect.

Two days later the native arrived from the main camp with more provisions, and brought an interesting letter from Blake. It seemed that some Englishmen who had been hunting in these hills just before us had driven the big rams to the other end of the range, where my friend had been most fortunate in finding them. He strongly advised my leaving my present camp and coming to the country which he had just left, having got six excellent heads. This was the limit which we had decided upon as the number of sheep that we each wanted.

It was now apparently clear that I had been hunting at a great disadvantage in my district. On receiving Blake's letter I at once determined to retrace my steps to the main camp, go to the head of the lake and follow up the trail which he had laid out upon the mountains.

Therefore the next morning (September 7) we shouldered our packs and went over the hills to our main camp. Instead of following the trail by which we had come, we decided to push straight across country, hoping in this way to reach our main camp in one march. Our change of route was unfortunate, and this day I can easily put down as the hardest one I ever passed in the mountains.

In order to bring out all our belongings in one trip we had extra heavy packs, and the country over which we marched was very trying. About noon I spied sheep on one of the outlying hills, and as we came nearer I made out through the glasses that this was a bunch of five rams, and that three of them carried exceptionally good heads. My only chance was to push ahead of my men, and this I did, but stalking sheep over a rough country with a heavy pack on your back is very trying work, and I failed to connect with these rams.

About five o'clock in the afternoon we came down over the mountains on to the high plateau above our main camp. We were all too used up to go any further, or even put up our light tent, although it soon began to rain. We made a rude camp in a patch of stunted hemlocks, and as I sat before the fire having my tea, I chanced to look up on the hills before me, and there was the bunch of five rams I had tried so hard to stalk early in the afternoon. They were at no great distance, but it was rapidly growing dark, and there was not time to get within range while it would be light enough to shoot. So I sat and studied these sheep through the glasses, determined to find them later, even if it took me a month.

One of them had a most beautiful head, with long and massive horns well over the full turn. Another had a head which would have been equally good if the left horn had not been slightly broken at the tip. The third also had an excellent head, and although not up to the other two, his horns made the full turn. The remaining two rams were smaller. I watched them until darkness came on, and all this while they fed slowly back toward the mountains on which my friend had been hunting the week before. I am convinced that this bunch of sheep had been driven out of these hills by Blake, and had been turned back again by me.

It rained hard that night, and the next morning the clouds were so low that it was impossible to go in search of the rams I had seen the evening before. I, therefore, determined to push immediately to the main camp, which we reached three hours later. We at once lunched, and, putting our light outfit in one of the boats, rowed up to the head of the lake.

This range of hills is surrounded by a mighty glacier, and at the foot of the glacier is a moraine some ten miles long extending down to Kenai Lake. On one side of this moraine you can walk by skirting the shore and using care, but on the other side the quicksands are deep and dangerous. We camped for the night in a place which my friend had used as his base of supplies.

The next morning opened dull, and I felt the effects of my hard work and did not greatly relish the idea of shouldering a fifty-pound pack. But my time was now getting short. In two weeks the rutting season of the moose would begin, and in the meantime I wanted four more fine specimens of the white sheep. Any day we might expect a heavy fall of snow, for the northern winter had already begun in the hills.

We soon found the tracks of Blake's party, which led up the moraine, and carried us over quicksand and through glacial streams, icy cold. Finally we came to where Blake had started up the mountain side, and with all due regard to my friend, his trail was not an easy one. About noon it began to rain, but we pushed upward, although soon soaked to the skin, and came out above timber just at dark. We were all fagged out and shaking with cold by the time we reached Blake's old camp.

The next morning broke dismally with the floodgates of the heavens open and the rain coming down in torrents. I lay among my rugs and smoked one pipe after another in order to keep down my appetite, for there was little chance of making a fire to cook with. In fact, most of the day was passed in this way, for all the wood had become thoroughly water-soaked.

Late in the afternoon we succeeded in getting a fire started and had a square meal. While we were crouched around the blaze the natives saw sheep on the hills just above us, but it was raining so hard that it was impossible to tell if they were rams. In fact, when sheeps' coats are saturated with water they do not show up plainly when seen at any distance, and might easily be mistaken for wet rocks.

The next day opened just as dismally, with the storm raging harder than ever, but by eleven o'clock it began to let up, and we soon had our things drying in the wind, for the clouds looked threatening, and we feared the rain would begin again at any time.

As we were short of provisions and depended almost entirely upon meat, my head man and I started at once for the hills. The little stream by our camp was swollen into a rushing torrent, and we were obliged to go almost to its source-- a miniature glacier--before we could wade it. Climbing to the crest of the mountains on which we had seen the sheep the evening before, and following just under the sky line, we soon saw a large and two small rams feeding on a sheltered ledge before us.

We much feared that they would get: our scent, but by circling well around we succeeded in making a fair approach. I should have had an excellent shot at the big ram had not one of the smaller ones given the alarm. The gale was coming in such gusts that it was difficult to take a steady aim, and at my first shot the bullet was carried to one side. I fired again just as the sheep were passing from view, and succeeded in breaking the leg of the big ram. Hunter and I now raced after him, but the hillside was so broken that it was impossible to locate him, so my man went to the valley below where he could get a good view and signal to me.

It is always well in hill shooting to have an understood code of signals between your man and yourself. The one which I used and found most satisfactory provided that if my man walked to the right or left it meant that the game was in either of these directions; if he walked away from the mountain, it was lower down; if he approached the mountain, it was higher up.

As Hunter, after reaching the valley and taking a look with the glasses, began to walk away, I knew that the sheep was below me, and I suddenly came close upon the three, which had taken shelter from the gale behind a large rock. Very frequently sheep will remain behind with a wounded companion; especially is this so when it is a large ram. Now, unfortunately, one of the smaller rams got between me and the big one, and as I did not want to kill the little fellow the big ram was soon out of range. But he was too badly wounded to go far over such grounds, and I soon stalked up near, when I fired, breaking another leg, and then ran up and finished him off. This ram carried a very pretty head 13-1/2 inches around the butts and 36-1/4 inches along the curve, but unfortunately the left horn was slightly broken at the tip. It was undoubtedly an old sheep, as his teeth, worn to the gums, and the ten rings around his horns indicated.

When a ram's constitution has been undermined by the rutting season, the horns cease to grow, nor do they begin again until the spring of the year with its green vegetation brings nourishing food, and this is the cause of the rings, which, therefore, indicate the number of winters old a sheep is. This was my head man's theory, and is, I believe, a correct one, for in the smaller heads which I have examined these rings coincided with the age of the sheep as told by the teeth. Up to five years, the age of a sheep can always be determined by the incisor teeth; a yearling has but two permanent incisors, a two-year-old four, a three-year-old six, and a four-year-old or over eight teeth, or a full set.

It was unpleasantly cold upon the mountains this day, and as no other sheep could be seen, we returned to camp by five o'clock. This was the easiest day's shooting that I had had.

As we sat by the camp-fire that evening, four sheep were seen on the hills above us, two of which I recognized as the small rams that had been with the one I had just killed. We felt quite certain that these were the bunch of five rams which we had seen when we were packing out from our first hill camp. In fact, this was the only good band of rams which I saw during the entire hunt. If these were the same sheep, the two newcomers carried good heads, for, as previously stated, I had studied this lot carefully through the glasses.

The next day, the thirteenth and Friday, opened dismally enough, but by the time we had finished breakfast the mountains Were clear of clouds and there was no wind to mar one's shooting. Such conditions were to be taken advantage of, and Hunter and I were soon working up the ridge well to leeward of the place where we had seen the sheep the night before. Reaching the crest we scanned the grounds on all sides, and also the rugged mountain tops about us.

The white coats of these sheep against the dark background of black moss-covered rocks render them easily seen, but we now failed to sight any even on the distant hills. Therefore we pushed ahead, going stealthily up wind and keeping a careful watch on all sides. We crossed over the ridge and worked our way just below the sky-line on the other side of the mountain from our camp, never supposing that the sheep would work back, for they had seen our camp-fire on the night before. We traveled nearly to the end of the ridge, and were just about to cross and work down to a sheltered place where we expected to find our game, when Hunter chanced to look back, and instantly motioned me to drop out of sight.

While we had been working around one side of the summit the sheep had been working back on the other side, and we had passed them with the mountain ridge between. Fortunately they were all feeding with their heads away or they must have seen us as we came out on the sky-line. My man had the glasses and assured me that there were two excellent heads. We now felt quite certain that these were the sheep we knew so well.

We cautiously dropped out of sight and worked back, keeping the mountain ridge between us. We were well above and had a favorable wind and the entire day before us. It was the first and only time upon these hills that the conditions had all been favorable for a fair stalk and good shooting. Hunter did his part well, and brought me up to within one hundred and twenty-five yards of the rams, which were almost directly below us. They had stopped feeding and were lying down. Only one of the smaller sheep was visible, and my man advised me to take a shot at him, and then take the two large ones as they showed themselves. Aiming low, I fired, and then as one of the big rams jumped up I fired again, killing him instantly. The smaller one that I had first shot at went to the left, while the one remaining large ram and the second smaller one went to the right. The latter were instantly hidden from view, for the mountain side was very rough and broken and covered with large slide rock. I raced in the same direction, knowing well that they would work up hill. But hurrying over such ground is rather dangerous work.

Soon the two sheep came into view, offering a pretty quartering shot at a little under a hundred yards. The old ram fell to my first bullet, and I allowed the smaller one to go and grow up, and I hope offer good sport to some persevering sportsman five years hence.

While Hunter climbed down and skinned out the heads I turned in pursuit of the one which I had first fired at, for we both thought he had been hit, having seen hair fly. I soon located him in the distance, but he showed no signs of a bad wound, and as his head was small I was truly glad that my shot had only grazed him. Both the rams which I killed carried excellent heads with unbroken points, and we were safely back in camp with the trophies shortly after two o'clock that afternoon--an easy and a pleasant day.

The larger ram measured 13-1/4 inches around the base of the horns, and 37-7/8 inches along the outer curves. These were the longest horns of the Ovis dalli that I killed. The other ram measured 13 inches around the horns and 34-

1/2 inches along the outer curve.

While we were having tea that afternoon, we chanced to look up on the hills, and there, near the crest of the ridge, was one of the small rams from the bunch we had stalked that morning. He offered a very easy chance had I wanted his head. It is worthy of note that these sheep seem to have no fear of the smell of blood or dead comrades, and on several occasions I have observed them near the carcass of some ram which I had shot.

The next day opened perceptibly cooler, and the angry clouds overhead told us to beware of a coming storm. As I now had seven heads, five of which were very handsome trophies, I concluded to take Hunter's advice and leave the high hills.

Our sheep shooting for the year was now practically over. Had the weather been fine it would have been an ideal trip; but with the exception of the third and thirteenth of September every day passed upon the mountains was not only disagreeable, but with conditions so unfavorable that it had been almost impossible to stalk our game properly, for when I had been once wet to the skin the cold wind from the glaciers soon chilled me to such a degree that I was unable to remain quietly in one place and allow the game to get in a favorable position for a stalk. I had been obliged to keep constantly going, and this frequently meant shooting at long range. With the exception of the rams shot on the eleventh and thirteenth of September, I had killed nothing under three hundred yards. Therefore much of the sport in making a careful and proper stalk had been lost.

My success with the white sheep had come only with the hardest kind of work, but I now had five really fine heads--which I later increased to six, my limit. I was quite satisfied with the measurements of these horns along the curve, but had hoped to have shot at least one which would tape over 14 inches around the butts, although this would be extreme, for the horns of the white sheep do not grow so large as the common Rocky Mountain variety. They are also much lighter in color. I believe that large and perfect heads will be most difficult to find a few years hence in this section, and the sportsman who has ambitions in this direction would do well not to delay his trip too long; for this range of hills is not over large, and unless these sheep have some protection, it is only a question of time before they will be almost entirely killed off.

V.

HUNTING THE GIANT MOOSE

On September 17 we packed up and moved down the lake several miles, where we made another base of supplies, for we were now going upon the moose range.

The rutting season of the moose begins on the Kenai Peninsula about the 15th of September, and lasts, roughly speaking, for one month. At this time the bulls come from the remote places where they have passed the summer and seek the cows, and the country which they now roam is generally the high tablelands which lie at the base of the mountains just below the timber line. We had timed our hunt to be in the moose range during this season, for then the bulls are bold, and not so difficult to find.

Bull moose differ from the rest of the deer family in not getting together a big band of cows, but pair off. The female remains with the bull only a short time, and then slips away, and then the bulls roam the forest in search of other partners. They are now very fearless, and if they come upon a female accompanied by another bull, fight gallantly to get possession of her. Their sense of smell is rather dulled at this time, for I have often seen their tracks following the trail which my native was constantly traveling.

The calves are born in May or June, and are weaned during the rutting season, for the bulls are very apt to drive them away from their mothers.

The antlers are hardly out of the velvet before the rutting season begins. They are then a light yellowish color, but are later stained dark brown by constant rubbing and scraping against bushes and tree trunks.

The moose of Alaska undoubtedly carry heads far grander than those found in the East. In fact, the antlers of the Kenai Peninsula moose equal, if they do not exceed in size, those from any other part of the world, and it was my ambition to kill by still-hunting a good example of one of these.

Calling moose I have never looked upon as true sport, unless the hunter does his own calling, and I am glad to see that many feel in the same way about this mode of hunting.

After we had made our base of supplies on the shore of the lake, we shouldered our packs and climbed up through the forest for several hours, until we came to the shore of a small lake, where we made camp. The scrubby woods were very thick, and extended up the sides of the mountains for some distance; then came a broad belt of thick alders, and beyond that the high open tablelands, which rolled back to the base of the sheep hills. In all directions deep game trails, traveled by the moose for many years, wound through the forest.

In the afternoon my man and I took our first hunt. Fresh tracks were seen in the much-used runways, which were often worn two feet deep by constant travel. Late in the afternoon I saw five sheep feeding on some low hills at no great distance, and as there were no lambs among the lot, we supposed that this was a band of rams, but we had not time to reach them before dark.

We were just about to return to camp when Hunter saw glistening in the sun among the thick alders, just above the timber line, the massive antlers of a moose. There was no time to be lost if we meant to come up with him, and so my man and I raced the entire way through the woods, and then up the steep ascent, but failed to reach him.

When I started on this hunt I had a thorough understanding with Hunter and my native that no one was to carry a rifle but myself, for I was determined not to allow my natives to molest the game. Indians do not like to wander through the forests without a gun, and my native had lately borrowed a rifle from one of Blake's men, but I insisted upon his leaving it at our base of supplies.

That afternoon, as Hunter and I started from camp, we sent the native back to the lake to bring us more provisions. He told us that he had no sooner reached the shore than he had heard a splash in the water near him, and looking up had seen a large moose swimming across to a neck of land at no great distance. He described this moose as at times being completely submerged by the weight of his antlers, and said that he had apparently great difficulty in swimming.

This temptation was too great for Lawroshka, and, as his rifle was at hand, he pushed off in the boat, and coming up close to the moose, shot him just as he was leaving the water. He offered to give me the head, and seemed greatly surprised when I refused it, and told him I did not wish to bring out any trophies which I had not shot myself. I was sorry to learn that some men who have hunted in this region did not hesitate to class among their trophies the heads which had been shot by their men.

I went to sleep that night with the expectation of a fair day and good sport on the morrow, but woke next morning to find it raining hard. Since reaching our hunting grounds on the 22d of August, we had had only five pleasant days, and three of these were used up in marching from one camp to another. It was now raining so hard that I determined not to hunt, and turned in among my blankets with my pipe, but after a time this failed to satisfy me, and by 11 o'clock Hunter and I decided that even a thorough wetting was preferable to doing nothing.

The five sheep which we had seen the evening before were still in view from our camp. One bunch of three lay in a commanding position on an open hillside, and were unapproachable, but the other two had left the main mountain range and were feeding on one of the outlying foothills. These offered an excellent chance, and Hunter and I started in their direction.

Nothing so thoroughly wets one as passing through thick underbrush which is ladened with raindrops, and we were both soon drenched, but we were now quite used to this discomfort, and had expected it.

After coming out above timber, we reached the belt of alders through which we were working upward, when one of the sheep appeared upon the rugged sky-line some half mile above us. The glasses showed that he was a young ram with a head not worth shooting, but as his mate followed, we could see at a glance that his horns made the full turn, and were well up to the standard that I had set.

The smaller one soon wandered down the hill to our left, but the old fellow was more wary, and kept to the rocky summit. We gradually worked nearer and nearer as his head was turned, or as he slowly fed behind some rocks. In this way we had almost reached a dip in the hillside which would hide us from view until I could approach near enough for a shot, when the ram suddenly appeared on the sky-line above. We both crouched to the ground and kept perfectly still, while he stood in bold relief against the clouds intently gazing in all directions. For almost a half hour he never moved, except to slowly turn his head. It was evident that he was restless, and missed his young companion which had wandered away. Then he gradually moved off and sank behind a rock, and as Hunter and I had seen his hindquarters disappear last, we knew he was lying down, for a sheep goes down on his front knees first. This was our chance, and we hastened to take advantage of it. In fact, Hunter had crossed the last open and I was half way over, when the ram suddenly appeared again on the crest of the hill, and by his side was his young companion. Again I dropped to the ground, while the sheep gazed down at me. I was almost tempted to take the shot, for the distance was now not over 400 yards, and I had killed several sheep at this range. But hoping that they had not made me out, I kept perfectly still. I could see Hunter crouching behind a bush a short distance ahead, and soon he beckoned. I now looked up only to find that the sheep had vanished.

As I was wearing a dark green shooting suit, I do not think they quite made me out, but their suspicions were aroused, and they headed for the main range of mountains. In order to reach this they would be obliged to cross nearly half a mile of open tableland. We hastened after them, and soon saw the rams, as we had expected, heading for the other hills. We yet hoped to stalk them when they had reached the level, for they had not been greatly alarmed, and were going leisurely along, now and again stopping to munch some of their favorite black moss from the rocks. On reaching the last hill they seemed to change their minds, for after gazing in all directions they lay down in an absolutely unapproachable position.

Hunter and I were caught on a bald hillside exposed to a biting north wind, with no chance of a nearer approach without being seen. Finally, as a last resort, we determined upon a drive.

While I lay perfectly still, Hunter advanced boldly across the open in a big circle, getting between the hill and the main range. When the rams' attention was fixed on him, I cautiously worked back and around, taking up a position which commanded the ridge over which the sheep had just gone. When Hunter had got between them and the other mountains, he began to approach. The rams now sprang to their feet, and evidently fully realized their dangerous position. They came, as we had expected, to the other end of the range from where I had taken my stand, but seemed reluctant to go back further on the isolated foothills.

It was too far for an accurate shot, and I waited, hoping for a better chance. As Hunter now worked up over the summit, the sheep broke back below him, and in another second would have had a clear field across the flat to the main range. Running up as quickly as the nature of the ground would permit, I lessened the distance some fifty yards, and, just as they were about to disappear from view, I fired twice, carefully aiming at the larger sheep, which I knew to be the big ram.

There was a strong wind blowing, and accurate shooting at such a long distance was out of the question, so I must regard it as an exceptionally lucky shot which broke his leg.

Hunter now signaled me to continue around the hill, and I soon came upon the old fellow lying down. I seated myself well within range, intending to catch my breath before shooting, when he suddenly sprang to his feet and bounded down the hill. I fired and missed, and started in pursuit. Although a sheep with a broken leg finds it hard to go up hill over rough ground, it is surprising how fast they can go down hill or across the open.

When this ram came to the base of the mountain he started in a straight line across the tableland, and led me a long chase before I ran him down and shot him. He carried quite a pretty head, measuring 13-1/2 inches around the butts and 32 inches along the curve.

I had now reached the limit I had set on sheep, and although I saw some later, I did not go after them.

It stormed hard all that night, and we woke the next morning to another wet and dismal day. I, therefore, determined to remain in camp, and was mending my much-worn knickerbockers by the fire when a moose was sighted on the mountain above timber, making for the thick belt of alders. He was soon hidden from view, and as we could not see that he passed through any of the open patches lower down, we hoped that he had chosen this secure retreat to lay up in.

The rain was coming down in torrents, but the bull carried a large and massive pair of antlers, and as I did not want to allow a chance to go by, Hunter and I were soon in pursuit. We circled well around in order to get the wind, and then forced our way through the heavy underbrush for some hours until we finally came to the belt of alders where we had last seen him. I now climbed a tree at the edge of the timber, hoping that from a lofty position I should be able to locate him, but met with no success.

It was now my intention to take a stand upon the hillside above timber, hoping that the moose would show himself toward evening, but in our wet clothes we were soon too chilled to remain inactive. As a last resort, Hunter forced his way back into the alders, while I kept in the open above. After going some distance my man turned to the right for the purpose of driving him out in my direction, but our hard and disagreeable hunt was to no purpose, and we returned to camp just before dark, having passed a wetter and more uncomfortable day than any yet.

Both Hunter and I thought this was the same bull which we had twice seen before, as he carried rather an unusual head, and had come from the same direction and to the same place.

The next day it rained even harder, and the clouds were so low that we could not see the mountain side, and therefore had no temptation to leave camp. My patience was by this time nearly exhausted, for the continual rain was very depressing, and detracted much from the pleasure of being in such a grand game country.

About noon I was sitting before the fire when Lawroshka went to the lake, only some ten steps away, for a pail of water. Here he saw a bull moose standing on the other side. He beckoned to me, and I seized my rifle and cautiously approached the native. The moose offered an easy shot at 250 yards, and my first bullet rolled him over. His head was disappointing, but it is often difficult to tell the size of a moose's antlers when they are half hidden in the trees.

We woke next morning to the usual dismal surroundings, and remained in camp all that day. Late that afternoon the fog lifted and we saw the same large moose in his accustomed place among the alders, but it was too late in the day to try for him.

That night the wind veered to the west, and just as I was about to turn in, the rain stopped and a few stars shone faintly in the heavens. The weather had been so constantly bad that even these signs failed to cheer me, and I had decided that we would break camp the next day no matter what the conditions might be. But the morning (September 22) opened bright and clear, with the first good frost in two weeks. We were most anxious for a cold snap, for the leaves were still thick upon the trees, which made it next to impossible to sec game in the woods at any distance.

After breakfast we shouldered our packs and were soon on the march, expecting to reach our permanent quarters in the moose range before noon, and have the afternoon to hunt. Bright days had been so rare with us that we meant to make the most of this one.

The heavy rains had flooded the woods, and the deep worn game trails that we followed were half full of water, while the open meadows and tundra that we occasionally crossed were but little better than miniature lakes. We had made about half of our march and my pack had just begun to grow doubly heavy from constant floundering around in the mire, when we came out into a long and narrow meadow. There were a few dwarf spruce at our end, but the rest of the small opening was free of underbrush.

Hunter was leading and I was close behind with Stereke at heel, while the native was a few steps further back. I had noticed my dog a short time before sniffing the air, and was therefore keeping a constant watch on all sides, hoping that we might come upon game, but little expecting it, when suddenly I caught sight of a large bull moose standing in the middle of the opening. He was about 300 yards away, and almost directly down wind. I do not see how he could have failed to get our scent, and he must have been indifferent to us rather than alarmed.

My first thought was of Stereke. I knew that he would break at the sight of game, and realized for the hundredth time my mistake in bringing a bear dog into the moose range. Quickly giving him to the native to hold, I dropped my pack and was instantly working my way toward the moose. I had got to within rather less than 200 yards when I saw the moose turn his head and look in my direction. A nearer approach was impossible, so I gave him at once two shots, and at the second he fell.

My dog, having bitten himself free from the native, made for the moose, and savagely attacked his haunches. Seeing that the bull was trying to regain his feet, I gave him another shot, and running up drove off the dog.

Now, for the first time, I had a good chance to see my trophy. I knew that it was a good head, but hardly expected such large and massive antlers. They were malformed and turned in, or the spread would have been considerably larger, but even then they went over sixty inches, with forty-four well defined points. I am quite sure that this was the same bull that we had seen so often among the alders, and which I had twice before unsuccessfully stalked.

Our march was delayed until we skinned out the head, cleaned the scalp, and hung the meat in some near-by trees for future use. It was therefore late that afternoon when we reached our new camp. We now settled ourselves comfortably, for we meant to stay in these quarters for the remainder of the hunt.

The next week my friend Blake joined me, and we scoured the country around this camp most diligently, but with no further success. Daily we came upon cows and small bulls, but it seemed as if all the large males had left the neighborhood. Stamp holes and unmistakable signs of the rutting season were found everywhere, but with the most careful hunting I was unable to get another shot.

There were a few bull moose in the dense woods, but not a sufficient number to warrant the hope of my getting another head such as I had already shot. At this time of the year moose are such restless animals, and are so constantly on the move that it is not difficult to distinguish their presence.

I had now hunted this entire range most thoroughly, and was reluctantly forced to the conclusion that there were not sufficient signs to warrant my remaining another month. I talked the matter over with my friend, and told him that if he cared to wait until the next monthly steamer we could combine our forces and start into a new country which we knew was good; but Blake did not want to delay his departure so long, and as he now decided to return to the coast, I made up my mind to go out with him, take the steamer to Seattle, and thence go to British Columbia, where I would finish my long hunt by a trip after Rocky Mountain sheep.

Shortly after this we broke camp and started back to Cook Inlet, which we reached October 2. A few days later the steamer arrived, and that same night I was on my way from Alaska.

Unfortunately, my hunting for the year was over, for on my arrival at Seattle I found that I had been too much pulled down by the hard work upon the hills to make it wise for me to go into British Columbia.[7]

[Transcriber's Note: Footnote numbered in the text, but no associated text.]

Jas. H. Kidder.

The Kadiak Bear and his Home

In 1901 the opportunity came to me to make a trip to the island which the Kadiak bear inhabits, and to become slightly acquainted with this largest of all carnivora. My companion was A. W. Merriam, of Milton, Mass.

We were under great obligations to Dr. C. Hart Merriam, of the Biological Survey, Washington, who, before we left home, gave us valuable information about the large game of Alaska. He told us of investigations which might prove of scientific value, and helped us to place our trip on a much broader base than a mere shooting expedition. One of the pleasantest features of such a trip was to see how freely information came in from all sides from those who could help in rounding out our work.

In order to find the Alaskan bears in their best pelage one must be on the ground in April, and this made it necessary for us to sail from Seattle April 1, on the Pacific Steam Whaling Company's boat, Excelsior. Seattle proved a very good outfitting place, and before sailing we had safely stowed away below, in waterproof canvas bags, the provisions necessary to last us three months, in the most condensed and evaporated form.

Most of our fellow passengers were miners. One of them interested me particularly. He was a Finn, one of the pioneer white hunters in the Aleutian country, and his drawn face and stooping shoulders told the tale of trails too long and packs too heavy. I passed much time with him, and learned a good deal about the habits of the big, brown, barren bear, and his methods of fighting when hard pressed.

Our first Alaskan port was Hunter's Bay, Prince of Wales Island, interesting because here is Clincon, one of the old settlements of the Haida Indians, famed for their wonderful totem poles, which tell in striking symbolic language the family histories of the tribe. There were many good faces among these people, and we asked ourselves and others the puzzling question, are they Aztecs, New Zealanders, or Japanese in origin? Among these people families with the same totem pole may not intermarry. An old man, the special wood carver of the tribe, does wonderful work.

An offshoot of the tribe inhabits Annette Island, under the kindly governorship of an old priest named Duncan. At first he founded his colony on the mainland, in British territory, but was there so hampered by religious rules that, with almost all his followers, he moved to Annette, where he is still beloved by the natives, to whom he has taught right living and many valuable arts of civilization.

We kept the inland route until Icy Straits took us away from Glacier Bay, and out into the open ocean. Early the next morning Yakutat came into view, and our boat was quickly surrounded by canoes filled with Indians, their wives, and woven baskets. These natives, supposed to belong to the Tlinkits, were distinctly less advanced than the Haida Indians.

In Yakutat we thought we were lucky in buying three Siwash bear dogs, but were not long in discovering our mistake. One of the dogs was so fierce we had to shoot him. Another was wild and ran away at the first opportunity, and the "last of the Siwash," though found wanting in every hunting instinct, had a kindly disposition and staid with us. We could not bring ourselves to the shooting point. Finally we found a Creole, who kept a store in a remote village on Kadiak Island, willing to take him off our hands.

The sight of the massive snow face of Mt. St. Elias, rising 18,002 feet above the immense stretches of the Malaspina glacier, called to mind the successful Abruzzi expedition, which reached the top of this mountain a few years ago. Looking at the rough sides of the grand old mountain, more impressive than any snow peak in Europe, one unconsciously plans an attack, as the climbing instinct is aroused.

Abruzzi has taken Mt. St. Elias out of the field of the mountain climber looking for new peaks, but a glance at the map shows us Mt. Logan, 19,000 feet, backing up Mt. St. Elias from the north, and Mt. McKinley, 20,000 feet, the highest known peak we have, placed nearer the center of the big peninsula. These should now claim the attention of some good mountaineer, with time and money at his command. They demand both.

We did not fail to inquire at Yakutat about that rare animal, the blue or St. Elias bear, and were told that two or three skins were secured every year. I was later much disappointed in being unable to return to this coast early enough in the year to look up this bear, which has never been killed by a white man, and as its skull has never been brought in by the Indians, it remains practically unknown.

The island of Kayak, the next calling place for boats, played a very important part in the early history of Alaska. This is the first land that Bering sighted, and where he landed after the memorable voyage of his two boats, the St. Peter and St. Paul, from Kamtschatka.

The early Russian adventurers of this part of the world have, it seems, been lost sight of, and have not had justice done them. The names of the Dane Bering, the Russians Shelikoff and Baranoff, should mean to us something more than the name of a sea, strait or island. A man who fitted out his expedition in Moscow, carried much of the building material for his two boats across Siberia to the rough shores of Kamtschatka, and sailed boldly eastward, deserves our warmest admiration. Bering never reached home. He died on the return voyage, and was buried on the small island of the Commander group which bears his name. The story of the expedition is one of extreme hardship and of splendid Russian courage.

At Orca we were transferred to the Newport, with Captain Moore in command, and, as on the Excelsior, everything was done for our comfort. We looked with envious eyes on Montague Island as we passed it in Prince William Sound, for we were told that the natives avoid fishing and shooting here, claiming that the big Montague brown bear are larger and fiercer than any others.

Our boat made a brief call at Homer, in Cook Inlet, one of the starting points for the famous Kenai shooting grounds. This inlet was named for the renowned voyager, who hoped that it would furnish a water passage for him to Hudson's Bay.

The trees stop at Cook Inlet, there being only a few on the western shore. To the south the wooded line intersects the Kadiak group of islands, and we find the northeastern part of Kadiak, as well as the whole of Wood and Afognak, except the central portion of the last, well covered with spruce.

The absence of forests makes it often possible to see for miles over the country, and explains why the Barren Grounds of Alaska offer such wonderful opportunities for bear hunting. There are bears all along the southern coast of the peninsula, but in the timber there, as elsewhere, the bears have all the best of it.

On leaving Cook Inlet, we kept a southerly course through the gloomy Barren Islands which mark the eastern boundary of the much-dreaded Shelikoff Straits, and early one morning passed Afognak, and made Wood Island landing, where we were most hospitably received by the North American Fur Company's people. Wood Island, about 1-1/2 miles from Kadiak, is small and well covered with spruce. It has some two hundred people, for the most part natives, and under Russian rule was used for a huge ice-storing plant. Kadiak Island, 100 miles by 30, is thickly studded with mountains, and extremely picturesque, with the white covering of early spring, as we found it, or when green with heavy grass dotted with wild flowers in July.

The Kadiak group looks as if it might have fallen out of Cook Inlet, and one of the native legends tells us that once the Kadiak Islands were so near the Alaskan shore that a mammoth sea otter, while trying to swim through the narrow straits, got wedged between the rocks, and his tremendous struggles to free himself pushed the islands out into their present position. The sea otter and bear have always been most intimately connected with the lives of the

Kadiakers, and have exercised a more important influence on their characters than any of their surroundings except the sea. It is no wonder, then, that the natives endowed these animals with a strength and size which easily takes them into the realm of mythology. The sea otter being nearly extinct, the bear is now made to shoulder all the large stories, and, strong as he is, this is no light burden.

The Kadiak coast line is roughly broken by deep bays, running inland from a half mile to fifteen or twenty miles. Some are broad, others narrow, but all are walled in by serrated, mountainous sides, much resembling the fjords of Norway. The highest peaks are about 4,000 feet.

The portions of Kadiak Island uncovered by spruce and the barren lands of the mainland, are not absolutely devoid of trees or bushes. Often there is a considerable growth of cottonwood trees along the bottom lands of the streams, and large patches of alder bushes are common, so that when the leaves are well out, one's view of the bottoms and lower hillsides is much obscured. The snowfall must be heavy on the upper reaches of the mountains, as there are great white patches to be seen well into the summer time. The climate is not what one would expect, unless he should look at the map, and note the warm Kuro Siwo (Japan current) sweeping along the southern Alaskan coast. Zero weather is uncommon, and except for the great rainfall the island is a very comfortable place of existence; existence, because that is the limit reached by most of the people. The few connected with the mission and the two fur companies are necessarily busy people, the latter especially so on steamer days, but a deep, unbroken peacefulness permeates the island and its people; it is a place so apart that outside happenings awaken but little interest, and time is not weighed in the balance. Some of the rare old Kadiak repose seems to have come down to the present people from the time when Lisiansky first visited the island and found the natives sitting on their mud houses, or on the shore, gazing into space, with apparent satisfaction.

On the other hand, if there is any sailing, fishing or shooting to be done, you will find the Kadiakers keen enough, and in trying situations they will command your respect, and will quite reverse your impression of them, gathered in the village life. The Eskimo inhabitants of the old times are gone, and the population is now made up of Russians, Creoles (part Russian and part Aleut), and a handful of Americans.

The natives are good-natured but not prepossessing in looks or cleanly. They live in dwellings kept very hot, and both men and women injure themselves by immoderate indulgence in the banya, a small Turkish bath, often attached to the barabaras, or native huts. It is made like a small barabara, except there is no smoke hole, has a similar frame, is thatched with straw, and can be made air-tight. The necessary steam is furnished by pouring water on stones previously heated very hot.

The women are frail and many die of consumption. When once sick, they appear to have no physical or mental resistance. They must be attractive, however, as there is a considerable population of white men here who have taken native wives. From a condition of comparative wealth, eight or ten years ago, when fur was plenty and money came easily, and was as promptly spent on all sorts of unnecessary luxuries, these people are now rapidly coming down to salmon, codfish and potatoes. When a native wants anything, he will sell whatever he owns for it, even to his rifle or wife. They almost all belong to the Greek Church, the Russians, when we bought Alaska, having reserved the right to keep their priests in the country.

The baidarka, the most valuable possession of the native in a country so cut up by waterways that little traveling is done by land, deserves a word. These are trusted in the roughest water more than any other craft, except the largest. A trip from Kadiak to Seattle in a baidarka is in fact on record. With a light framework of wood, covered, bottom and deck, excepting the hatches, with the skin of the hair seal, it is lighter than any other canoe, pliable, but very staunch, and works its way over the waves more like a snake than a boat. The lines are such that friction is done away with, and driven through the water by good men, it is the most graceful craft afloat. It has a curious split prow, so made for ease in lifting with one hand, and may have one, two, or three hatches, according to its size. The paddles used are curiously narrow and pointed.

What still remains unexplained is the native one-sided method of paddling; that is to say, in a two-hatch baidarka, both natives make six or seven short strokes on one side together, and then change to the other side. An absolutely straight course is thus impossible, but the Aleut is a creature of habit, and smiles at all new suggestions.

In the canoe is plenty of room for provisions and live stock. I speak of the latter because a native will often carry his wife, children, and dog inside a one-hatch baidarka while he paddles.

Water is kept out of the hatches by the kamlaykas which the natives wear. This is a long jacket made of bears' intestines, very light and water tight, and when the neck and sleeve bands are made fast, and the skirts secured about the hatch with a thong, man and canoe alike are dry as a chip.

In the early days, Shelikoff's severe rule in Kadiak actively encouraged the hunting instinct, and the first Russian fur post was established at St. Paul, named after one of Bering's boats, the present town of Kadiak, by far the largest village of the island, and situated on the eastern coast, opposite Wood Island. It is said that the Russians, after a few very prosperous years of indiscriminate slaughter, recognized the great importance of carrying on the fur industry in a systematic manner, in order to prevent entire extinction of the game, and divided the lands and waters into large districts. They made laws, with severe penalties attached, and enforced them. Certain districts were hunted and trapped over in certain years. Fur animals were killed only when in good pelage, and the young were spared. In this way hunted sections always had considerable intervals in which to recover from attacks.

A solitary sea otter skin hanging up in the fur company's store, at the end of the season, told us plainer than words that these animals, formerly so plentiful east of Kadiak Island, and along the coast of Cook's Inlet, were almost extinct. Two of our hunters were famous shots, and they liked to talk of the good old days, when sea otter and bear were plenty. One of them, Ivan, it is claimed, made $3,000 in one day. The amount paid a native is $200 or more for each sea otter pelt. They are much larger than a land otter, a good skin measuring six feet in length and three feet in width when split and stretched.

When fishing is allowed from schooners, the natives leave Kadiak for the grounds early in May. Each schooner carries thirty or forty baidarkas and twice as many men. Otters are often found at some distance from shore, and can be seen only when the water is quiet. The natives prefer the bow and arrow to the .40-65 Winchesters the company have given them, even claiming that otter are scarce because they have been driven from their old grounds by the noise of firearms. The bows, four feet long, are very stout, and strongly reinforced with cords of sinew along the back. The arrows, a little under a yard in length, are tipped with a well-polished piece of whalebone. A sharp and barbed piece of whale's tooth fits into a hole bored in the end of the bone, and a cord of considerable length is tied to the detachable arrow head, the other end of the cord being wound around and fastened to the middle of the shaft.

The advantages of this arrow are obvious. When the game is struck, its struggles disengage the arrow head, and the shaft being dragged by the cord attached to its middle, soon tires the otter out. The seal spears, used for the finishing coup, are made in the same way, and in addition have attached to the long shaft a bladder, which continually draws the animal to the surface. So expert are the natives, that, after shooting several arrows, they gather them all up together in one hand as they sweep by in a baidarka. The arrow is not sent straight to the mark, but describes a considerable curve. Good bows are valued very highly, and on an otter expedition will not be swapped even for a rifle.

On a favorable morning the baidarkas leave the schooners, and, holding their direction so as to describe a large fan, can view a good piece of water. A paddle held high in air shows that game has been sighted, and a large circle, perhaps a mile in circumference, is at once formed around the otter, each baidarka trying to get in the first successful shot. To the man who first hits home belongs the skin, but as an otter can stay under water twenty minutes, and when rising for air exposes only his nose, a long and exciting chase follows.

Some natives patrol the small island shores, and during the winter make a good harvest picking up dead otters which have washed ashore. This happens in winter, because it is during severest weather that the otter freezes his nose, which means death. The pelts from these frozen animals, however, bring only a small price.

In earlier days nets were spread beneath the water around rocks shown by the hair rubbings to be resting places of otter. The method was often successful, as the poor beast swam over the trap in gaining his rock, but when leaving dove well below the surface, and was caught. This barbarous custom, together with the netting of ducks in narrow passageways, has, fortunately, long been a thing of the past.

In Kadiak Village, we met a Captain Nelson, the first man down from the north that spring, who had sledded from Nome to Katmai on Shelikoff Straits in two months. At Katmai he was held up several days, his men refusing to cross the straits until the local weather prophet, or astronom, as he is called, gave his consent. Seven hours of hard paddling carried them over the twenty-seven miles, the most treacherous of Alaskan narrows.

These astronoms are relics of an interesting type, who formerly held firm sway over the natives. They are supposed to know much about the weather from reading the sunrises, sunsets, stars, moon and tides, and often sit on a hilltop for hours studying the weather conditions. They are still absolutely relied upon to decide when sea otter parties may start on a trip, and are looked up to and trusted as chiefs by the people of the villages in which they live.

At Wood Island we heard of Messrs. Kidder and Blake, two other sportsmen from Boston, who had already left for their hunting grounds in Kaluda Bay.

The spring was backward, and the bears still in their dens, but Merriam and I decided to take the North American Company's schooner Maksoutoff on its spring voyage around the island, when it carries supplies and collects furs from the natives. We were to sail as far as Kaguiac, a small village on the south shore, and were here promised a 30-foot sloop by the company. We added to our equipment two native baidarkas for hunting and a bear dog belonging to an old Russian hunter, Walter Matroken. Tchort (Russian for Devil) looked like a cross between a water spaniel and a Newfoundland, and though old and poorly supplied with teeth, many of which he had lost during his acquaintance with bears, he proved a good companion, game in emergencies, and a splendid retriever.

Our rifle and camera batteries were as follows:

Merriam had a.45-70 and a.50-110 Winchester, both shooting half-jacketed bullets. My rifles were a.30-40 Winchester, a double .577, and a double .40-93-400, kindly lent me by Mr. S.D. Warren, of Boston, and on which I relied. Besides the pocket cameras and a small Goerz, I carried one camera with double lenses of 17-1/2-inch focus, and one with single lense of 30-inch focus. The last two were, of course, intended for animals at long range.

Hoping to prove something in regard to the weight of the Kadiak bear, I brought a pair of Fairbanks spring scales, weighing up to 300 pounds, and some water-tight canvas bags for weighing blood and the viscera.

We selected two good men as hunters for the trip, Vacille and Klampe.

On the second day out from Wood Island a storm came on, and though the Maksoutoff was staunch, we could not hold for our port, owing to the exposed coast, where squalls come sweeping without warning from the mountain tops, driving the snow down like smoke, the so-called "wollies." It was wild and wintry enough when we turned into the sheltered protection of Steragowan Harbor.

A few mallards and a goose were here added to the ship's store next morning from the flats, and the weather clearing, we made Kaguiac, and found our sloop in good condition. In addition we took along an otter boat, a large rowboat, from here, as our baidarkas proved rather unseaworthy. Besides Mr. Heitman, the fur company's man, there was one other white settler in Kaguiac named Walch, who came to Kadiak twenty-seven years ago at the time of the first American military occupation, and though he had served in many an exciting battle in the Civil War, the Kadiak calm appealed to him. He married, settled down among the natives contentedly, and has never moved since. This, curiously, is the case of many men who come to the North, after leading wandering and adventurous lives.

Unfavorable winds at Kaguiac delayed our sailing, so we passed the time in excursions after ptarmigans and mallards. We also secured here another native, a strong, willing worker, who knew the coast.

The weather cleared suddenly, the wind shifting from northeast to northwest, and enabled us to make a run to our first good hunting ground in Windy Bay, a large piece of water five miles long by three wide, and surrounded by rock mountains covered with snow, the only bare ground to be seen at this time being on the low foothills, and in the sunny ravines. We made ourselves at home at the only good anchorage in a small cove with high crags on two sides and a ravine running off toward the east.

The following morning--April 28--opened bright and calm, and we were soon viewing the snow slopes with our glasses. Ivan, the new man, was the first to call our attention to a streak on a distant mountain side, and although perhaps 2-1/2 miles away, we could make out, even with the naked eye, a deep furrow in the snow running down diagonally into the valley below, undoubtedly a bear road. I took a five-cent piece from my pocket, tossed for choice of shot, and lost to Merriam.

Once on land, we found the going very bad, and often wallowed in the snow mid-thigh deep. Then was the time for snowshoes, which we had been told were unnecessary. Floundering along in this soft snow began to tell a little on the keenness of the party, when Vacille and Ivan, who were off on one side, suddenly waved, and hunting on to them we were shown the bear far up the valley in some bushes. As he lay on his side in the snow he looked much like a cord of wood, and very large. The wind came quartering down the valley, and made a stalk difficult, so it was thought best to wait, as the bear would probably come down nearer the water in the evening. We watched nearly four hours, and during that time the bear made perhaps 150 yards in all, crawling, rolling over, lapping his paws, occasionally trying a somersault, and finally landing in a patch of alders.

As night was upon us, we decided to chance the situation, and approached along a ridge on one side of the valley until almost above the bear. At this point Tchort, the dog, caught the scent, broke away, and raced down over the bluff out of sight. Almost immediately the bear appeared in the open 200 yards away, legging as fast as he could in the snow, and headed for the hillside. Merriam made a good shot behind the shoulder with his fifty. The bear fell, caught his feet again, and was in and over a small brook, leaving a bloody road behind him, which Tchort was quick in following. The dog was soon nipping the bear's heels, and giving him a good deal of trouble. Up the side of the hill they raced, Merriam firing when the dog gave him opportunity. The bear, angry and worried, suddenly whipped around and made for the dog, which in the soft snow at such close quarters could not escape. But Tchort, a born fighter, accepted the only chance and closed in. He disappeared completely between the forelegs of the bear, and we felt that all was over. To our great wonder in a few seconds he crawled out from beneath the hindquarters of his enemy, and engaged him again. One more shot and the bear lay quiet. The skin was a beauty--dark brown, with a little silvering of gray over the shoulders, without any rubbed spots, such as are common on bears only just out of their dens. Some brush was thrown over the bear, and we rowed back to the sloop, well content. The next day, which was foggy and rainy, was spent in getting off the skin, measuring and weighing the animal piecemeal, and carrying all back to the sloop.

Contrary to expectation, the bear was found to be still covered with a thin layer of fat, even after his long hibernation. Before weighing, our men, who had killed some thirty bear among them, said that this one was two-thirds as large as any they had seen.

The measurements and weights were as follows: Height at shoulder, about 4 ft. Length in straight line from nose to root of tail, 6 ft. 8 in. Total weight, 625 lbs. Weight of middle piece, 260 lbs. Weight of skull (skin removed), 20 lbs. Weight of skin, 80 lbs. The right forearm weighed 50 lbs., and the left 55. This supports the theory that a bear is left-handed. Right hind-quarter, 60 lbs.; left hindquarter, 60 pounds. The stomach was filled with short alder sticks, not much chewed, and one small bird feather. Organic acids were present in the stomach, but no free hydrochloric for digestion of flesh.

It was a great satisfaction to see that none of the bear was wasted, which fact brings up one very good trait of the Creole hunters. They dislike to go after bear into a district situated far from the coast, because in so rough a country it is almost impossible to get all the meat out. They sell the skin, eat the meat, and make the intestines into kamlaykas for baidarka work.

April 30 a strong wind kept us from trying the head of the bay, and a short trip was made up into a low lying valley, near the sloop, but without results.

Our men had already proved themselves good. Vacille was the best waterman and a good cook; Klampe the best hunter, and Ivan a glutton for all sorts of work.

The underlying principle on which the Aleut hunter works was brought out on our short bear hunt. After sighting the game, he waits until he is sure of his wind, then takes a stand where the bear will pass close by, and shows himself a monument of patience. Almost all the viewing is done from the water, a small hill near the shore being occasionally used for a lookout. They get up at daylight, and two men in a baidarka patrol both sides of a big bay, watching carefully for bear tracks on the mountain sides, as this is the surest indication of their presence. As soon as the bears come from their dens they always make a climbing tour, the natives claiming that this exercise is taken to strengthen them. Personally I believe the Kadiak bear has very good reasons for keeping on the move continually outside of his hibernating season.

If the natives find no sign on their morning tour, they rest all day, perhaps taking a Turkish bath in a banya, which is not infrequently attached to the hunting barabara. Another trip of inspection is made again in the afternoon at four or five o'clock, as the bear usually lies up between nine and three. A bay is watched for several days in this way, and if nothing is seen the natives return to their village, or hunt the hair seal, which are still to be found in fair numbers, especially on Afognak Island.

When you are with these men you must either conduct the shooting trip on your own lines or give yourself entirely into the native's hands, and do as he thinks best. You must leave him alone, and not bother him with many questions, and in any case you usually get Nish naiou ("I don't know") for answer. The native gives this reply without thinking; it is so much easier. The most you can do is to cheer him on when luck is bad, as he is easily discouraged and becomes homesick.

During the bad weather that followed we had plenty of opportunity to use our ingenuity in extracting information from our men on the subject of bear.

It seems that the Kadiak bear hibernates, as a rule, from December to April, depending on the season somewhat, and the young are supposed to be born in March in the dens. Although the skins are good in the late fall, they are finest when the bear first comes out in early spring, as it is then that the hide is thinnest and the hair longest. On the other hand, in summer, when the hair is very thin, the hide becomes extremely thick and heavy; this condition changing again as fall comes on. The total amount of epidermis, in other words, does not vary so much as one would suppose, and whether the hide or the hair is responsible for most of the weight depends on the time of year.

When the animal leaves his den he finds food scarce, and has to go on the principle that a full stomach is better than an empty one, even if the filling is made of alder twigs. It is not long, however, before green grass begins to sprout along the small streams, low down, and grass and the roots of the salmon berry bushes carry the bear along until the fish run.

The running of the salmon varies, and the bears make frequent prospecting trips down the streams in order to be sure to be on hand for the first run, which usually occurs during the latter part of May. During the salmon season the bears have opportunity to fill themselves full every night, and put on a tremendous weight of fat in the late fall, when they become saucy and lazy, and more inclined to show fight. Berries--especially the salmon berry--help out the fish diet in summer time. As soon as salmon becomes their food the pelts deteriorate, but unless living near a red salmon stream, with shallow reaches, the bears do not get much fish diet until the second run early in July, so that fair skins are sometimes obtained even up to June 15, although by this time the hair is usually much faded in color.

The bear makes a zigzag course down the salmon stream from one shallow rapid to another, standing immovable while fishing, and throwing out his catch with the left paw. The numerous fishing beds give a false idea of the number of bear present in a district, as it takes but a few days for a single bear to cover the sides of a stream for a long distance with such places. One finds fish skeletons scattered all along a salmon stream, and it is generally easy to tell whether a bear or eagle has made the kill. An eagle usually carries the whole fish away with him, leaving only scales behind. A bear, on the other hand, eats his fish where he catches him, preferring the belly and back, and usually discarding the skeleton, and always the under jaw.

The Finn hunter whom I met on my way north, said he had seen an old cow bear when fishing with her cubs, rush salmon in toward the shore and scoop them out for the young. Generally they watch on a low bank, or in the shallow water, while fishing.

During the rutting season, supposed to be in June, the female travels ahead, the male bringing up the rear to furnish protection from that quarter. Then if one kills the female the male gives trouble, often charging on sight.

The Finn thought that, as a rule, the cow bear comes on at a gallop and a bull rises on his hind legs when getting in close. When wounded the bear usually strikes the injured spot, or if it is a cow and cubs, the old one cuffs her young soundly, thinking them the cause of pain. The nose is the main source of protection, as, like all bears, these are followed to their very dens in the fall by the keenest of hunters, and their only restful sleep is the long winter one. Fortunately some excellent game laws for Alaska have been passed, and by making a close season for several years, followed by severe restrictions, we may yet hope that the perpetual preservation of this grand brown bear will be assured on the Kadiak group, which, from its situation, fitly offers him, when well guarded, his best chance of making a successful stand against his enemies.

The fact that the natives make a profit from the bear skins, and that his flesh furnishes them with food is not to be considered, as at the present rate of extermination there will soon be no bear left for discussion.

The natives certainly could and should be helped out in their living, as competition in the fur trade of late has so exterminated fur-bearing animals that hunting and trapping bring them in little, and their diet is indeed low. One of my hunters during last fall only secured one bear, one silver gray fox, and two land otter.

A good way to help out the food question, and compensate the native for his loss of bear meat, would be to transport a goodly number of Sitka deer to the three islands, and allow them to multiply. There has been a Sitka deer on Wood Island for several years, and he has lived through the winters without harm, as his footprints scattered over the island testify. Afognak and Wood Island are especially suitable for such a purpose, being well wooded and furnishing plenty of winter food for deer in willows, alders and black birch. The clement winters make the plan feasible, and it ought not to be an expensive experiment.

We had a very bad time of it on the night of April 30, which showed me what I had long felt, that the dangers of Kadiak were not centered in the bear, but in the tremendous wind blows and tide rips in its fjords. A strong wind came on from the east, and fairly howled through the ravine opposite our anchorage, catching our little sloop with full force. We could not change our position, as we occupied the only anchorage. Vacille, who had turned in, felt the anchor dragging, and we found ourselves being blown out into the large bay, where we could not have lived for any time in the big seas, and, should we continue to drag, our only chance was to try to beach her on a sand shore some half mile away.

When the boat was not dragging she was wallowing in cross seas, and being hammered by the otter boat, which was difficult to manage. The anchors held firmly, much to our relief, and after a disagreeable night of watching we beat back to our mooring at the head of the little cove. The mountains being covered with fresh snow in the morning, there was nothing to do but eat and sleep.

The bear meat improved with age, and hours of boiling rid it of its bitter flavor. The whole cabin--and its occupants--smelled of bear's grease. The thermometer registered 30.

On May 2, as the wind was unsuitable for bear hunting, we made a photographing trip to a cliff across the bay, where two bald-headed eagles had built their nest. Merriam and I had a very interesting stalk with a camera. We landed near the cliff, and the eagles, becoming disturbed, flew away. The men were sent out in the boat, and we kept in hiding until signalled that the birds had quieted down. We gained the top of the cliff, a mere knife edge in places, where we worked our way along, straddling the rock. The birds had selected a splendid place, straight up from the water, where they had built their nest firmly into a bush on the side of the cliff.

I stalked the eagle within about 75 feet and caught her with the camera, as she was leaving her nest. The earth forming the center of the nest was frozen and three eggs lay in a little hollow of hay on top. The big birds circled about us all the time, but did not offer to attack. Bald-headed eagles are very common on Kadiak, and are always found about the salmon streams later, during the run, being good fishermen. It seems they, of all the birds here, are the first to lay their eggs, and their young are the last to leave the nest.

We secured some eagle eggs on these trips, of which we made several, and found the cliff nests much the easier to approach, as it was very difficult to get above nests built in trees.

In connection with the eagle, the magpie should not be forgotten. Of these black and white birds there were many about, and there seemed to be a bond of sympathy between the widely separated species of marauders. Bold enough we knew the smaller bird to be, but to believe that he would actually steal an eagle's fish breakfast from under his very nose one must see the act. The eagle appeared to mind but little, occasionally pecking the thief away when he became offensive.

The magpie, on the other hand, seemed to have a warm feeling for his big friend, and once at least we saw him flying about an eagle's nest and warning the old birds of our approach with his harsh cry.

One good day among many bad ones showed no more bear signs, so we soaped the seams of the otter boat, which leaked badly, and set sail for Three Saints Bay, named after Shelikoff's ship. This proved to be a narrow piece of water running far inland, with snow-covered mountain sides, and by far the most beautiful fjord on the island.

There were no bear signs, however, and a favorable wind carried us eastward toward Kaluda Bay, where Kidder and Blake were hunting. On our way we stopped at Steragowan, an interesting little village, bought a few stores, and secured some interesting stone lamps, and whale spears, with throwing sticks.

Once in Kaluda Bay, we found Kidder's and Blake's barabara where they made headquarters, and their cook informed us that both sportsmen were many miles up the bay after bear.

Several years ago there was a flourishing colony of natives at the entrance to Kaluda Bay, but now there are only two hunting barabaras, a broken down chapel, and a good-sized graveyard. The village prospered until one day a dead whale was reported not far from land. All the inhabitants gorged themselves on the putrid blubber, and they died almost to a man.

The Kadiakers show a good deal of courage in whale hunting. With nothing but their whale spears tipped with slate, two men will run close up to a whale, drive two spears home with a throwing stick, and make off again. The slate is believed in some way to poison the animal, and he often dies within a short time. The natives go home, return in a few days, and, if lucky, find the whale in the same bay. Whales are plenty, and were sometimes annoying to us, playing too near our otter boat. On one occasion we tried a shot at one that was paying us too much attention, and persuaded the big chap to leave us in peace.

Bad weather held us fast several days, but we finally made the southeast corner of the island, and from there had good wind to Kadiak. On our way we passed Uyak, one of the blue fox islands. Raising these animals for their fur has become a regular business, and when furs are high it pays well. The blue fox has been found to be the only one that multiplies well in comparative captivity, and he thrives on salmon flesh.

At Wood Island, news came to us through prospectors, of a bear in English Bay, south of Kadiak village. This bay is well known as a good bear ground, and at the end of the bay there are some huge iron cages weighing tons which were used as bear traps, some years ago, by men working for the Smithsonian Institution.

We found bear tracks coming into the valley, down one mountain side, and leading out over the opposite mountain, and were obliged to return to Wood Island empty handed.

Merriam now decided to return home on the next boat, and after a few days I started off for the north side of Kadiak in an otter boat fitted with sail, picking up on the way a white man, Jack Robinson, and a native hunter, Vacille, at Ozinka, a small village on Spruce Island. My men proved a good combination, but we were all obliged to work hard for two months before a bear was finally secured.

We tried bay after bay, and were often held up, and for days at a time kept from good grounds by stormy weather and bad winds. The inability to do anything for long periods made these months the most wearing I have ever passed. Our little open boat went well only before the wind, but, as somebody has said, the prevailing winds in Alaska are head winds, and we spent many long hours at the oars.

Although we had a good tent with us, we used, for the most part, the native hunting barabara for shelter. These are fairly clean and comfortable, and are found in every bay of any size.

The natives inherit their hunting grounds, and are apparently scrupulous in observing each other's rights. In fact, it is dangerous to invade another man's trapping country, as one may spring a Klipse trap set for fox and otter, and receive a dangerous gash from the blade that makes these contrivances so deadly.

On the way to the hunting grounds Vacille pointed out to us a cliff where he once had an exciting bear hunt.

There were two hunters, and they were fortunate enough to locate an inhabited den in early spring. Two bears were killed through crevices in the rocks, but the men suspected there was still one inside, and Vacille crawled in to make sure. He found himself in a fair sized chamber with a bear at the other end, and a lucky shot tumbled the animal at his feet.

This story brought up others of bear hunting with the lance. Before firearms came into common use, boys were given lessons in fighting the bear with the lance, and became very expert at it. Their method was to approach a bear as closely as possible, without being seen, then show themselves suddenly, and as the bear reared strike home. The lance was held fast by the native, and the bear was often mortally wounded by forcing the lance into himself in his struggles to reach his enemy.

This class of native no longer exists on Kadiak, but it is said there is one famous old Aleut near Iliamna Lake on the mainland who scorns any but this method of hunting.

High above the den where the three bears were killed was a scoop out of the cliff called the shaman's barabara. Here, before Russian times, the shamans or witches were buried, and here also were kept the masks used in certain ceremonial rites. The Russians removed the mummies and masks long ago.

The shamans were considered oracles. It was claimed they could prevent a whale from swimming out of a bay by dragging a bag of fat, extracted from the dead body of a newly born infant, across the entrance. Their instructions were unfailingly obeyed, as it was supposed they could cause death as a punishment for their enemies.

One evening at our first halting place beyond Ozinka, we found tracks in the snow on one side of our valley, and early in the morning came upon a two-year-old bear, not far from camp. The bear was grubbing about on the hillside, and we took our position so that he crossed us under a hundred yards. Unbeknown to me, and just as I was about to fire, my native gave the caw of a raven to hold the bear up. He whipped around and faced us, my bullet entering the brush on one side of him. Off he rushed into the woods with the dog after him. I followed, and on coming out into a clearing saw the dog being left far behind on the mountain side. Old Tchort was not in condition. This was sad and illustrated the fact that it is sometimes best to be alone.

We next tried Kaguiac Bay and here spent many days. Two bears had been killed by the natives near the barabara where we camped, and there was plenty of sign.

Before sunrise we were watching from a good position, and it was scarcely light when Vacille made out a big bear, two miles or more away. He was traveling the snow ar 陟 e of the mountain opposite, and trying to find a good descent into our valley. One could see the huge body and head plainly with the naked eye against the sky-line as he made his way rapidly through the deep snow. Finally he found a place somewhat bare of snow and gave us a splendid exhibition of rock climbing. It took little time for him to get down into the alders, where he apparently dropped asleep. To our astonishment he woke up about 10 o'clock and worked down toward the bottom land. We stalked him in the woods and alders, which were very thick, within 300 yards, and here I should have risked a shot at his hindquarters showing up brown against the hillside, and seemingly as large as a horse.

We chanced a nearer approach, though the wind was treacherous, and coming up to a spot where we could have viewed him found the monster had decamped. All attempts to locate him again were fruitless.

The bear paths around this bay were a very interesting study. They are hammered deep into the earth, and afford as good means of traveling as the New Brunswick moose paths.

Sometimes instead of a single road we have a double one, the bear using one path for the legs of each side of his body. Again, on soft mossy side hills, instead of paths we find single footprints which have been used over and over, and made into huge saucers, it being the custom of the bear to take long strides on the side hills, and to step into the impressions made by other animals which had traveled ahead of it.

The red salmon were beginning to run, and some fishermen in another part of the bay supplied us, from time to time, from their nets. Especially good were the salmon heads roasted.

Bear sign failed, and Afognak Island, where Vacille shot and trapped, had been so much talked about, that I determined to see it for myself, and with a good wind we rowed across the straits and sailed twelve miles into the island by Kofikoski Bay.

Scattered along up the bay were small islands, and these furnished us with a good supply of gulls' eggs, which lasted many days.

The Afognak coast is heavily wooded with spruce, while a large plateau in the interior is almost barren, and gave good opportunity for using the glasses.

During several days at the head of Kofikoski Bay nothing was seen, so we packed up and crossed a large piece of the island by portages and a chain of lakes, where our Osgood boat was indispensable. The country crossed was like a beautiful park of meadows, groves and lakes, and one could scarcely believe it was uncultivated.

The Red Salmon River of Seal Harbor, to which we were headed, could not fail us, for bear could scoop out the salmon in armfuls below the lower falls, so Vacille said, and he was honest, and now as keen as anything while traveling his own hunting grounds.

For a whole week a northeast storm blew directly toward the bay, and kept us in camp. It was fishing weather, however, and my fly-rod, with a Parmachenee belle, kept us well supplied with steelheads and speckled trout, which were plentiful in the clear waters of a wandering trout brook running through a meadow below the camp.

A calm evening came finally, and we paddled down the last lake, some three miles, to the famous pool.

There were the salmon swarming below the fall, and many constantly in the air on their upward journey, but the eagles perched high on the dark spruces, closing in the swirling water, were all they had to fear. There were no bears and no fresh bear signs. It was an ideal spot, this salmon pool, but a feast for the eyes only, as the red salmon will not rise to a fly. Even Tchort looked disconsolate on our track back to Ozinka.

About July 10 there is usually a run of dog salmon, and not much later another of humpbacks. The dog salmon grow to be about twice as large as the red salmon, and often weigh 12 pounds. They are much more sluggish than the red fish, and as they prefer the small shallow streams, become an easy prey for the bear. The humpback fish are fatter and better eating even than the red salmon, but are somewhat smaller.

The red fish never ascend a stream which has not a lake on its upper waters for spawning. The dog and humpback, on the contrary, are not so particular, and are found almost everywhere. In September there is a run of silver salmon, which, like the red salmon, will only swim a stream with a lake at its head. They run up to 40 pounds, and the bears grow fat on them before turning into winter quarters. The skeletons of this big fish, cleaned by bear, are found along every small stream running from the lakes.

The large canneries, like the one at Karluk, on Karluk River, near the western end of Kadiak, put up only the red salmon. They are not nearly as good eating as the humpback or silver salmon, but are red, and this color distinction the market demands. The catches at Karluk run up into the tens of thousands, and one thinks of this with many misgivings, remembering the fate of the sea otter and bear. Good hatcheries are constantly busy, keeping up the supply, but it appears that though one in every ten thousand of these fish is marked before being set free, so far as known no marked fish have ever been captured.

On our return to Kadiak Island, we found the streams still free of salmon, and the vegetation had become so rank as to interfere a good deal with traveling and sighting game. The whole party looked serious, and the strain was beginning to tell, no game having been seen for seven long weeks. This, with the swarms of gnats and mosquitoes, made time pass heavily.

Other places proving barren, we finally brought up at Wesnoi Leide, half an hour's row from Ozinka, and found the dog fish just beginning to run up stream, at the head of the bay. Better still, there were fresh bear tracks.

The wind was favorable, and we stationed ourselves the first evening on a bluff overlooking a long meadow, on the lower part of the stream. Hardly had we sat down, when Vacille said: "If that brown spot on the hillside were not so large, I would take it for a bear." The brown spot promptly walked into the woods, half a mile away. We were keen enough again, but our watching proved fruitless, as nothing came down on the meadow, showing that there was good fishing well up the stream.

We rowed back to Ozinka, and left the country undisturbed, determined to get well into the woods the following night, before the bear came down to feed.

The next evening we made an early start, and walking up the stream into the woods found plenty of fresh tracks, and finally halted by some big trees. The men placed themselves on some high limbs, where they could watch, and I stood in deep grass, some six or eight feet from a well-traveled path used by the bear in fishing the stream. The magpies were calling all about, and seemed to be saying, _Midwit, midwit_, Aleut for bear. The air was dead calm. Hardly were the men on their perches, before they saw a bear walk into the brush on one side of the valley. We waited quietly, in the midst of mosquitoes, but nothing came in sight. It was already after 10 o'clock, and so dark that the men gave up their watch, and came down to join me. Suddenly we heard a sharp screech up the stream, and when it was repeated, Vacille said it must be a young bear crying because its mother would not feed it fast enough. Here Vacille did some good work.

We walked rapidly up stream, through the thick brush, and before we had gone 100 yards heard a large animal, just ahead, moving about in the brush, and making a good deal of noise. I started ahead to get a view, thinking we had disturbed the bear, but Vacille held me back. We walked on noiselessly to a little bare point in the stream, and just then the bear appeared, bent on fishing, thirty feet away. She lumbered down into the stream, and when I fired fell into the water, the ball just missing her shoulder. She was up again, and this time I shot hurriedly, and a little behind the ribs. She ran, crossing up about forty feet away, and a trial with the .30-40 scored, but made no impression.

Tchort caught up with her just as she fell, after running a hundred feet or more, and gave us to understand that he was the responsible party. We tried immediately to capture the cub, which would have been a rare prize, but had no success at all in the thicket. The old one, though of considerable age, was not a large specimen, and, with the exception of the head, the hair was in bad condition. Length about 6 feet 4 inches; height at shoulder 44 inches; weight 500 pounds. The stomach was full of salmon, gleaned from the fishing beds made all along the stream. The Ozinka people did not enjoy my killing a bear just outside the village.

I caught the boat about a week later, after a few pleasant days with Kidder and Blake, who had turned up at Wood Island, after a very successful hunt on the mainland.

A word in regard to the Kadiak bear. Dr. Merriam has proved that he is distinct from other bear. That he ever reached 2,000 pounds is doubtful in my mind, but, by comparing measurements of skins, we can be sure he comes up to 1,200, or a little over. Whether the Kadiak bear is bigger than the big brown bear of the mainland is doubtful. At present the growth of these bears is badly interfered with by the natives, and they rarely reach the old bear age, when these brutes become massive in their bony structure, and accumulate a vast amount of fat, just before denning up.

W. Lord Smith.

The Mountain Sheep and its Range

The mountain sheep is, in my estimation, the finest of all our American big game. Many men have killed it and sheep heads are trophies almost as common as moose heads, and yet among those who have hunted it most and know it best, but little is really understood as to the life of the mountain sheep, and many erroneous ideas prevail with regard to it. It is generally supposed to be an animal found only among the tops of the loftiest and most rugged mountains, and never to be seen on the lower ground, and there are still people interested in big game who now and then ask one confidentially whether there really is anything in the story that the sheep throw themselves down from great heights, and, striking on their horns, rebound to their feet without injury.

Each one of us individually knows but little about the mountain sheep, yet each who has hunted them has observed something of their ways, and each can contribute some share to an accumulation of facts which some time may be of assistance to the naturalist who shall write the life history of this noble species. But unless that naturalist has already been in the field and has there gathered much material, he is likely to be hard put to it when the time comes for his story to be written, since then there may be no mountain sheep to observe or to write of. The sheep is not likely to be so happy in its biographer as was the buffalo, for Dr. Allen's monograph on the American bison is a classic among North American natural history works.

The mountain sheep is an inhabitant of western America, and the books tell us that it inhabits the Rocky Mountains from southern California to Alaska. This is sufficiently vague, and I shall endeavor a little further on to indicate a few places where this species may still be found, though even so I am unable to assign their ranges to the various forms that have been described.

For this species seems to have become differentiated into several species and sub-species, some of which are well marked, and all of which we do not as yet know much about. These as described are the common sheep of the Rocky Mountains _(Ovis canadensis_); the white sheep of Alaska _(Ovis dalli)_, and its near relative, _O. dalli kenaiensis_; the so-called black sheep of northern British Columbia (_O. stonei_), described by Dr. Allen; Nelson's sheep of the southwest (_O. nelsoni_) and _O. mexicanus_, both described by Dr. Merriam. Besides these, Mr. Hornaday has described Ovis fannini of Yukon Territory, about which little is known, and Dr. Merriam has given the sheep of the Missouri River bad lands sub-specific rank under the title _O.c. auduboni_. Recently Dr. Elliot has described the Lower California sheep as a sub-species of the Rocky Mountain form under the name _O.c. cremnobates_. For twenty-five years I heard of a black sheep-like animal in the central range of the Rocky Mountains far to the north, said to be not only black in color, but with black horns, something like those of an antelope, but in shape and ringed like a female mountain sheep. From specimens recently examined at the American Museum of Natural History, I now know this to be the young female of Ovis stonei. That several species of sheep should have been described within the last three or four years shows, perhaps as well as anything, how very little we know about the animals of this group.

The sheep of the Rocky Mountains and of the bad lands (_O. canadensis_ and _O. canadensis auduboni_) are those with which we are most familiar. Both forms are called the Rocky Mountain sheep, and from this it is commonly inferred that they are confined to the mountains, and live solely among the rocks. In a measure this belief is true today, but it was not invariably so in old times. As in Asia, so in America, the wild sheep is an inhabitant of the high grass land plateaus. It delights in the elevated prairies, but near these prairies it must have rough or broken country to which it may retreat when pursued by its enemies. Before the days of the railroad and the settlements in the West, the sheep was often found on the prairie. It was then abundant in many localities where to-day farmers have their wheat fields, and to some extent shared the feeding ground of the antelope and the buffalo. Many and many a time while riding over the prairie, I have seen among the antelope that loped carelessly out of the way of the wagon before which I was riding, a few sheep, which would finally separate themselves from the antelope and run up to rising ground, there to stand and call until we had come too near them, when they would lope off and finally be seen climbing some steep butte or bluff, and there pausing for a last look, would disappear.

Those were the days when if a man had a deer, a sheep, an antelope, or the bosse ribs of a buffalo cow on his pack or in his wagon, it did not occur to him to shoot at the game among which he rode. I have seen sheep feeding on the prairies with antelope, and in little groups by themselves in North Dakota, Montana, and Wyoming, and men whose experience extends much further back than mine--men, too, whose life was largely devoted to observing the wild animals among which they lived--unite in telling me that they were commonly found in such situations. Personally I never saw sheep among buffalo, but knowing as I do the situations that both inhabited and the ways of life of each, I am confident that sheep were often found with the buffalo, just as were antelope.

The country of northwestern Montana, where high prairie is broken now and then by steep buttes rising to a height of several hundred feet, and by little ranges of volcanic uplifts like the Sweet Grass Hills, the Bear Paw Mountains, the Little Rockies, the Judith, and many others, was a favorite locality for sheep, and so, no doubt, was the butte country of western North Dakota, South

Dakota and Nebraska, this being roughly the eastern limit of the species. In general it may be said that the plains sheep preferred plateaus much like those inhabited by the mule deer, a prairie country where there were rough broken hills or buttes, to which they could retreat when disturbed. That this habit was taken advantage of to destroy them will be shown further on.

To-day, if one can climb above timber line in summer to the beautiful green alpine meadows just below the frowning snow-clad peaks in regions where sheep may still be found, his eye may yet be gladdened by the sight of a little group resting on the soft grass far from any cover that might shelter an enemy. If disturbed, the sheep get up deliberately, take a long careful look, and walking slowly toward the rocks, clamber out of harm's way. It will be labor wasted to follow them.

Such sights may be witnessed still in portions of Montana and British Columbia, Idaho, Wyoming and Colorado, where bald, rolling mountains, showing little or no rock, are frequented by the sheep, which graze over the uplands, descending at midday to the valleys to drink, and then slowly working their way up the hills again to their illimitable pastures.

Of Dall's sheep, the white Alaskan form, we are told that its favorite feeding grounds are bald hills and elevated plateaus, and although when pursued and wounded it takes to precipitous cliffs, and perhaps even to tall mountain peaks, the land of its choice appears to be not rough rocks, but rather the level or rolling upland.

The sheep formerly was a gentle, unsuspicious animal, curious and confiding rather than shy; now it is noted in many regions for its alertness, wariness, and ability to take care of itself.

Richardson, in his "Fauni-Boreali Americana," says: "Mr. Drummond informs me that in the retired part of the mountains, where hunters had seldom penetrated, he found no difficulty in approaching the Rocky Mountain sheep, which there exhibited the simplicity of character so remarkable in the domestic species; but that where they had been often fired at they were exceedingly wild, alarmed their companions on the approach of danger by a hissing noise, and scaled the rocks with a speed and agility that baffled pursuit." The mountain men of early days tell precisely the same thing of the sheep. Fifty or sixty years ago they were regarded as the gentlest and most unsuspicious animal of all the prairie, excepting, of course, the buffalo. They did not understand that the sound of a gun meant danger, and, when shot at, often merely jumped about and stared, acting much as in later times the elk and the mule deer acted.

We may take it for granted that, before the coming of the white man, the mountain sheep ranged over a very large portion of western America, from the Arctic Ocean down into Mexico. Wherever the country was adapted to them, there they were found. Absence of suitable food, and sometimes the presence of animals not agreeable to them, may have left certain areas without the sheep, but for the most part these animals no doubt existed from the eastern limit of their range clear to the Pacific. There were sheep on the plains and in the mountains; those inhabiting the plains when alarmed sought shelter in the rough bad lands that border so many rivers, or on the tall buttes that rise from the prairies, or in the small volcanic uplifts which, in the north, stretch far out eastward from the Rocky Mountains.

While some hunters believe that the wild sheep were driven from their former habitat on the plains and in the foothills by the advent of civilized man, the opinion of the best naturalists is the reverse of this. They believe that over the whole plains country, except in a few localities where they still remain, the sheep have been exterminated, and this is probably what has happened. Thus Dr. C. Hart Merriam writes me:

"I do not believe that the plains sheep have been driven to the mountains at all, but that they have been exterminated over the greater part of their former range. In other words, that the form or sub-species inhabiting the plains (_auduboni_) is now extinct over the greater part of its range, occurring only in the localities mentioned by you. The sheep of the mountains always lived there, and, in my opinion, has received no accession from the plains. In other words, to my mind it is not a case of changed habit, but a case of extermination over large areas. The same I believe to be true in the case of elk and many other animals."

That this is true of the elk--and within my own recollection--is certainly the fact. In the early days of my western travel, elk were reasonably abundant over the whole plains as far east as within 120 miles of the city of Omaha on the Missouri River, north to the Canadian boundary line--and far beyond--and south at least to the Indian Territory. From all this great area as far west as the Rocky Mountains they have disappeared, not by any emigration to other localities, but by absolute extermination.

A few years ago we knew but one species of mountain sheep, the common bighorn of the West, but with the opening of new territories and their invasion by white men, more and more specimens of the bighorn have come into the hands of naturalists, with the result that a number of new forms have been described covering territory from Alaska to Mexico. These forms, with the localities from which the types have come, are as follows:

Ovis canadensis, interior of western Canada. (Mountains of Alberta.)

Ovis canadensis auduboni, Bad Lands of South Dakota. (Between the White and Cheyenne rivers.)

Ovis nelsoni, Grapevine Mountains, boundary between California and Nevada. (Just south of Lat. 37 deg.)

Ovis mexicanus, Lake Santa Maria, Chihuahua, Mexico.

Ovis stonei, headwaters Stikine River (Che-o-nee Mountains), British Columbia.

Ovis dalli, mountains on Forty-Mile Creek, west of Yukon River, Alaska.

Ovis dalli kenaiensis, Kenai Peninsula, Alaska (1901).

Ovis canadensis cremnobates, Lower California.

The standing of Ovis fannini has been in doubt ever since its description, and recent specimens appear to throw still more doubt on it. Those most familiar with our sheep do not now, I believe, acknowledge it as a valid species. It comes from the mountains of the Klondike River, near Dawson, Yukon Territory.

What the relations of these different forms are to one another has not yet been determined, but it may be conjectured that _Ovis canadensis, O. nelsoni_, and

O. dalli differ most widely from one another; while _O. stonei_ and _O. dalli_, with its forms, are close together; and _O. canadensis_, and _O.c. auduboni_ are closely related; as are also _O. nelsoni, O. mexicanus_, and _O.c. cremnobates_. The sub-species auduboni is the easternmost member of the American sheep family, while the sheep of Chihuahua and of Lower California are the most southern now known.

PRIMITIVE HUNTING.

At many points in the Rocky Mountains and the Sierra Nevadas the Indians were formerly great sheep hunters, and largely depended on this game for their flesh food. That it was easily hunted in primitive times cannot be doubted, and is easily comprehended when we remember the testimony of white observers already quoted. In certain places in the foothills of the mountains, or in more or less isolated ranges in Utah, Nevada, Montana, and other sections, the Indians used to beat the mountains, driving the sheep up to the summits, where concealed bowmen might kill them. On the summits of certain ranges which formerly were great resorts for sheep, I have found hiding places built of slabs of the trachyte which forms the mountain, which were used by the Indians for this purpose in part, as, later, they were also used by the scouting warrior as shelters and lookout stations from which a wide extent of plain might be viewed. The sheep on the prairie or on the foothills of such ranges, if alarmed, would of course climb to the summit, and there would be shot with stone-headed arrows.

Mr. Muir has seen such shelters in Nevada, and he tells us also that the Indians used to build corrals or pounds with diverging wings, somewhat like those used for the capture of antelope and buffalo on the plains, and that they drove the sheep into these corrals, about which, no doubt, men, women, and children were secreted, ready to destroy the game.

Certain tribes made a practice of building converging fences and driving the sheep toward the angle of these fences, where hunters lay in wait to kill them, as elsewhere mentioned by Mr. Hofer. In fact, sheep in those old times shared with all the other animals of the prairie that tameness to which I have often adverted in writing on this subject, and which now seems so remarkable.

The Bannocks and Sheep Eaters depended for their food very largely on sheep. In fact, the Sheep Eaters are reported to have killed little else, whence their name. Both these tribes hunted more or less in disguise, and wore on the head and shoulders the skin and horns of a mountain sheep's head, the skin often being drawn about the body, and the position assumed a stooping one, so as to simulate the animal with a considerable closeness. The legs, which were uncovered, were commonly rubbed with white or gray clay, and certain precautions were used to kill the human odor.

A Cheyenne Indian told me of an interesting happening witnessed by his grandfather very many years ago. A war party had set out to take horses from the Shoshone. One morning just at sunrise the fifteen or sixteen men were traveling along on foot in single file through a deep canon of the mountains, when one of them spied on a ledge far above them the head and shoulders of a great mountain sheep which seemed to be looking over the valley. He pointed it out to his fellows, and as they walked along they watched it. Presently it drew back, and a little later appeared again further along the ledges, and stood there on the verge. As the Indians watched, they suddenly saw shoot out from another ledge above the sheep a mountain lion, which alighted on the sheep's neck, and both animals fell whirling over the cliff and struck the slide rock below. The fall was a long one, and the Cheyennes, feeling sure that the sheep had been killed, either by the fall or by the lion, rushed forward to secure the meat. When they reached the spot the lion was hobbling off with a broken leg, and one of them shot it with his arrow, and when they made ready to skin the sheep, they saw to their astonishment that it was not a sheep, but a man wearing the skin and horns of a sheep. He had been hunting, and his bow and arrows were wrapped in the skin close to his breast. The fall had killed him. From the fashion of his hair and his moccasins they knew that he was a Bannock.

A reference to the hunting methods of the Sheep Eaters reminds one very naturally of that pursued by the Blackfeet, when sheep were needed, for their skins or for their flesh. These animals were abundant about the many buttes which rise out of the prairie on the flanks of the Rocky Mountains, in what is now Montana, and when disturbed retreated to the heights for safety.

Hugh Monroe, a typical mountain man of the old time, who reached Fort Edmonton in the year 1813, and died in 1893, after eighty years spent upon the prairie in close association with the Indians, has often told me of the Blackfoot method of securing sheep when their skins were needed for women's dresses. On such an occasion a large number of the men would ride out from the camp to the neighborhood of one of these buttes, and on their approach the sheep, which had been feeding on the prairie, slowly retreated to the heights above. The Indians then spread out, encircling the butte by a wide ring of horsemen, and sending three or four young men to climb its heights, awaited results. When the men sent up on the butte had reached its summit, they pursued the sheep over its limited area, and drove them down to the prairie below, where the mounted men chased and killed them. In this way large numbers of sheep were procured.

Of the hunting of the sheep by the Indians who inhabited the rough mountains in and near what is now the Yellowstone National Park, Mr. Hofer has said to me:

"It is supposed that when the Sheep Eater Indians inhabited the mountains about the Park they kept the sheep down pretty close, but after they went away the sheep increased in that particular range of country, the whole Absaroka range; that is to say, the country from Clark Fork of the Yellowstone down to the Wind River drainage.

"The greatest number of sheep in recent years was pretty well toward the head of Gray Bull, Meeteetse Creek and Stinking Water. In those old times the Indians used to build rude fences on the sides of the mountains, running down a hill, and these fences would draw together toward the bottom, and where they came nearly together the Indians would have a place to hide in. Fifteen years ago there was one such trap that was still quite plainly visible. One fence follows down pretty near the edge of a little ridge, draining steeply down from Crandle Creek divide to Miller Creek. There was no pen at the bottom, and no cliff to run them off, so that the Indians could not have killed them in that way, but near where the fences came together there was a pile of dead limbs and small rocks that looked to me as if it had been used by a person lying in wait to shoot animals which were driven down this ridge; and it was near enough to the place that they must pass to shoot them with arrows. These Indians had arrows, and hunted with them; and up on top of the ridges you will find old stumps that have been hacked down with stone hatchets. Some of the tree trunks have been removed, but others have been left there. I think that some Indians would go around the sheep and start them off, and gradually drive them to the pass where the hunter lay. I remember following along this ridge, and then on another ridge that went on toward the Clark Fork ridge to quite a high little peak, and on top of this peak was quite a large bed for a man to lie in. He could watch there until the sheep should pass through, and then he could come out and drive them on."

AGENTS OF DESTRUCTION.

The settling up of much of their former range, with pursuit by skin-hunters, head-hunters, and meat-hunters, has had much to do with the reduction in numbers of the mountain sheep, but more important than these have been the ravages by diseases brought in to their range by the domestic sheep, and then spread by the wild species among their wild associates. For many years it has been known that the wild sheep of certain portions of the Rocky Mountain region are afflicted with scab, a disease which in recent years seems to have attacked the elk as well. Testimony is abundant that wild sheep are killed by scab as domestic sheep are. On a few occasions I have seen animals that appeared to have died from this cause, but Mr. Hofer, to be quoted later, has had a much broader experience.

More sweeping and even more fatal has been the introduction among the wild sheep of an anthrax, of which, however, very little is known.

Aside from man, the most important enemies of the sheep in nature are the mountain lion and eagles of two species. These last I believe to be so destructive to newly born sheep and goats that I think it a duty to kill them whenever possible.

Dr. Edward L. Munson, at that time Assistant Surgeon, U.S. Army, but whose services in more recent years have won him so much credit, and such well deserved promotion, wrote me in 1897 the following interesting paragraphs with relation to disease among sheep. He said:

"The Bear Paw Mountains were full of mountain sheep a dozen years ago. One was roped last summer, and this is the only representative which has been seen or heard of there in ten years. The introduction of tame sheep early in the '80's was followed by a most destructive anthrax, which not only destroyed immense numbers of tame sheep, but also exterminated the wild ones, which appeared to be especially susceptible to this disease. In going through these mountains one often finds the skeletons of a number huddled together, and the above is the explanation given by some of the older settlers. The mountains are small, and the wild sheep could not climb up out of the infected zone. Immediate contact is, of course, not necessary in the propagation of anthrax, and the bacilli and spores left on soil grazed over by an infected band would readily infect another animal feeding over such a country even a long time afterward.

"I have also heard that the introduction of dog distemper played havoc with wolves, coyotes, and Indian dogs, when it first came into the country. This is the case with regard to any disease introduced into a virgin human population, in which there is no immunity due to the prevalence of such a disease for hundreds of years previously."

Mr. Elwood Hofer, discussing this subject in conversation, says:

"There are not a great many sheep in the Park now, anywhere; they have died off from sickness--the scab. This is a fact known to everyone living in the neighborhood of the Park. I have killed only one that had the disease badly, but I used to see them every day, and pay no attention to them. I did not hunt for them, for I did not want them in that condition. I remember that once a man came out to Gardiner who did not know that the sheep were sick. He saw some when he was hunting, and rushed up in great excitement and killed three of them. They seemed to be weak and were pretty nearly dead with scab before he saw them. Sometimes they become so weak from this disease that they lie down and die.

"I first noticed sheep with the scab around the canyon by the Yellowstone. I never saw any troubled with this disease around Meeteetsee or Stinking Water. I have been there in winter, and hunted them as late as November, and Col. Pickett used to kill some still later. I never heard him speak of the scab."

In spring and early summer, when the young sheep are small, the eagles are constantly on the watch for them, and unquestionably capture many lambs. I have been told by my friend, Mr. J.B. Monroe, who has several times captured lambs alive, that when they heard the rope whistling as he threw it toward them, they would run directly toward him, seeming to fear some enemy from above. He believes that they took the sound of the rope flying through the air for the sound of the eagle's wings.

While, of course, the mountain lions cannot overtake the sheep in fair chase, they lie in wait for them among the rocks, killing many, because the sheep range on ground suitable for the lions to stalk them on; that is to say, among the rocks on steep mountain sides, or at the edges of canyons.

A conversation had with Mr. Hofer a year or two since is so interesting that I offer no apology for giving the gist of it here. It has to do with the enemies of the sheep, especially the mountain lion, and with some of the sheep's ways. In substance, Mr. Hofer said:

"One day about the first of January I was in my cabin looking through the window, and up through the Cinnabar Basin, over the snow-covered mountains. As I was looking, I saw a dark patch disappear in the snow and then rise out of it again. The snow was deep and fluffy. The animal that I was watching would disappear in the snow with a plunge, and then would come up with a jump. It made several wonderful flights. It was so far off I could not tell what it was, and when I looked at it through the glasses I saw that it was a big ram breaking a trail. I was watching him closely and at first did not notice that others were with him. Soon, however, I discovered that there were four or five other sheep following him.

"The big ram came down from the side of the mountain, and, to pass over to the other mountain, he had to cross the valley. There were a number of knolls or ridges in this valley, where the snow was not so deep as in the hollows. The ram broke a trail to a knoll, and stopped and looked back, and pretty soon I saw the rest of the sheep coming along. They followed his trail and passed him while he was standing there looking back, always looking up at the mountain. While he stood on this knoll where the snow was not deep--for it had blown off--and the other sheep had passed him, one of them took the lead to the next knoll, breaking the trail, but here the snow was not so deep as that the ram had come through. No sooner had the sheep got to this knoll than the old ram started. He took the trail the others had made, and joined them at the next knoll, and then plunging in, went on ahead and broke a fresh trail to the next rise of ground. The ram did most of the trail-breaking, but sometimes one of the others went ahead; there was always one in the rear, on guard, as it were, until they had crossed the valley to a steep ridge on the next mountain. As they went, they stopped every little while and stood for some time looking back.

"Knowing the habits of the animal, I felt sure that something had driven them off the mountain. They looked back as if to see whether anything was following, or perhaps to look again at what had frightened them. I thought it was a mountain lion. Soon afterward I took my snowshoes and went up that way and found the track of a mountain lion. From the size of the track it seemed as if the animal must have been enormous. On soft snow, though, tracks spread and look big, and besides that, these cats commonly spread out their toes. There was no mistake about its being a mountain lion, for I could see where the tail had struck the soft snow and made holes in it.

"Mountain lions were around there a good deal, and E. De Long, who had a cabin a little further up in the valley, told me that three times in his experience of hunting up there he had come on a place where a mountain lion had just killed a sheep. In each case he found the sheep in nearly the same place, and in each case the sheep was freshly killed, and he dressed it and took it home.

"This seemed to be a favorite place for the lions to kill sheep. They are great hands to kill sheep in about the same place. Far up on the Boulder--way up near the head--Col. Pickett and I found nineteen or twenty skulls of sheep by one rock. There was a wonderful lot of them. They had been killed at various times, and in a place where they never could have been killed by snowslides. It was under a very high rock, fifteen feet perpendicular on one side, and in the valley a game trail passed close under this side. On the other side the rock was not so high, but sloped off to the side of the hill. A lion could easily lie there without being seen, but could himself see both ways. The game trail was so close that he could jump right down on to it. The number of skulls that we saw here was so remarkable that Col. Pickett and I counted them; there were more than eighteen.

"The skulls were most of them old--killed a good while before. None of them had the shells of the horns. They were old skulls, and the oldest were almost in fragments, very much weathered. It was the accumulation of a number of years, probably ten or fifteen. To my mind it showed clearly that this was a favorite place for lions to lie for mountain sheep. I have known of something similar to that in Cinnabar Basin, where I have seen a number of skulls scattered along the gulch. There was a heavy trail there which led up to a valley where there is a pass by which we used to wind down to the Yellowstone and Tom Miner Creek and Trapper Creek.

"Lions are quite bad along the Yellowstone here, and sometimes in a hard winter they seem to be driven out of the mountains, and a considerable number have been killed on Gardiner River and Reese Creek.

"If mountain lions are after the sheep, the sheep leave the mountain they are on and go to another; they will not stay there, and will not return until something drives them back."

SOME WAYS OF THE SHEEP.

Mr. Hofer said:

"In old times it was sometimes possible to get a 'stand' on sheep, and, in my opinion, sheep often, even to-day, are the least suspicious of all the mountain animals. A mountain sheep always seems to fear the thing that he sees under him. If a man goes above him he does not seem to know what to do. I could never understand why, when one is above him, he stands and looks. I have sometimes been riding around in the mountains, and have come on sheep right below me. I have often thrown stones at them, and sometimes it was quite a while before I could get them to start. Finally, however, they would run off. They acted as if they were dazed.

"On the other hand, when I carried the mail down in San Juan county, Colorado, in the winter of 1875-'76, going across from Animas Forks by way of the Grizzly Pass to Tellurium Fork, I was the only person in that section of the country all through the winter, and yet, although the sheep saw only me, and saw me every day, they always acted wild. Sometimes a ram would see me and stand and look for a long time, and then presently all along the mountain side I would see sheep running as if they were alarmed. On the other hand, if I met any of them on top of the mountain, they scarcely ever ran, they just stood and looked at me.

"Once, when on a hunting trip, I had my horses all picketed in sight, just above the basin where we were camped. The boy that had the care of the horses had been up to change the picketed animals, and when he came in he said: 'There's a sheep up there close by the horses. He saw me and was not afraid.' We went out of the tent and presently I could see the sheep, a small one about four years old. We went up toward it, and I saw the sheep moving about. It went out to a little flat place on the slide rock, where the slide rock had pushed out a little further, making a little low butte, or flat-topped table; it was loose rock, with snow. Here the sheep lay down.

"I went around to station my man where he could get a rest for his rifle, and when I had done this, I went around above to make the sheep get up to drive him out, so that the man could shoot him. After I got well up the gulch, above him, the sheep could see me plainly, and I could see his eyes. I hesitated about making him get up, thinking perhaps it was somebody's tame sheep, but we were the first ones up there that spring, and of course it was not a tame sheep. If we had not been out of meat I would not have disturbed the animal. I walked toward it to make it get up, but it would not, and still lay there. When I was within thirty feet of it I took up a stone and threw it, and called at him. The sheep stood up and looked at me. I said, 'Go on, now,' and he started in the direction I wished him to take. When he came in sight, the man fired two or three shots at him, but did not hurt him, and the sheep again lay down in sight of camp. Afterward I fired at him about 300 yards up the side of the mountain, but I did not touch him. However, he was disturbed by the shooting, and moved away.

"It is often difficult to find a reason for the way sheep act. It is possible that this young ram, which was in the Sunlight Mining District, had seen many miners, and that they had not disturbed him, and that so he had lost his fear of man. He was not at all afraid of horses, perhaps because he was accustomed to seeing miners' horses; or he may have taken them for elk. I do not see why our wind did not alarm him. At all events, for some reason, this one showed no fear.

"Along the Gardiner River, inside the northern boundary of the Yellowstone Park, there are always a number of sheep in winter, and they become very tame, having learned by experience that people passing to and fro will not injure them. Men driving up the road from Mammoth Hot Springs to Gardiner, constantly see these sheep, which manifest the utmost indifference to those who are passing them. Sometimes they stand close enough to the road for a driver to reach them with his whip. One winter the surgeon at the post, driving along, came upon a sheep standing in the road, and as it did not move, he had to stop his team for it. He did not dare to drive his horse close up to it. Finally the ram jumped out to one side of the road, and the surgeon drove on. He said he could have touched it with his whip."

One winter when Mr. Hofer made an extended snowshoe trip through the Park, he passed very close to sheep. It appeared to him that they fear man less along the wagon roads than when he is out on the benches and in the mountains. They seem to care little for man, but if a mountain lion appears in the neighborhood, the sheep are no longer seen. Just where they go is uncertain, but it is believed that they cross the Yellowstone River by swimming.

In winter, and especially late in the winter, sheep frequent southern and southwestern exposures, and spend much of their time there. I have seen places on the St. Marys Lake, in northern Montana, where there were cartloads of droppings, apparently the accumulation of many years, and have seen the same thing in the cliffs along the Yellowstone River. On the rocks here there were many beds among the cliffs and ledges. Often such beds are behind a rock, not a high one, but one that the sheep could look over. In places such as this the animals are very difficult to detect.

Although the wild sheep was formerly, to a considerable extent, an inhabitant of the western edge of the prairies of the high dry plains, it is so no longer. The settling of the country has made this impossible, but long before its permanent occupancy the frequent passage through it by hunters had resulted in the destruction of the sheep or had driven it more or less permanently to those heights where, in times of danger, it had always sought refuge.

To the east of the principal range of the wild sheep in America to-day there are still a few of its old haunts not in the mountains which are so arid or so rough, or where the water is so bad that as yet they have not to any great extent been invaded by the white man. Again to the south and southwest, in portions of Arizona, Old Mexico, and Lower California, there rise out of frightful deserts buttes and mountain ranges inhabited by different forms of sheep. In that country water is extremely scarce, and the few water holes that exist are visited by the sheep only at long intervals. There are many men who believe that the sheep do not drink at all, but it is chiefly at these water holes that the sheep of the desert are killed.

At the present day the chief haunts of the mountain sheep are the fresh Alpine meadows lying close to timber line, and fenced in by tall peaks; or the rounded grassy slopes which extend from timber line up to the region of perpetual snows. Sitting on the point of some tall mountain the observer may look down on the green meadows, interspersed perhaps with little clumps of low willows which grow along the tiny watercourses whose sources are the snow banks far up the mountain side, and if patient in his watch and faithful in his search, he may detect with his glasses at first one or two, and gradually more and more, until at length perhaps ten, fifteen or thirty sheep may be counted, scattered over a considerable area of country. Or, if he climbs higher yet, and overlooks the rounded shoulders which stretch up from the passes toward the highest pinnacles of all--he will very likely see far below him, lying on the hill and commanding a view miles in extent in every direction, a group of nine, ten or a dozen sheep peacefully resting in the midday sun. Those that he sees will be almost all of them ewes and young animals. Perhaps there may be a young ram or two whose horns have already begun to curve backward, but for the most part they are females and young.

The question that the hunter is always asking himself is where are the big rams? Now and then, to be sure, more by accident than by any wisdom of his own, he stumbles on some monster of the rocks, but of the sheep that he sees in his wanderings, not one in a hundred has a head so large as to make him consider it a trophy worth possessing. It is commonly declared that in summer the big rams are "back along the range," by which it is meant that they are close to the summits of the tallest peaks. It is probable that this is true, and that they gather by twos and threes on these tall peaks, and, not moving about very much, escape observation.

During the spring, summer, and early fall the females and their young keep together in small bands in the mountains, well up, close under what is called the "rim rock," or the "reefs," where the grass is sweet and tender, the going good, and where a refuge is within easy reach. While hunting in such places in September and October, when the first snows are falling, one is likely to find the trail of a band of sheep close up beneath the rock. If the mountain is one long inhabited by sheep, they have made a well-worn trail on the hillside, and the little band, while traveling along this in a general way, scatters out on both sides feeding on the grass heads that project above the snow, and often with their noses pushing the light snow away to get at the grass beneath. I have never seen them do this, nor have I seen them paw to get at the grass, but the marks in the snow where they have fed showed clearly that the snow was pushed aside by the muzzle.

Like most other animals, wild and tame, sheep are very local in their habits, and one little band will occupy the same basin in the mountains all summer long, going to water by the same trail, feeding in the same meadows and along the same hillsides, occupying the same beds stamped out in the rough slide rock, or on the great rock masses which have fallen down from the cliff above. Even if frightened from their chosen home by the passage of a party of travelers, they will go no further than to the tops of the rocks, and as soon as the cause of alarm is removed will return once more to the valley.

I saw a striking instance of this some years ago, when, with a Geological Survey party, I visited a little basin on the head of one of the forks of Stinking Water in Wyoming, where a few families of sheep had their home.

Our appearance alarmed the sheep, which ran a little way up the face of the cliff, and then, stopping occasionally to look, clambered along more deliberately. When we reached the head of the basin we found that there was no way down on the other side, and that we must go back as we had come. The afternoon was well advanced and the pack train started back and camped only a mile or two down the valley, while I stopped among some great rocks to watch the movements of the sheep. Though at first not easy to see, the animals' presence was evident by their calling, and at length several were detected almost at the top of the cliff, but already making their way back into the valley.

I was much interested in watching a ewe, which was coming down a steep slope of slide rock. There was apparently no trail, or if there was one, she did not use it, but picked her way down to the head of the slope of slide rock, stood there for a few moments, and then, after bleating once or twice, sprang well out into the air and alighted on the slide rock, it seemed to me, twenty-five feet below where she had been. A little cloud of dust arose and she appeared to be buried to her knees in the slide rock. I could not see how it was possible for her to have made this jump without breaking her slender legs, yet she repeated it again and again, until she had come down about to my level and had passed out of sight. Nor was this ewe the only one that was coming down. From a number of points on the precipice round about I could hear rocks rolling and sheep calling, and before very long eight or ten ewes and four or five lambs had come together in the little basin, and presently marched almost straight up to where I lay hid. There was meat in the camp, and so no reason for shooting at these innocents. Later when I returned to camp, one of the packers informed me that for an hour or two before a yearling ram had been feeding in the meadow with the pack animals, close to the camp.

The sheep now commonly shows himself to be the keenest and wariest of North American big game. Yet we may readily credit the stories told us by older men of his former simplicity and innocence, since even to-day we sometimes see these characteristics displayed. I remember riding up a narrow valley walled in on both sides by vertical cliffs and at its head by a rock wall which was partly broken down, and through which we hoped to find a way into the next valley to the northward. As we rode along, a mile or more from the cliff at the valley's head, I saw one or two sheep passing over it, and a few minutes later was electrified by hearing my companion say: "Oh, look at the sheep! Look at the sheep! Look at the sheep!" And there, charging down the valley directly toward us, came a bunch of thirty or forty sheep in a close body, running as if something very terrifying were close behind them, and paying not the slightest attention to the two horsemen before them. I rolled off my horse and loaded my gun. The sheep came within twenty-five or thirty steps and a little to one side, and passed us like the wind, but they left behind one of their number, which kept us in fresh meat for several days thereafter.

The first shot I fired at this band gave me a surprise. I drew my sight fine on the point of the breast of the leading animal and pulled the trigger, but instead of the explosion which should have followed I heard the hammer fall on the firing-pin. There was a slow hissing sound, a little puff at the muzzle of the rifle, and I distinctly heard the leaden ball fall to the ground just in front of me. In a moment I had reloaded and had killed the sheep before it had passed far beyond me; but for a few seconds I could not comprehend what had happened. Then it came back to me that a few days before I had made from half a dozen cartridges a weight to attach to a fish line for the purpose of sounding the depth of a lake. Evidently a lubricating wad had been imperfect, and dampness had reached the powder.

Like others of our ungulates, wild sheep are great frequenters of "licks"--places where the soil has been more or less impregnated with saline solutions. These licks are visited frequently--perhaps daily--during the summer months by sheep of all ages, and such points are favorite watching places for men who need meat, and wish to secure it as easily as possible. At a certain lick in northern Montana, shots at sheep may be had almost any day by the man who is willing to watch for them. In the summer of 1903 a bunch of nine especially good rams visited a certain lick each day. The guide of a New York man who was hunting there in June--of course in violation of the law--took him to the lick. The first day nine rams came, and the New Yorker, after firing many shots, frightened them all away. Perhaps he hit some of them, for the next day only seven returned, of which three were killed. In British Columbia I have seen twenty-five or thirty sheep working at a lick, from which the earth had been eaten away, so that great hollows and ravines were cut out in many directions from the central spring.

Examination of such licks in cold--freezing--weather, seems to show that the sheep do not then visit them. I have seen mule deer and sheep nibbling the soil in company, and have seen white goats visit a lick frequented also by sheep.

Of Dall's sheep, Mr. Stone declares that it is rapidly growing scarcer, and this statement is based not only on his own observation, but on reports made to him by the Indians. Mr. Stone describes it as possessing wonderful agility, endurance, and vitality, and gives many examples of their ability to get about among most difficult rocks when wounded. He adds: "From my experience with these animals, I believe they seek quite as rugged a country in which to make their homes as does the Rocky Mountain goat. They brave higher latitudes and live in regions in every way more barren and forbidding." He reports the females with their lambs as generally keeping to the high table lands far back in the mountains. Among the specimens which he recently collected, broken jaw bones reunited were so frequent among the females killed as to excite comment. Notwithstanding Mr. Stone's gloomy view of the future of this species, we may hope that the enforcement of the game laws in Alaska will long preserve this beautiful animal.

Our knowledge of the habits of the Lower California sheep inhabiting the San Pedro Martir Mountains has been slight. Mr. Gould's admirable account of a hunting trip for them--"To the Gulf of Cortez," published in a preceding volume of the Club's book--will be remembered, and the curious fact stated by his Indian guide that the sheep break holes in the hard, prickly rinds of the venaga cactus with their horns, and then eat out the inside.

Recently, however, a series of thirteen specimens collected by Edmund Heller were received by Dr. D.G. Elliot, and described, as already stated, and he gives from Mr. Heller's note-book the following notes on their habits:

"Common about the cliffs, coming down occasionally to the water holes in the valley. Most of the sheep observed were either solitary or in small bands of three to a dozen. Only one adult ram was seen, all the others, about thirty, being either ewes or lambs. The largest bunch seen consisted of eleven, mostly ewes and a few young rams." The sheep, as a rule, inhabit the middle line of cliffs where they are safe from attack above and can watch the valley below for danger. Here about the middle line of cliffs they were observed, and the greater number of tracks and dust wallows, where they spend much of their time, were seen. A few were seen on the level stretches of the mesas, and a considerable number of tracks, but these were made by those traveling from one line of cliffs to another.

"They are constantly on guard, and very little of their time is given to browsing. Their usual method is to feed about some high cliffs or rocks, taking an occasional mouthful of brush, and then suddenly throwing up the head and gazing and listening for a long time before again taking food. They are not alarmed by scent, like deer or antelope, the direction of the wind apparently making no difference in hunting them. A small bunch of six were observed for a considerable time feeding. Their method seemed to be much the same as individuals, except that when danger was suspected by any member, he would give a few quick leaps, and all the flock would scamper to some high rock and face about in various directions, no two looking the same way. These maneuvers were often performed, perhaps once every fifteen minutes.

"Their chief enemy is the mountain lion, which hunts them on the cliffs, apparently never about watering places. Lion tracks were not rare about the sheep runs. They are extremely wary about coming down for water, and take every precaution. Before leaving the cliffs to cross the valley to water they usually select some high ridge and descend along this, gazing constantly at the spring, usually halting ten or more minutes on every prominent rocky point. When within a hundred yards or less of the water, a long careful search is made, and a great deal of ear-work performed, the head being turned first to one side and then to the other. When they do at last satisfy themselves, they make a bolt and drink quickly, stopping occasionally to listen and look for danger.

"If, however, they should be surprised at the water they do not flee at once, but gaze for some time at the intruder, and then go a short way and take another look, and so on until at last they break into a steady run for the cliffs. At least thirty sheep were observed at the water, and none came before 9:30 A.M. or later than 2:30 P.M., most coming down between 12:00 M. and 1:00 P.M. This habit has probably been established to avoid lions, which are seldom about during the hottest part of the day. A few ewes were seen with two lambs, but the greater number had only one. Most of the young appeared about two months old. Their usual gait was a short gallop, seldom a walk or trot."

The great curving horns of the wild sheep have always exercised more or less influence on people's imagination, and have given rise to various fables. These horns are large in proportion to the animal, and so peculiar that it has seemed necessary to account for them on the theory that they had some marvelous purpose. The familiar tale that the horns of the males were used as cushions on which the animal alighted when leaping down from great heights is old. A more modern hypothesis which promises to be much shorter lived is that advanced a year or two ago by Mr. Geo. Wherry, of Cambridge, England, who suggested that "The form of the horn and position of the ear enables the wild sheep to determine the direction of sound when there is a mist or fog, the horn acting like an admiralty megaphone when used as an ear trumpet, or like the topophone (double ear trumpet, the bells of which turn opposite ways) used for a fog-bound ship on British-American vessels to determine the direction of sound signals."

It is, of course, well understood, and, on the publication of Mr. Wherry's hypothesis, was at once suggested, that there are many species of wild sheep, and that the spiral of the horn of each species is a different one. Moreover, within each species there are of course different ages, and the spiral may differ with age and also at the same age to some extent with the individual. In some cases, the ear perhaps lies at the apex of a cone formed by the horn, but in others it does not lie there. Moreover this hypothesis, like the other and older one, in which the horns were said to act as the jumping cushion, takes no account of the females and young, which in mists, fogs, and at other times, need protection quite as much as the adult males. The old males with large and perfect horns have to a large extent fulfilled the function of their lives-- reproduction--and their place is shortly to be taken by younger animals growing up. Moreover they have reached the full measure of strength and agility, and through years of experience have come to a full knowledge of the many dangers to which their race is exposed. It would seem extraordinary that nature should have cared so well for them, and should have left the more defenseless females and young unprotected from the dangers likely to come to them from enemies which may make sounds in a fog.

The old males with large and perfect horns have come to their full fighting powers, and do fight fiercely at certain seasons of the year. And it is believed by many people that the great development of horns among the mountain sheep is merely a secondary sexual character analogous to the antlers of the deer or the spurs of the cock.

Most people who have hunted sheep much will believe that this species depends for its safety chiefly on its nose and its eyes. And if the observations of hunters in general could be gathered and collated, they would probably agree that the female sheep are rather quicker to notice danger than the males, though both are quick enough.

PROTECTION.

It is gratifying to note that the rapid disappearance of the mountain sheep has made some impression on legislators in certain States where it is native. Some of these have laws absolutely forbidding the killing of mountain sheep; and while in certain places in all of such States and Territories this law is perhaps lightly regarded, and not generally observed, still, on the whole, its effect must be good, and we may hope that gradually it will find general observance. The mountain sheep is so superb an animal that it should be a matter of pride with every State which has a stock of sheep within its borders to preserve that stock most scrupulously. It is said that in Colorado, where sheep have long been protected, they are noticeably increasing, and growing tamer. I have been told of one stock and mining camp, near Silver Plume, where there is a bunch of sheep absolutely protected by public sentiment, in which the miners, and in fact the whole community, take great pride and delight.

It is fitting that on the statute books the mountain sheep should have better protection than most species of our large game, since there is no other species now existing in any numbers which is more exposed to danger of extinction. Destroyed on its old ranges, it is found now only in the roughest mountains, the bad lands, and the desert, and it is sufficiently desirable as a trophy to be ardently pursued wherever found.

Several States have been wise enough absolutely to protect sheep; these are North Dakota, California, Arizona, Montana, Colorado (until 1907), Utah, New Mexico (until March 1, 1905), and Texas (until July, 1908). Three other States, South Dakota, Wyoming and Idaho, permit one mountain sheep to be killed by the hunter during the open season of each year. Oregon, which has a long season, from July 15 to November 1, puts no limit on the number to be killed, while in Nevada there appears to be no protection for the species.

If these protective laws were enforced, sheep would increase, and once more become delightful objects of the landscape, as they have in portions of Colorado and in the National Park, where, as already stated, they are so tame during certain seasons of the year that they will hardly get out of the way. On the other hand, in many localities covered by excellent laws, there are no means of enforcing them. Montana, which perhaps has as many sheep as any State in the Union, does not, and perhaps cannot, enforce her law, the sheep living in sections distant from the localities where game wardens are found, and so difficult to watch. In some cases where forest rangers are appointed game wardens, they are without funds for the transportation of themselves and prisoners over the one hundred or two hundred miles between the place of arrest and the nearest Justice of the Peace, and cannot themselves be expected to pay these expenses. In the summer of 1903 sheep were killed in violation of law in the mountains of Montana, and also in the bad lands of the Missouri River.

On the other hand, in Colorado there are many places where the law protecting the sheep is absolutely observed. Public opinion supports the law, and those disposed to violate it dare not do so for fear of the law. Near Silver

Plume, already mentioned, a drive to see the wild sheep come down to water is one of the regular sights offered to visitors, and while there may be localities where sheep are killed in violation of the law in Colorado, it is certain that there are many where the law is respected.

There are still a few places where sheep may be found to-day, living somewhat as they used to live before the white men came into the western country. Such places are the extremely rough bad lands of the Missouri River, between the Little Rocky Mountains and the mouth of Milk River, where, on account of the absence of water on the upper prairie and the small areas of the bottoms of the Missouri River, there are as yet few settlements. The bad lands are high and rough, scarcely to be traversed except by a man on foot, and in their fastnesses the sheep--protected formally by State law, but actually by the rugged country--are still holding their own. They come down to the river at night to water, and returning spend the day feeding on the uplands of the prairie, and resting in beds pawed out of the dry earth of the washed bad lands, just as their ancestors did.

In old times this country abounded in buffalo, elk, deer of two species, sheep, and antelope, and if set aside as a State park by Montana, it would offer an admirable game refuge, and one still stocked with all its old-time animals, except the elk and the buffalo.

* * * * *

RANGE.

The present range of the different forms of mountain sheep extends from Alaska and from the Pacific Ocean east to the Rocky Mountains--with a tongue extending down the Missouri River as far as the Little Missouri--south to Sonora and Lower California. The various forms from north to south appear to be Dall's sheep, the saddleback sheep, Stone's sheep, the common bighorn, with the Missouri River variety, existing to the east, in the bad lands, and with Nelson's, the Mexican and the Lower California sheep running southward into Mexico.

Among the experienced hunters of both forms of Dall's sheep are Messrs. Dali DeWeese, of Colorado, and A.J. Stone, Collector of Arctic Mammals for the American Museum of Natural History. Mr. Stone gives two distinct ranges for this sheep, (1) the Alaska Mountains and Kenai Peninsula, and (2) the entire stretch of the Rocky Mountains north of latitude 60 degrees to near the Arctic coast just at the McKenzie, reaching thence west to the headwaters of the Noatak and Kowak rivers that flow into Kotzebue Sound.

Stone's sheep, which was described by Dr. Allen in 1897, came from the head of the Stickine River, and two years after its description Dr. J.A. Allen quotes Mr. A.J. Stone, the collector, as saying: "I traced the _Ovis stonei_, or black sheep, throughout the mountainous country of the headwaters of the Stickine, and south to the headwaters of the Nass, but could find no reliable information of their occurrence further south in this longitude. They are found throughout the Cassiar Mountains, which extend north to 61 degrees north latitude and west to 134 degrees west longitude. How much further west they may be found I have been unable to determine. Nor could I ascertain whether their range extends from the Cassiar Mountains into the Rocky Mountains to the north of Francis and Liard River. But the best information obtained led me to believe that it does not. They are found in the Rocky Mountains to the south as far as the headwaters of the Nelson and Peace rivers in latitude 56 degrees, but I proved conclusively that in the main range of the Rocky Mountains very few of them are found north of the Liard River. Where this river sweeps south through the Rocky Mountains to Hell's Gate, a few of these animals are founds as far north as Beaver River, a tributary of the Liard. None, however, are found north of this, and I am thoroughly convinced that this is the only place where these animals may be found north of the Liard River.

"I find that in the Cassiar Mountains and in the Rocky Mountains they everywhere range above timber line, as they do in the mountains of Stickine, the Cheonees, and the Etsezas.

"Directly to the north of the Beaver River, and north of the Liard River below the confluence of the Beaver, we first meet with Ovis dalli."

A Stony Indian once told me that in his country--the main range of the Rocky Mountains--there were two sorts of sheep, one small, dark in color, and with slender horns, which are seldom broken, and another sort larger and pale in color, with heavy, thick horns that are often broken at the point. He went on to say that these small black sheep are all found north of Bow River, Alberta, and that on the south side of Bow River the big sheep only occur. The country referred to all lies on the eastern slope of the Rocky Mountains. The hunting ground of the Stonies runs as far north as Peace River, and it is hardly to be doubted that they know Stone's sheep. The Brewster Bros., of Banff, Alberta, inform me that Stone's sheep is found on the head of Peace River.

A dozen or fifteen years ago one of the greatest sheep ranges that was at all accessible was in the mountains at the head of the Ashnola River, in British Columbia, and on the head of the Methow, which rises in the same mountains and flows south into Washington. This is a country very rough and without roads, only to be traversed with a pack train.

Mr. Lew Wilmot writes me that there are still quite a number of sheep ranging from Mt. Chapacca, up through the Ashnola, and on the headwaters of the Methow. Indeed, it is thought by some that sheep are more numerous there now than they were a few years ago. In Dyche's "Campfires of a Naturalist" a record is given of sheep in the Palmer Lake region, at the east base of the Cascade range in Washington.

The Rev. John McDougall, of Morley, Alberta, wrote me in 1899, in answer to inquiries as to the mountain sheep inhabiting the country ranged over by the Stony Indians, "that it is the opinion of these Indians that the sheep which frequent the mountains from Montana northward as far as our Indians hunt, are all of one kind, but that in localities they differ in size, and somewhat in color.

"They say that from the 49th parallel to the headwaters of the Saskatchewan River, sheep are larger than those in the Selkirks and coast ranges; and also that as they go north of the Saskatchewan the sheep become smaller. As to color, they say that the more southerly and western sheep are the lighter; and that as you pass north the sheep are darker in color. These Stonies report mountain sheep as still to be found in all of the mountain country they roam in. Their hunting ground is about 400 miles long by 150 broad, and is principally confined to the Rocky Mountain range."

In an effort to establish something of the range of the mountain sheep, during the very last years of the nineteenth century, I communicated with a large number of gentlemen who were either resident in, or travelers through, portions of the West now or formerly occupied by the mountain sheep, and the results of these inquiries I give below:

Prof. L.V. Pirsson, of Yale University, who has spent a number of years in studying the geology of various portions of the northern Rocky Mountains, wrote me with considerable fullness in 1896 concerning the game situation in some of the front ranges of the Rockies, where sheep were formerly very abundant. In the Crazy Mountains he says he saw no sheep, and that while it was possible they might be there, they must certainly be rare. In 1880 there were many sheep there. In the Castle Mountains none were seen, nor reported, nor any traces seen. The same is true of the Little Belt, Highwood, and Judith Mountains. He understood that sheep were still present in the bad lands; immediately about the mountains and east of them the country was too well settled for any game to live. Earlier, however, in the summer of 1890, passing through the Snowy Mountains, which lie north of the National Park, sheep were seen on two occasions; a band of ten ewes and lambs on Sheep Mountain, and a band of seven rams on the head of the stream known as the Buffalo Fork of the Lamar River. In 1893 an old ram was killed on Black Butte, at the extreme eastern end of the Judith Mountains, near Cone Butte, and it is quite possible that this animal had strayed out of the bad lands on the lower Musselshell, or on the Missouri. Even at that time there were said to be no sheep on the Little Rockies, Bearpaws, or Sweetgrass Hills.

All the ranges spoken of were formerly great sheep ranges, and on all of them, many years ago, I saw sheep in considerable numbers.

There are a very few sheep in the Wolf Mountains of Montana.

There are still mountain sheep among the rough bad lands on both sides of the Missouri River, between the mouth of the Musselshell and the mouth of Big Dry. It is hard to estimate the number of these sheep, but there must be many hundreds of them, and perhaps thousands. As recently as August, 1900, Mr. S.C. Leady, a ranchman in this region, advised me that he counted in one bunch, coming to water, forty-nine sheep.

Mr. Leady further advised me that in his country, owing to the sparse settlement, the game laws are not at all regarded, and sheep are hunted at all times of the year. The settlers themselves advocate the protection of the game, but there is really no one to enforce the laws. Recent advices from this country show that the conditions there are now somewhat improved.

It is probable that in suitable localities in the Missouri River bad lands sheep are still found in some numbers all the way from the mouth of the Little Missouri to the mouth of the Judith River.

Mr. O.C. Graetz, now, or recently, of Kipp, Montana, advised me, through my friend, J.B. Monroe, that in 1894, in the Big Horn Mountains, Wyo., on the head of the Little Horn River, in the rough and rolling country he saw a band of eleven sheep. The same man tells me that also in 1894, in Sweetwater county, in Wyoming, near the Sweetwater River, south of South Pass, on a mountain known as Oregon Butte, he twice saw two sheep. The country was rolling and high, with scattering timber, but not much of it. In this country, and at that time, the sheep were not much hunted.

Mr. Elwood Hofer, one of the best known guides of the West, whose home is in Gardiner, Park county, Mont., has very kindly furnished me with information about the sheep on the borders of the Yellowstone National Park. Writing in May, 1898, he says: "At this time sheep are not numerous anywhere in this country, compared with what they were before the railroad (Northern Pacific Railroad) was built in 1881. In summer they are found in small bands all through the mountains, in and about the National Park. I found them all along the divide, and out on the spurs, between the Yellowstone and Stinking Water rivers, and on down between the Yellowstone and Snake rivers, on one side, and the south fork of Stinking Water River and the Wind River on the east. I found sheep at the extreme headwaters of the Yellowstone, and of the Wind River, and the Buffalo Fork of Snake River. There are sheep in the Tetons, Gallatin-Madison range, and even on Mount Holmes. I have seen them around Electric Peak, and so on north, along the west side of the Yellowstone as far as the Bozeman Pass; but not lately, for I have not been in those mountains for a number of years. All along the range from the north side of the Park to within sight of Livingston there are a few sheep.

"On the Stinking Water, where I used to see bands of fifteen to twenty sheep, now we only see from three to five. Of late years I have seen very few large rams, and those only in the Park. Last summer Mr. Archibald Rogers saw a large ram at the headwaters of Eagle Creek, very close to the Park. In winter there are usually a few large rams in the Gardiner Canyon. I hear that there are a few sheep out toward Bozeman, on Mt. Blackmore, and the mountains near there.

"I believe that some of the reasons for the scarcity of mountain sheep in this country are these: First, the settlement of the plains country close to the mountains, prevents their going to their winter ranges, and so starves them; secondly, the same cause keeps them in the mountains, where the mountain lions can get at them; and thirdly, the scab has killed a good many. I do not think that the rifle has had much to do with destroying the sheep."

Sheep were formerly exceedingly abundant in all the bad lands along the Yellowstone and Missouri rivers, and in the rough, broken country from Powder River west to the Big Horn. The Little Missouri country was a good sheep range, and also the broken country about Fort Laramie. In the Black Hills of Dakota they were formerly abundant, and also along the North Platte River, near the canons of the Platte, in the Caspar Mountain, and in all the rough country down nearly to the forks of the Platte.

The easternmost locality which I have for the bighorn is the Birdwood Creek in Nebraska. This lies just north of O'Fallon Station on the Union Pacific Railroad and flows nearly due south into the North Platte River. It is in the northwestern corner of Lincoln county, Nebraska, just west of the meridian of 101 degrees. Here, in 1877, the late Major Frank North, well known to all men familiar with the West between the years 1860 and 1880, saw, but did not kill, a male mountain sheep. The animal was only 100 yards from him, was plainly seen and certainly recognized. Major North had no gun, and thought of killing the sheep with his revolver, but his brother, Luther H. North, who was armed with a rifle, was not far from him, and Major North dropped down out of sight and motioned his brother to come to him, so that he might kill it. By the time Luther had come up, the sheep had walked over a ridge and was not seen again, but there is no doubt as to its identification. It had probably come from Court House Rock in Scott's Bluff county, Nebraska, where there were still a few sheep as recently as twenty-five years ago.

These animals were also more or less abundant along the Little Missouri River as late as the late '80's, and perhaps still later. This had always been a favorite range for them, and in 1874 they were noticed and reported on by Government expeditions which passed through the country, and the hunters and trappers who about that time plied their trade along that river found them abundant. Mr. Roosevelt has written much of hunting them on that stream.

The low bluffs of the Yellowstone River--in the days when that was a hostile Indian country, and only the hunter who was particularly reckless and daring ventured into it--were a favorite feeding ground for sheep. They were reported very numerous by the first expeditions that went up the river, and a few have been killed there within five or six years, although the valley is given over to farming and the upper prairie is covered with cattle. This used to be one of the greatest sheep ranges in all the West; the wide flats of the river bottom, the higher table lands above, and the worn bad lands between, furnishing ideal sheep ground. The last killed there, so far as I know, were a ram and two ewes, which were taken about forty miles below Rosebud Station, on the river, in 1897 or 1898.

Of Wyoming, Mr. Wm. Wells writes: "I have only been up here in northwestern Wyoming for a year, but from what I have seen, sheep are holding their own fairly well, and may be increasing in places. In 1897, Mr. H.D. Shelden, of Detroit, Mich., and myself were hunting sheep just west of the headwaters of Hobacks River. There was a sort of knife-edge ridge running about fifteen miles north and south, the summit of which was about 2,000 feet above a bench or table-land. The ridge was well watered, and in some places the timber ran nearly up to the top of the ridge. On this ridge there were about 100 sheep, divided into three bands. Each band seemed to make its home in a cup-like hollow on the east side of the ridge, about 500 feet below the crest, but the members of the different bands seemed to visit back and forth, as the numbers were not always the same.

"We could take our horses up into either one of the three hollows, and some of the sheep were so tame that we have several times been within fifty yards in plain sight, and had the sheep pay very little attention to us. In one instance two ewes and lambs went on ahead of us at a walk for several hundred yards, often stopping to look back; and in another a sheep, after looking at us, two horses and two dogs, across a canyon 200 yards wide, pawed a bed in the slide rock and lay down. In another case I drove about thirty head of ewes and lambs to within thirty-five yards of Mr. Shelden, and when he rose up in plain sight, they stood and looked at him. When he saw that there was no ram there, he yelled at them, upon which they ran off about 400 yards, and then stood and looked at us.

"I do not think that these sheep had been hunted, until this time, for several years. As nearly as I could tell, they ranged winter and summer on nearly the same ground. At the top of the range, facing the east, were overhanging ledges of rock, and under these the dung was two feet or more deep.

"Either during the winter or early spring the sheep had been down in the timber on the east side of the ridge, as I found the remains of several, in the winter coat, that had been killed by cougars."

Mr. D.C. Nowlin, of Jackson, Wyo., was good enough to write me in 1898, concerning the sheep in the general neighborhood of Jackson's Hole; that is to say, in the ranges immediately south of the National Park, a section not far from that just described. He says: "In certain ranges near here sheep are comparatively plentiful, and are killed every hunting season.

"Occasionally a scabby ram is killed. I killed one here which showed very plainly the ravages of scab, especially around the ears, and on the neck and shoulders. Evidently the disease is identical with that so common among domestic sheep, and I have heard more than one creditable account of mountain sheep mingling temporarily with domestic flocks and thus contracting the scab. I am confident that the same parasite which is found upon scabby domestic sheep is responsible for the disease which affects the bighorn. It is not difficult to account for the transmission of the disease, as western sheep-men roam with their flocks at will, from the peach belt to timber line, regardless alike of the legal or inherent rights of man or beast. Partly through isolation, and partly through moral suasion by our people, no domestic sheep have invaded Jackson's Hole."

Mr. Ira Dodge, of Cora, Wyo., in response to inquiries as to the sheep in his section of the country, says: "Mountain sheep are, like most other game, where you find them; but their feeding grounds are mainly high table-lands, at the foot of, or near, high rocky peaks or ranges. These table-lands occur at or near timber line, varying one or two thousand feet either way. In this latitude timber line occurs at about 11,500 feet. In all the ranges in this locality, namely, the Wind River, Gros Ventre, and Uintah, water is found in abundance, and, as a rule, there is plenty of timber. I think I have more often found sheep in the timber, or below timber line, than at higher altitudes, although sometimes I have located the finest rams far above the last scrubby pine.

"The largest bunch of sheep that I have seen was in the fall of 1893. I estimated the band at 75 to 100. In that bunch there were no rams, and they remained in sight for quite a long time; so that I had a good opportunity to estimate them.

"I do not profess to know where the majority of these sheep winter, but, undoubtedly, a great number winter on the table-lands before mentioned, where a rich growth of grass furnishes an abundance of feed. At this altitude the wind blows so hard and continuously, and the snow is so light and dry, that there would be no time during the whole winter when the snow would lie on the ground long enough to starve sheep to death. Several small bunches of sheep winter on the Big Gros Ventre River. These, I think, are the same sheep that are found in summer time on the Gros Ventre range. I have occasionally killed sheep that were scabby, but I have no positive knowledge that this disease has killed any number of sheep. In the fall of 1894 I discovered eleven large ram skulls in one place, and since that time found four more near by. My first impression was that the eleven were killed by a snowslide, as they were at the foot of one of those places where snowslides occur, but finding the other four within a mile, and in a place where a snowslide could not have killed them, it rather dispelled my first theory. As mountain sheep can travel over snow drifts nearly as well as a caribou, I do not believe that they were stranded in a snowstorm and perished, and no hunter would have killed so great a number and left such magnificent heads. The scab theory is about the only solution left. The sheep are not hunted very much here, and I believe their greatest enemy is the mountain lion.

"There is one isolated bunch of mountain sheep on the Colorado Desert, situated in Fremont and Sweetwater counties, Wyo., which seems to be holding its own against many range riders, meat and specimen hunters, as well as coyotes. They are very light in color, much more so than their cousins found higher up in the mountains, and locally they are called ibex, or white goats. The country they live in is very similar to the bad lands of Dakota, and I dare say that their long life on the plains has created in them a distinct sub-species of the bighorn."

The Colorado Desert is situated in Wyoming, between the Green River on the west, and the Red Desert on the east. The sheep are seen mostly on the breaks on Green River. They are sometimes chased by cowboys, but I have never known of one being caught in that way.

I am told that in some bad lands in the Red Desert, locally known as Dobe Town, there is a herd of wild sheep, which are occasionally pursued by range riders. Rarely one is roped.

Mr. Fred E. White, of Jackson, Wyo., advised me in 1898 of the existence of sheep in the mountains which drain into Gros Ventre Fork, the heads of Green River and Buffalo Fork of Snake River. Mr. White was with the Webb party, some years ago, when they secured a number of sheep. The same correspondent calls attention to the very large number of sheep which in 1888, and for a few years thereafter, ranged in the high mountains between the waters of the Yellowstone and the Stinking Water. This is one of the countries from which sheep have been pretty nearly exterminated by hunters and prospectors.

Within the past twenty or thirty years mountain sheep have become very scarce in all of their old haunts in Wyoming and northern Colorado. This does not seem to be particularly due to hunting, but the sheep seem to be either moving away or dying out. Mr. W.H. Reed, in 1898, wrote me from Laramie, Wyo., saying: "At present there are perhaps thirty head on Sheep Mountain, twenty-two miles west of Laramie, Wyo.; on the west side of Laramie Peak there are perhaps twenty head; on the east side of the Peak twelve to fifteen head, and near the Platte Canon, at the head of Medicine Bow River, there are fifteen. In 1894 I saw at the head of the Green River, Hobacks River, and Gros Ventre River, between two and three hundred mountain sheep. There are sheep scattered all through the Wind River, and a very few in the Big Horn Mountains; but all are in small bunches, and these widely separated. Some of the old localities where they were very abundant in the early '70's, but now are never seen, are Whalen Canon, Raw Hide Buttes, Hartville Mountains, thirty miles northwest of Ft. Laramie, Elk Mountains, and the adjacent hills fifteen miles east of Fort Steele, near old Fort Halleck. They seem to have disappeared also from the bad lands along Green River, south of the Union Pacific Railroad, from the Freezeout Hills, Platte Canyon, at the mouth of Sweetwater River, from Brown's Canyon, forty miles northwest of Rawlins, from the Seminole and Ferris Mountains, and from many other places in the middle and northeastern part of Wyoming."

In Colorado, the mountains surrounding North Park and west to the Utah line, had many mountain sheep twenty-five years ago, but to-day old hunters tell me that there are only two places where one is sure to find sheep. These are Hahn's Peak and the Rabbit Ears, two peaks at the south end of North Park.

There were sheep in and about the Black Hills of Dakota as late as 1890, for Mr. W.S. Phillips has kindly informed me that about June of that year he saw three sheep on Mt. Inyan Kara. These were the only ones actually seen during the summer, but they were frequently heard of from cattle-men, and Mr. Phillips considers it beyond dispute that at that time they ranged from Sundance, Inyan Kara and Bear Lodge Mountains--all on the western and southwestern slope of the Black Hills, on and near the Wyoming-Dakota line-- on the east, westerly at least to Pumpkin Buttes and Big Powder River, and in the edge of the bad lands of Wyoming as far north as the Little Missouri Buttes, and south to the south fork of the Cheyenne River, and the big bend of the north fork of the Platte, and the head of Green River. This range is based on reports of reliable range riders, who saw them in passing through the country. It is an ideal sheep country--rough, varying from sage brush desert, out of which rises an occasional pine ridge butte, to bad lands, and the mountains of the Black Hills. There are patches of grassy, fairly good pasture land. The country is well watered, and there are many springs hidden under the hills which run but a short distance after they come out of the ground and then sink. Timber occurs in patches and more or less open groves on the pine ridges that run sometimes for several miles in a continuous hill, at a height of from one to three or four hundred feet above the plain. The region is a cattle country.

In 1893 and '97 fresh heads and hides were seen at Pocotello, Idaho, and at one or two other points west of there in the lava country along Snake River and the Oregon short line. The sheep were probably killed in the spurs and broken ranges that run out on the west flank of the main chain of the Rockies toward the Blue Mountains of Oregon.

Mr. William Wells, of Wells, Wyo., has very kindly given me the following notes as to Colorado, where he formerly resided. He says: "During 1890, '91, '92, there were a good many mountain sheep on the headwaters of Roan Creek, a tributary of Grand River, in Colorado. Roan Creek heads on the south side of the Roan or Book Plateau, and flows south into Grand River. The elevation of Grand River at this point is about 5,000 feet, and the elevation of the Book Plateau is about 8,500 feet. The side of the plateau toward Grand River consists of cliffs from 2,000 to 3,000 feet high, and as the branches of Roan Creek head on top of the plateau they form very deep box canyons as they cut their way to the river. It is on these cliffs and in these canyons that the sheep were found. I understand that there are some there yet, but I have not been in that section since 1892. On all the cliffs are benches or terraces--a cliff of 300 to 1,000 feet at the top, then a bench, then another cliff, and so on to the bottom. The benches are well grassed, and there is more or less timber, quaking asp, spruce and juniper in the side canyons. There are plenty of springs along the cliffs, and as they face the south, the winter range is good. The top of the plateau is an open park country, and at that time was, and is yet, for that matter, full of deer and bear, but I never saw any sheep on top, though they sometimes come out on the upper edge of the cliffs.

"There were, and I suppose are still, small bands of sheep on Dome and Shingle Peaks, on the headwaters of White River, in northwestern Colorado.

"There was also a band of sheep on the Williams River Mountains which lie between Bear River and the Williams Fork of Bear River, in northwestern Colorado, but these sheep were killed off about 1894 or '95. The Williams River Mountains are a low range of grass-covered hills, well watered, with broken country and cliffs on the south side, toward the Williams Fork.

"It is also reported that there is a band of sheep in Grand River Canyon, just above Glenwood Springs, Colo., and sheep are reported to be on the increase in the Gunnison country, and other parts of southwestern Colorado, as that State protects sheep."

Mr. W.J. Dixon, of Cimarron, Kan., wrote me in May, 1898, as follows: "In 1874 or '75 I killed sheep at the head of the north fork of the Purgatoire, or Rio de las Animas, on the divide between the Spanish Peaks and main range of the Rocky Mountains, southwest by west from the South Peak. I was there also in November, 1892, and saw three or four head at a distance, but did not go after them. They must be on the increase there."

In 1899 there was a bunch of sheep in east central Utah, about thirty miles north of the station of Green River, on the Rio Grande Western Railroad, and on the west side of the Green River. These were on the ranch of ex-member of Congress, Hon. Clarence E. Allen, and were carefully protected by the owners of the property. The ranch hands are instructed not to kill or molest them in any manner, and to do nothing that will alarm them. They come down occasionally to the lower ground, attracted by the lucerne, as are also the deer, which sometimes prove quite a nuisance by getting into the growing crops. The sheep spend most of their time in the cliffs not far away. When first seen, about 1894, there were but five sheep in the bunch, while in 1899 twenty were counted. This information was very kindly sent to me by Mr. C.H. Blanchard, at one time of Silver City, but more recently of Salt Lake City, in Utah.

Mr. W.H. Holabird, formerly of Eddy, New Mexico, but more recently of Los Angeles, Cal., tells me that during the fall of 1896 a number of splendid heads were brought into Eddy, N.M. He is told that mountain sheep are quite numerous in the rugged ridge of the Guadeloupe Mountains, bands of from five to twelve being frequently seen. As to California, he reports: "We have a good many mountain sheep on the isolated mountain spurs putting out from the main ranges into the desert. I frequently hear of bands of two to ten, but our laws protect them at all seasons."

My friend, Mr. Herbert Brown, of Yuma, Ariz., so well known as an enthusiastic and painstaking observer of natural history matters, has kindly written me something as to the mountain sheep in that Territory. He says: "Under the game law of Arizona the killing of mountain sheep is absolutely prohibited, but that does not prevent their being killed. It does, however, prevent their being killed for the market, and it was killing for the market that threatened their extermination. So far as I have ever been able to learn, these sheep range, or did range, on all the mountains to the north, west, and south of Tucson, within a hundred miles or so. I know of them in the Superstition Mountains, about a hundred miles to the north; in the Quijotoas Mountains, a like distance to the southwest, and in the mountains intermediate; I have no positive proof of their existence in the Santa Ritas, but about twenty-three years ago I saw a pair of old and weather-beaten horns that had been picked up in that range near Agua Caliente, that is about ten or twelve miles southwest of Mt. Wrightson. I never saw any sheep in the range, nor do I know of any one more fortunate than myself in that respect. In days gone by the Santa Catalinas, the Rincon, and the Tucson Mountains were the most prolific hunting grounds for the market men. So far as I can remember, the first brought to the market here were subsequent to the coming of the railroad in 1880. They were killed in the Tucson Mountains by the 'Logan boys,' well known hunters at that time. Later the Logans made a strike in the mines and disappeared. For several years no sheep were seen, but finally Mexicans began killing them in the Santa Catalinas, and occasionally six or eight would be hung up in the market at the same time. Later the Papago Indians in the southwest began killing them for the market. These people, as did also the Mexicans, killed big and little, and the animals, never abundant, were threatened with extermination. Those killed by the Logans came from the Tucson Mountains; those killed by the Mexicans from the Santa Catalinas, and those killed by the Indians probably from the Baboquivari or Comobabi ranges. I questioned the hunters repeatedly, but they never gave me a satisfactory answer.

"Although I never saw the sheep, I have repeatedly seen evidence of them in both the ranges named. Inasmuch as I have not seen one in several years past, I feel very confident that there are not many to see. Last year I learned of a large ram being killed in the Superstition Mountains which was alone when killed. About three years ago the head of a big ram was brought to this city. It is said to have weighed seventy pounds. I did not see it, nor did I learn where it came from.

"The Superstition and the Santa Catalinas are the very essence of ruggedness, but notwithstanding this I am constrained to believe that the days of big game are nearly numbered in Arizona. The reasons for this are readily apparent. The mountain ranges are more or less mineralized. To this there is hardly an exception. There is no place so wild and forbidding that the prospector will not enter it. If 'pay rock' or 'pay dirt' is struck, then good-by solitude and big game. A second cause is to be found in the cattle industry, which, as a rule, is very profitable. One of the most successful cattle growers in the country once told me that cattle in Arizona would breed up to 95 per cent. These breeders during the dry season leave the mesas and climb to the top of the very highest mountains, and, of course, the more cattle the less game. A year ago I was in the Harshaw Mountains, and was told by a young man named Sorrell that a bunch of wild cattle occupied a certain peak, and that on a certain occasion he had seen a big mountain sheep with the cattle.

"So far as I know, I never saw or heard of a case of scab among wild sheep."

Later, but still in 1898, Mr. Brown wrote me that, according to Mr. J. D. Thompson, mountain sheep are common in all the mountains bordering the Gulf Coast in Sonora, and also in Lower California. Mr. Thompson is operating mines in the Sierra Pinto, Sonora, 180 miles southeast of Yuma. This range is about six miles long and 800 feet high. The mule deer and sheep are killed according to necessity. Indians do the killing. A mule deer is worth two dollars, Mexican money, and a sheep but little more, although the former are much more abundant than the latter. The last sheep taken to camp was traded off for a pair of overalls.

"It is reasonably certain that with sheep in southern Arizona and southern Sonora, every mountain range between the two must be tenanted by this species.

"During the August feast days the Papago Indians living about Quitovac generally have a Montezuma celebration, in which live deer are employed. For this purpose several are caught. Subsequently they are killed and eaten. They are taken by relays of men or horses, sometimes both."

In northern Arizona sheep are still common. Dr. C. Hart Merriam in his report on the San Francisco Mountain--"North American Fauna" III.--recorded the San Francisco herd, of which he saw eight or nine together. He also recorded their presence at the Grand Canyon, where they are still fairly common, though very wary.

Mr. A.W. Anthony, of California, wrote me in 1898 concerning sheep in southern California, and I am glad to quote his letter almost in full. He says: "In San Diego county, Cal., there are a few sheep along the western edge of the Colorado Desert. So far as I know, these are all in the first ranges above the desert, and do not extend above the pi 駒 n belt. These barren hills are dry, broken and steep, with very little water, and except for the stock men, who have herds grazing on the western edge of the desert, they are very seldom disturbed. Along the line of the old Carriso Creek stage road from Yuma to Los Angeles, between Warner Pass and the mouth of Carriso Creek--where it reaches the desert--are several water holes where sheep have, up to 1897, at least, regularly watered during the dry season.

"I have known of several being killed by stock men there during the past few years, by watching for them about the water. As a rule, the country is too dry, open and rough to make still-hunting successful. At the same time I think they would have been killed off long since except for reinforcements received from across the line in Lower California.

"Up to 1894 a few sheep were found as far up the range as Mt. Baldy, Los Angeles county, and they may still occur there, but I cannot be sure. One or two of the larger ranges west of the Colorado River, in the desert, were, two years ago, and probably are still, blessed with a few sheep. I have known of two or three parties that went after them, but they would not tell where they went; not far north of the Southern Pacific Railroad, I think.

"In Lower California sheep are still common in many places, but are largely confined to the east side of the peninsula, mostly being found in the low hills between the gulf and the main divide. A few reach the top of San Pedro Martir--12,000 feet--but I learn from the Indians they never were common in the higher ranges. The pi 駧 n belt and below seem to be their habitat, and in very dry, barren ranges. I have known a few to reach the Pacific, between 28 deg. n. lat. and 30 deg. n. lat.; but they never seem at home on the western side of the peninsula.

"Owing to their habitat, few whites care to bother them--it costs too much in cash, and more in bodily discomfort; but the natives kill them at all seasons; not enough, however, to threaten extermination unless they receive help from the north.

"I have no knowledge of any scab, or other disease, affecting the sheep, either in southern or Lower California."

For northern California, records of sheep are few. Dr. Merriam, Chief of the Biological Survey, tells me that sheep formerly occurred on the Siskiyou range, on the boundary between California and Oregon, and that some years ago he saw an old ram that had been killed on these mountains. On Mt. Shasta they were very common until recently. In the High Sierra, south of the latitude of Mono Lake, a few still occur, but there are extremely rare.

In Oregon records are few. Dr. Merriam informs me that he has seen them on Steen Mountain, in the southeastern part of the State, where they were common a few years ago. Mr. Vernon Bailey, of the Biological Survey, has seen them also in the Wallowa Mountains. The Biological Survey also has records of their occurrence in the Blue Mountains, where they used to be found both on Strawberry Butte and on what are called the Greenhorn Mountains. The last positive record from that region is in 1895. In 1897 Mr. Vernon Bailey reported sheep from Silver and Abert Lakes in the desert region east of the Cascade. They were formerly numerous in the rocky regions about Silver Lake, and a few still inhabited the ridges northeast of Abert Lake.

In Nevada Mr. Bailey found sheep in the Toyabe range.

Mr. Bailey found sheep in the Seven Devils Mountains, and he and Dr. Merriam found them in the Salmon River, Pahsimeroi and Sawtooth Mountains, all in Idaho. Mr. Bailey also found them in Texas in the Guadaloupe Mountains and in most of the ranges thence south to the boundary line in western Texas.

* * * * *

From what has already been said it will be seen that in inaccessible places all over the western country, from the Arctic Ocean south to Mexico, and at one or two points in the great plains, there still remain stocks of mountain sheep. Once the most unsuspicious and gentle of all our large game animals, they have become very shy, wary, and well able to take care of themselves. In the Yellowstone Park, on the other hand, they have reverted to their old time tameness, and no longer regard man with fear. There, as is told on other pages of this volume, they are more tame than the equally protected antelope, mule deer or elk.

Should the Grand Canyon of the Colorado be set aside as a national park, as it may be hoped it will be, the sheep found there will no doubt increase, and become, as they now are in the Yellowstone Park, a most interesting natural feature of the landscape. And in like manner, when game refuges shall be established in the various forest reservations all over the western country, this superb species will increase and do well. Alert, quick-witted, strong, fleet and active, it is one of the most beautiful and most imposing of North American animals. Equally at home on the frozen snowbanks of the mountain top, or in the parched deserts of the south, dwelling alike among the rocks, in the timber, or on the prairie, the mountain sheep shows himself adaptable to all conditions, and should surely have the best protection that we can give him.

I shall never forget a scene witnessed many years ago, long before railroads penetrated the Northwest. I was floating down the Missouri River in a mackinaw boat, the sun just topping the high bad land bluffs to the east, when a splendid ram stepped out, upon a point far above the water, and stood there outlined against the sky. Motionless, with head thrown back, and in an attitude of attention, he calmly inspected the vessel floating along below him; so beautiful an object amid his wild surroundings, and with his background of brilliant sky, that no hand was stretched out for the rifle, but the boat floated quietly on past him, and out of sight.

George Bird Grinnell.

Preservation of the Wild Animals of North America[8]

[Footnote 8: Address before the Boone and Crockett Club, Washington, January 23, 1904.]

The National and Congressional movement for the preservation of the Sequoia in California represents a growth of intelligent sentiment. It is the same kind of sentiment which must he aroused, and aroused in time, to bring about Government legislation if we are to preserve our native animals. That which principally appeals to us in the Sequoia is its antiquity as a race, and the fact that California is its last refuge.

As a special and perhaps somewhat novel argument for preservation, I wish to remind you of the great antiquity of our game animals, and the enormous period of time which it has taken nature to produce them. We must have legislation, and we must have it in time. I recall the story of the judge and jury who arrived in town and inquired about the security of the prisoner, who was known to be a desperate character; they were assured by the crowd that the prisoner was perfectly secure because he was safely hanging to a neighboring tree. If our preservative measures are not prompt, there will be no animals to legislate for.

SENTIMENT AND SCIENCE.

The sentiment which promises to save the Sequoia is due to the spread of knowledge regarding this wonderful tree, largely through the efforts of the Division of Forestry. In the official chronology of the United States Geological Survey--which is no more nor less reliable than that of other geological surveys, because all are alike mere approximations to the truth--the Sequoia was a well developed race 10,000,000 of years ago. It became one of a large family, including fourteen genera. The master genus--the _Sequoia_--alone includes thirty extinct species. It was distributed in past times through Canada, Alaska, Greenland, British Columbia, across Siberia, and down into southern Europe. The Ice Age, and perhaps competition with other trees more successful in seeding down, are responsible for the fact that there are now only two living species--the "red wood," or _Sequoia sempervirens_, and the giant, or Sequoia gigantea. The last refuge of the gigantea is in ten isolated groves, in some of which the tree is reproducing itself, while in others it has ceased to reproduce.

In the year 1900 forty mills and logging companies were engaged in destroying these trees.

All of us regard the destruction of the Parthenon by the Turks as a great calamity; yet it would be possible, thanks to the laborious studies which have chiefly emanated from Germany, for modern architects to completely restore the Parthenon in its former grandeur; but it is far beyond the power of all the naturalists of the world to restore one of these Sequoias, which were large trees, over 100 feet in height, spreading their leaves to the sun, before the Parthenon was even conceived by the architects and sculptors of Greece.

LIFE OF THE SEQUOIA AND HISTORY OF THOUGHT.

In 1900 five hundred of the very large trees still remained, the highest reaching from 320 to 325 feet. Their height, however, appeals to us less than their extraordinary age, estimated by Hutchins at 3,600, or by John Muir, who probably loves them more than any man living, at from 4,000 to 5,000 years. According to the actual count of Muir of 4,000 rings, by a method which he has described to me, one of these trees was 1,000 years old when Homer wrote the Iliad; 1,500 years of age when Aristotle was foreshadowing his evolution theory and writing his history of animals; 2,000 years of age when Christ walked upon the earth; nearly 4,000 years of age when the "Origin of Species" was written. Thus the life of one of these trees spanned the whole period before the birth of Aristotle (384 B.C.) and after the death of Darwin (A.D. 1882), the two greatest natural philosophers who have lived.

These trees are the noblest living things upon earth. I can imagine that the American people are approaching a stage of general intelligence and enlightened love of nature in which they will look back upon the destruction of the Sequoia as a blot on the national escutcheon.

VENERATION OF AGE.

The veneration of age sentiment which should, and I believe actually does, appeal to the American people when clearly presented to them even more strongly than the commercial sentiment, is roused in equal strength by an intelligent appreciation of the race longevity of the larger animals which our ancestors found here in profusion, and of which but a comparatively small number still survive. To the unthinking man a bison, a wapiti, a deer, a pronghorn antelope, is a matter of hide and meat; to the real nature lover, the true sportsman, the scientific student, each of these types is a subject of intense admiration. From the mechanical standpoint they represent an architecture more elaborate than that of Westminster Abbey, and a history beside which human history is as of yesterday.

SLOW EVOLUTION OF MODERN MAMMALS.

These animals were not made in a day, nor in a thousand years, nor in a million years. As said the first Greek philosopher, Empedocles, who 560 B.C. adumbrated the "survival of the fittest" theory of Darwin, they are the result of ceaseless trials of nature. While the Sequoia was first emerging from the Carboniferous, or Coal Period, the reptile-like ancestors of these mammals, covered with scales and of egg-laying habits, were crawling about and giving not the most remote prophecy of their potential transformation through 10,000,000 of years into the superb fauna of the northern hemisphere.

The descendants of these reptiles were transformed into mammals. If we had

had the opportunity of studying the early mammals of the Rocky Mountain region with a full appreciation of the possibilities of evolution, we should have perceived that they were essentially of the same stock and ancestral to our modern types. There were little camels scarcely more than twelve inches high, little taller than cotton-tail rabbits and smaller than the jackass rabbits; horses 15 inches high, scarcely larger than, and very similar in build to, the little English coursing hound known as the whippet; it is not improbable that we shall find the miniature deer; there certainly existed ancestral wolves and foxes of similarly small proportions. You have all read your Darwin carefully enough to know that neither camels, horses, nor deer would have evolved as they did except for the stimulus given to their limb and speed development by the contemporaneous evolution of their enemies in the dog family.

THE MIDDLE STAGE OF EVOLUTION.

A million and a half years later these same animals had attained a very considerable size; the western country had become transformed by the elevation of the plateaux into dry, grass-bearing uplands, where both horses and deer of peculiarly American types were grazing. We have recently secured some fresh light on the evolution of the American deer. Besides the _Palaeryx_, which may be related to the true American deer _Odocoileus_, we have found the complete skeleton of a small animal named _Merycodus_, nineteen inches high, possessed of a complete set of delicate antlers with the characteristic burr at the base indicating the annual shedding of the horn, and a general structure of skeleton which suggests our so-called pronghorn antelope, _Antilocapra_, rather than our true American deer, Odocoileus. This was in all probability a distinctively American type. Its remains have been found in eastern Colorado in the geological age known as Middle Miocene, which is estimated (_sub rosa_, like all our other geological estimates), at about a million and a half years of age. Our first thought as we study this small, strikingly graceful animal, is wonder that such a high degree of specialization and perfection was reached at so early a period; our second thought is the reverence for age sentiment.

THE AFRICAN PERIOD IN AMERICA.

The conditions of environment were different from what they were before or what they are now. These animals flourished during the period in which western America must have closely resembled the eastern and central portions of Africa at the present time.

This inference is drawn from the fact that the predominant fauna of America in the Middle and Upper Miocene Age and in the Pliocene was closely analogous to the still extant fauna of Africa. It is true we had no real antelopes in this country, in fact none of the bovines, and no giraffes; but there was a camel which my colleague Matthew has surnamed the "giraffe camel," extraordinarily similar to the giraffe. There were no hippopotami, no hyraces. All these peculiarly African animals, of African origin, I believe, found their way into Europe at least as far as the Sivalik Hills of India, but never across the Bering Sea Isthmus. The only truly African animal which reached America, and which flourished here in an extraordinary manner, was the elephant, or rather the mastodon, if we speak of the elephant in its Miocene stage of evolution. However, the resemblance between America and Africa is abundantly demonstrated by the presence of great herds of horses, of rhinoceroses, both long and short limbed, of camels in great variety, including the giraffe-like type which was capable of browsing on the higher branches of trees, of small elephants, and of deer, which in adaptation to somewhat arid conditions imitated the antelopes in general structure.

ELIMINATION BY THE GLACIAL PERIOD.

The Glacial Period eliminated half of this fauna, whereas the equatorial latitude of the fauna in Africa saved that fauna from the attack of the Glacial Period, which was so fatally destructive to the animals in the more northerly latitudes of America. The glaciers or at least the very low temperature of the period eliminated especially all the African aspects of our fauna. This destructive agency was almost as baneful and effective as the mythical Noah's flood. When it passed off, there survived comparatively few indigenous North American animals, but the country was repopulated from the entire northern hemisphere, so that the magnificent wild animals which our ancestors found here were partly North American and partly Eurasiatic in origin.

ELIMINATION BY MAN.

Our animal fortune seemed to us so enormous that it never could be spent. Like a young rake coming into a very large inheritance, we attacked this noble fauna with characteristic American improvidence, and with a rapidity compared with which the Glacial advance was eternally slow; the East went first, and in fifty years we have brought about an elimination in the West which promises to be even more radical than that effected by the ice. We are now beginning to see the end of the North American fauna; and if we do not move promptly, it will become a matter of history and of museums. The bison is on the danger line; if it survives the fatal effects of its natural sluggishness when abundantly fed, it still runs the more insidious but equally great danger of inbreeding, like the wild ox of Europe. The chances for the wapiti and elk and the western mule and black-tail deer are brighter, provided that we move promptly for their protection. The pronghorn is a wonderfully clever and adaptive animal, crawling under barb-wire fences, and thus avoiding one of the greatest enemies of Western life. Last summer I was surprised beyond measure to see the large herds of twenty to forty pronghorn antelopes still surviving on the Laramie plains, fenced in on all sides by the wires of the great Four-Bar Ranch, part of which I believe are stretched illegally.

RECENT DISAPPEARANCE.

I need not dwell on the astonishingly rapid diminution of our larger animals in the last few years; it would be like "carrying coals to Newcastle" to detail personal observations before this Club, which is full of men of far greater experience and knowledge than myself. On the White River Plateau Forest Reserve, which is destined to be the Adirondacks of Colorado, with which many of you are familiar, the deer disappeared in a period of four years. Comparatively few are left.

The most thoroughly devastated country I know of is the Uintah Mountain Forest Reserve, which borders between southwestern Wyoming and northern Utah. I first went through this country in 1877. It was then a wild natural region; even a comparatively few years ago it was bright with game, and a perfect flower garden. It has felt the full force of the sheep curse. I think any one of you who may visit this country now will agree that this is not too strong a term, and I want to speak of the sheep question from three standpoints: First, as of a great and legitimate industry in itself; second, from the economic standpoint; third, from the standpoint of wild animals.

GENERAL RESULTS OF GRAZING.

The formerly beautiful Uintah Mountain range presents a terrible example of the effects of prolonged sheep herding. The under foliage is entirely gone. The sheep annually eat off the grass tops and prevent seeding down; they trample out of life what they do not eat; along the principal valley routes even the sage brush is destroyed. Reforesting by the upgrowth of young trees is still going on to a limited extent, but is in danger. The water supply of the entire Bridger farming country, which is dependent upon the Uintah Mountains as a natural reservoir, is rapidly diminishing; the water comes in tremendous floods in the spring, and begins to run short in the summer, when it is most needed. The consequent effects upon both fish and wild animals are well known to you. No other animal will feed after the sheep. It is no exaggeration to say, therefore, that the sheep in this region are the enemies of every living thing.

BALANCE OF NATURE.

Even the owner cannot much longer enjoy his range, because he is operating against the balance of nature. The last stage of destruction which these innocent animals bring about has not yet been reached, but it is approaching; it is the stage in which there is no food left for the sheep themselves. I do not know how many pounds of food a sheep consumes in course of a year--it cannot be much less than a ton--but say it is only half a ton, how many acres of dry western mountain land are capable of producing half a ton a year when not seeding down? As long as the consumption exceeds the production of the soil, it is only a question of time when even the sheep will no longer find subsistence.

THE LAST STAGE TO BE SEEN IN THE ORIENT.

While going through these mountains last summer and reflecting upon the prodigious changes which the sheep have brought about in a few years, it occurred to me that we must look to Oriental countries in order to see the final results of sheep and goat grazing in semi-arid climates. I have proposed as an historical thesis a subject which at first appears somewhat humorous, namely, "The Influence of Sheep and Goats in History." I am convinced that the country lying between Arabia and Mesopotamia, which was formerly densely populated, full of beautiful cities, and heavily wooded, has been transformed less by the action of political causes than by the unrestricted browsing of sheep and goats. This browsing destroyed first the undergrowth, then the forests, the natural reservoirs of the country, then the grasses which held together the soil, and finally resulted in the removal of the soil itself. The country is now denuded of soil, the rocks are practically bare; it supports only a few lions, hyaes, gazelles, and Bedouins. Even if the trade routes and mines, on which Brooks Adams in his "New Empire" dwells so strongly as factors of all civilization, were completely restored, the population could not be restored nor the civilization, because there is nothing in this country for people to live upon. The same is true of North Africa, which, according to Gibbon, was once the granary of the Roman Empire. In Greece to-day the goats are now destroying the last vestiges of the forests.

I venture the prediction that the sheep industry on naturally semi-arid lands is doomed; that the future feeding of both sheep and cattle will be on irrigated lands, and that the forests will be carefully guarded by State and Nature as natural reservoirs.

COMMERCIALISM AND IDEALISM.

By contrast to the sheep question, which is a purely economic or utilitarian one, and will settle itself, if we do not settle it by legislation based on scientific observation, the preservation of the Sequoia and of our large wild animals is one of pure sentiment, of appreciation of the ideal side of life; we can live and make money without either. We cannot even use the argument which has been so forcibly used in the case of the birds, that the cutting down of these trees or killing of these animals will upset the balance of nature.

I believe in every part of the country--East, West, North, and South--we Americans have reached a stage of civilization where if the matter were at issue the majority vote would unquestionably be, _let us preserve our wild animals._

We are generally considered a commercial people, and so we are; but we are more than this, we are a people of ideas, and we value them. As stated in the preamble of the Sequoia bill introduced on Dec. 8, 1903, we must legislate for the benefit and enjoyment of the people, and I may add for the greatest happiness of the largest number, not only of the present but of future generations.

So far as my observation goes, preservation can only be absolutely insured by national legislation.

GOVERNMENT LEGISLATION BY ENGLAND, BELGIUM, GERMANY.

The English, a naturally law-abiding people, seem to have a special faculty for enforcing laws. By co-operation with the Belgian Government they have taken effective and remarkably successful measures for the protection of African game. As for Germany, in 1896 Mr. Gosselin, of the British Embassy in Berlin, reported as follows for German East Africa:

That the question of preserving big game in German East Africa has been under the consideration of the local authorities for some time past, and a regulation has been notified at Dar-es-Salaam which it is hoped will do something toward checking the wanton destruction of elephants and other indigenous animals. Under this regulation every hunter must take out an animal license, for which the fee varies from 5 to 500 rupees, the former being the ordinary fee for natives, the latter for elephant and rhinoceros hunting, and for the members of sporting expeditions into the interior. Licenses are not needed for the purpose of obtaining food, nor for shooting game damaging cultivated land, nor for shooting apes, beasts of prey, wild boars, reptiles, and all birds except ostriches and cranes. Whatever the circumstances, the shooting is prohibited of all young game--calves, foals, young elephants, either tuskless or having tusks under three kilos, all female game if recognizable--except, of course, those in the above category of unprotected animals. Further, in the Moschi district of Kilima-Njaro, no one, whether possessing a license or not, is allowed without the special permission of the Governor to shoot antelopes, giraffes, buffaloes, ostriches, and cranes. Further, special permission must be obtained to hunt these with nets, by kindling fires, or by big drives. Those who are not natives have also to pay 100 rupees for the first elephant killed, and 250 for each additional one, and 50 rupees for the first rhinoceros and 150 for each succeeding one. Special game preserves are also to be established, and Major von Wissmann, in a circular to the local officers, explains that no shooting whatever will be allowed in these without special permission from the Government. The reserves will be of interest to science as a means of preserving from extirpation the rarer species, and the Governor calls for suggestions as to the best places for them. They are to extend in each direction at least ten hours' journey on foot. He further asks for suggestions as to hippopotamus reserves, where injury would not be done to plantations. Two districts are already notified as game sanctuaries. Major von Wissmann further suggests that the station authorities should endeavor to domesticate zebras (especially when crossed with muscat and other asses and horses), ostriches, and hyaena dogs crossed with European breeds. Mr. Gosselin remarks that the best means of preventing the extermination of elephants would be to fix by international agreement among all the Powers on the East African coast a close time for elephants, and to render illegal the exportation or sale of tusks under a certain age.

In December, 1900, Viscount Cranborne in the House of Commons reported as follows:

* * * That regulations for the preservation of wild animals have been in force for some time in the several African Protectorates administered by the Foreign Office as well as in the Sudan. The obligations imposed by the recent London Convention upon the signatory Powers will not become operative until after the exchange of ratifications, which has not yet taken place. In anticipation, however, steps have been taken to revise the existing regulations in the British Protectorates so as to bring them into strict harmony with the terms of the convention. The game reserves now existing in the several Protectorates are: In (a) British Central Africa, the elephant marsh reserve and the Shirwa reserve; in (b) the East Africa Protectorate, the Kenia District; in (c) Uganda, the Sugota game reserve in the northeast of the Protectorate; in (d) Somaliland, a large district defined by an elaborate boundary line described in the regulations. The regulations have the force of law in the Protectorates, and offenders are dealt with in the Protectorate Courts. It is in contemplation to charge special officers of the Administrations with the duty of watching over the proper observance of the regulations. Under the East African game regulations only the officers permanently stationed at or near the Kenia reserve may be specially authorized to kill game in the reserve.

Other effective measures have been taken in the Soudan district. Capt. Stanley Flower, Director of the Gizeh Zoological Gardens, made a very full report, which is quoted in Nature for July 25, 1901, p. 318.

STATE LAWS.

The preservation of even a few of our wild animals is a very large proposition; it is an undertaking the difficulty of which grows in magnitude as one comes to study it in detail and gets on the ground. The rapidly increasing legislation in the Western States is an indication of rapidly growing sentiment. A still more encouraging sign is the strong sympathy with the enforcement of the laws which we find around the National Park in Wyoming and Montana especially. State laws should be encouraged, but I am convinced that while effective in the East, they will not be effective in the West _in time_, because of the scattered population, the greater areas of country involved, the greater difficulty of watching and controlling the killing, and the actual need of game for food by settlers.

When we study the operation of our State laws on the ground we find that for various reasons they are not fully effective. A steady and in some cases rapid diminution of animals is going on so far as I have observed in Colorado and Wyoming; either the wardens strictly enforce the laws with strangers and wink at the breaking of them by residents, or they draw their salaries and do not enforce the laws at all.[9]

[Footnote 9: Addendum.--There is no question as to the good intention of State legislation. The chief difficulty in the enforcement of the law is that officers appointed locally, and partly from political reasons, shrink from applying the penalties of the law to their own friends and neighbors, especially where the animals are apparently abundant and are sought for food. The honest enforcement of the law renders the officer unpopular, even if it does not expose him to personal danger. He is regarded as interfering with long established rights and customs. The above applies to conscientious officers. Many local game wardens, as in the Colorado White River Plateau, for example, give absolutely no attention to their duties, and are not even on the ground at the opening of the season. In the Plateau in August, 1901, the laws were being openly and flagrantly violated, not only by visitors, but by residents. At the same time the National forest laws were being most strictly and intelligently enforced. There is no question whatever that the people of various States can be brought to understand that National aid or co-operation in the protection of certain wild areas is as advantageous to a locality as National irrigation and National forest protection. It is to be sought as a boon and not as an infringement.]

THE VARIOUS CAUSES OF ELIMINATION.

The enemies of our wild animals are numerous and constantly increasing. (1) There is first the general advance of what we call civilization, the fencing up of country which principally cuts off the winter feeding grounds. This was especially seen in the country south of the National Park last winter. (2) The destruction of natural browsing areas by cattle and sheep, and by fire. (3) The destruction of game by sportsmen plays a comparatively small part in the total process of elimination, yet in some cases it is very reckless, and especially bad in its example. When I first rode into the best shooting country of Colorado in 1901, there was a veritable cannonading going on, which reminded me of the accounts of the battle of El Caney. The destruction effected by one party in three days was tremendous. In riding over the ground--for I was not myself shooting--I was constantly coming across the carcasses of deer. (4) The summer and winter killing for food; this is the principal and in a sense the most natural and legitimate cause, although it is largely illegal. In this same area, which was more or less characteristic and typical of the other areas, even of the conditions surrounding the national reserve in the Big Horn region, the destruction was, and is, going on principally during the winter when the deer are seeking the winter ranges and when they are actually shot and carted away in large numbers for food both for the ranchmen and for neighboring towns. Making all allowances for exaggeration, I believe it to be absolutely true that these deer were being killed by the wagonload! The same is true of the pronghorn antelope in the Laramie Plains district. The most forceful argument against this form of destruction is that it is extremely short-lived and benefits comparatively few people. This argument is now enforced by law and by public sentiment in Maine and New York, where the wild animals, both deer and moose, are actually increasing in number.

Granted, therefore, that we have both National and State sentiment, and that National legislation by co-operation with the States, if properly understood, would receive popular support, the carrying out of this legislation and making it fully effective will be a difficult matter.

It can be done, and, in my judgment, by two measures. The first is entirely familiar to you: certain or all of the forest reserves must be made animal preserves; the forest rangers must be made game wardens, or special wardens must be appointed. This is not so difficult, because the necessary machinery is already at hand, and only requires adaptation to this new purpose. It can probably be carried through by patience and good judgment. Second, the matter of the preservation of the winter supply of food and protection of animals while enjoying this supply is the most difficult part of the whole problem, because it involves the acquisition of land which has already been taken up by settlers and which is not covered by the present forest reserve machinery, and which I fear in many instances will require new legislation.

Animals can change their habits during the summer, and have already done so; the wapiti, buffalo, and even the pronghorn have totally changed their normal ranges to avoid their new enemy; but in winter they are forced by the heavy snows and by hunger right down into the enemy's country.

Thus we not only have the problem of making game preserves out of our forest reserves, but we have the additional problem of enlarging the area of forest reserves so as to provide for winter feeding. If this is not done all the protection which is afforded during the summer will be wholly futile. This condition does not prevail in the East, in Maine and in the Adirondacks, where the winter and summer ranges are practically similar. It is, therefore a new condition and a new problem.

Greater difficulties have been overcome, however, and I have no doubt that the members of this Club will be among the leaders in the movement. The whole country now applauds the development and preservation of the Yellowstone Park, which we owe largely to the initiative of Phillips, Grinnell, and Rogers. Grant and La Farge were pioneers in the New York Zoological Park movement. We know the work of Merriam and Wadsworth, and we always know the sympathies of our honored founder, member, and guest of this evening, Theodore Roosevelt.

What the Club can do is to spread information and thoroughly enlighten the people, who always act rightly when they understand.

It must not be put on the minutes of the history of America, a country which boasts of its popular education, that the _Sequoia_, a race 10,000,000 years old, sought its last refuge in the United States, with individual trees older than the entire history and civilization of Greece, that an appeal to the American people was unavailing, that the finest grove was cut up for lumber, fencing, shingles, and boxes! It must not be recorded that races of animals representing stocks 3,000,000 years of age, mostly developed on the American continent, were eliminated in the course of fifty years for hides and for food in a country abounding in sheep and cattle.

The total national investment in animal preservation will be less than the cost of a single battleship. The end result will be that a hundred years hence our descendants will be enjoying and blessing us for the trees and animals, while, in the other case, there will be no vestige of the battleship, because it will be entirely out of date in the warfare of the future.

Henry Fairfield Osborn.

Distribution of the Moose

Republished by permission from the Seventh Annual Report of the Forest, Fish and Game Commission of the State of New York.

The Scandinavian elk, which is closely related to the American moose, was known to classical antiquity as a strange and ungainly beast of the far north; especially as an inhabitant of the great Teutoborgian Forest, which spread across Germany from the Rhine to the Danube. The half mythical character which has always clung to this animal is well illustrated in the following quotation from Pliny's Natural History, Book 8, chapter 16:

"There is also the achlis, which is produced in the island of Scandinavia. It has never been seen in this city, although we have had descriptions of it from many persons; it is not unlike the elk, but has no joints in the hind leg. Hence it never lies down, but reclines against a tree while it sleeps; it can only be taken by previously cutting into the tree, and thus laying a trap for it, as, otherwise, it would escape through its swiftness. Its upper lip is so extremely large, for which reason it is obliged to go backwards when grazing; otherwise by moving onwards, the lip would get doubled up." Pliny's achlis and elk were the same animal.

The strange stiffness of joint and general ungainliness of the elk, however, were matters of such general observation as to apparently have become embodied in the German name _eland_, sufferer. Curiously enough this name eland was taken by the Dutch to South Africa, and there applied to the largest and handsomest of the bovine antelopes, Oreas canna.

In mediaeval times there are many references in hunting tales to the elk, notably in the passage in the Nibelungen Lied describing Siegfried's great hunt on the upper Rhine, in which he killed an elk. Among the animals slain by the hero is the "schelk," described as a powerful and dangerous beast. This name has been a stumbling block to scholars for years, and opinions vary as to whether it was a wild stallion--at all times a savage animal--or a lone survivor of the Megaceros, or Irish elk. In this connection it may be well to remark that the Irish elk and the true elk were not closely related beyond the fact that both were members of the deer family. The Irish elk, which was common in Europe throughout the glacial and post-glacial periods, living down nearly or quite to the historic period, was nothing more than a gigantic fallow deer.

The old world elk is still found in some of the large game preserves of eastern Germany, where the Emperor, with his somewhat remarkable ideas of sportsmanship, annually adds several to his list of slaughtered game. They are comparatively abundant in Scandinavia, especially in Norway, where they are preserved with great care. They still survive in considerable numbers in Russia and Siberia as far east as Amurland.

Without going into a detailed description of the anatomical differences between the European elk and the American moose, it may be said that the old world animal is much smaller in size and lighter in color. The antlers are less elaborate and smaller in the European animal, and correspond to the stage of development reached by the average three-year-old bull of eastern Canada. There is a marked separation of the main antler and the brow antlers. That this deterioration of both body and antlers is due partly to long continued elimination of the best bulls, and partly to inbreeding, is probable. We know that the decline of the European red deer is due to these causes, and that a similar process of deterioration is showing among the moose in certain outlying districts in eastern North America.

The type species of this group, known as _Alces machlis_, was long considered by European naturalists uniform throughout its circumpolar distribution, in the north of both hemispheres. The American view that practically all animals in this country represent species distinct from their European congeners is now generally accepted, and the name Alces americanus has been given to the American form. It would appear, however, that the generic name Alces must soon be replaced by the earlier form Paralces.

The comparatively slight divergence of the two types at the extreme east and west limits of their range, namely, Norway and eastern Canada, would indicate that the period of separation of the various members of the genus is not, geologically speaking, of great antiquity.

The name moose is an Algonquin word, meaning a wood eater or browser, and is most appropriate, since the animal is pre-eminently a creature of the thick woods. The old world term elk was applied by the English settlers, probably in Virginia, to the wapiti deer, an animal very closely related to the red deer of Europe. In Canada the moose is sometimes spoken of as the elk, and even in the Rocky Mountain region one hears occasionally of the "flat-horned elk." We are fortunate in possessing a native name for this animal, and to call it other than moose can only create confusion.

The range of the moose in North America extends from Nova Scotia in the extreme east, throughout Canada and certain of the Northern United States, to the limits of tree growth in the west and north of Alaska. Throughout this vast extent of territory but two species are recognized, the common moose, _Alces americanus_, and the Alaska moose, _Alces gigas_, of the Kenai Peninsula. What the limits of the range of the Alaska moose are, may not be known for some years. Specimens obtained in the autumn of 1902 from the headwaters of the Stikine River in British Columbia, appear to resemble closely, in their large size and dark coloration, the moose of the Kenai Peninsula. The antlers, however, are much smaller. These specimens also differ from the eastern moose in the same manner as does the Kenai Peninsula animal, except in the antlers, which approximate to those of the type species.

I have no doubt that the moose on the mainland along Cook Inlet will prove to be identical with those of the Kenai Peninsula itself, but how far their range extends we have at present no means of knowing. It is even possible that further exploration will bring to light other species in the Northwestern Provinces and in Alaska.

Taking up this range in detail, the Nova Scotia moose are to-day distinctly smaller than their kin in Ontario, but are very numerous when the settled character of the country is taken into consideration. I have seen very few good antlers come from this district, and in my opinion the race there is showing decided signs of deterioration.

These remarks apply, but with less force, to New Brunswick and to Maine, where the moose, though larger than the Nova Scotia animal, are distinctly inferior to those of the region north of the Great Lakes. This is probably due to killing off the big bulls, thus leaving the breeding to be done by the smaller and weaker bulls; and, also, to inbreeding.

In Maine the moose originally abounded, but by the middle of the last century they were so reduced in numbers as to be almost rare. Thanks to very efficient game laws, backed by an intelligent public opinion, moose have greatly increased during the last few days in Maine and also in New Brunswick. Their habits have been modified, but as far as the number of moose and deer are concerned, the protection of game in Maine has been a brilliant example to the rest of the country. During the same period, however, caribou have almost entirely disappeared.

Moose were found by the first settlers in New Hampshire and Vermont, appearing occasionally, as migrants only, in the Berkshire hills of Massachusetts. In the State of New York the Catskills appear to have been their extreme southern limit in the east; but they disappeared from this district more than a century ago. In the Adirondacks, or the North Woods, as they were formerly called, moose abounded among the hard wood ridges and lakes. This was the great hunting country of the Six Nations. Here, too, many of the Canadian Indians came for their winter supply of moose meat and hides. The rival tribes fought over these hunting grounds much in the same manner as the northern and southern Indians warred for the control of Kentucky.

Going westward in the United States we find no moose until we reach the northern peninsula of Michigan and northern Wisconsin, where moose were once numerous. They are still abundant in northern Minnesota, where the country is extremely well suited to their habits. Then there is a break, caused by the great plains, until we reach the Rocky Mountains. They are found along the mountains of western Montana and Idaho as far south as the northwest corner of Wyoming in the neighborhood of the Yellowstone Park, the Tetons and the Wind River Mountains being their southern limit in this section.[10] The moose of the west are relatively small animals with simple antlers, and have adapted themselves to mountain living in striking contrast to their kin in the east.

[Footnote 10: William Roland, an old-time mountaineer, states that he once killed a moose about ten miles north of old Ft. Tetterman, in what is now Wyoming.--EDITOR.]

North of the Canadian boundary we may start with the curious fact that the great peninsula of Labrador, which seems in every way a suitable locality for moose, has always been devoid of them. There is no record of their ever appearing east of the Saguenay River, and this fact accounts for their absence from Newfoundland, which received its fauna from the north by way of Labrador, and not from the west by way of Cape Breton. Newfoundland is well suited to the moose, and a number of individuals have been turned loose there, without, as yet, any apparent results. Systematic and persistent effort, however, in this direction should be successful.

South of the St. Lawrence River, the peninsula of Gasp?was once a favorite range, but the moose were nearly killed off in the early '60's by hide-hunters. Further west they are found in small numbers on both banks of the St. Lawrence well back from the settlements, until on the north shore we reach Trois Riviers, west of which they become more numerous.

The region of the upper Ottawa and Lake Kippewa has been in recent years the best moose country in the east. The moose from this district average much heavier and handsomer antlers than those of Maine and the Maritime Provinces. However, the moose are now rapidly leaving this country and pushing further north. Twenty-five years ago they first appeared, coming from the south, probably from the Muskoka Lake country, into which they may have migrated in turn from the Adirondacks. This northern movement has been going on steadily within the personal knowledge of the writer. Ten years ago the moose were practically all south and east of Lake Kippewa, now they are nearly all north of that lake, and extend nearly, if not quite, to the shores of James Bay. How far to the west of that they have spread we do not know; but it is probable that they are reoccupying the range lying between the shores of

Lake Superior and James Bay, which was long abandoned. Northwest of Lake Superior, throughout Manitoba and far to the north, is a region heavily wooded and studded with lakes, constituting a practically untouched moose country.

No moose, of course, are found in the plains country of Assiniboia, Saskatchewan, and Alberta; but east in Keewatin, and to the north in Athabaska, northern British Columbia, and northwest into Alaska we have an unbroken range, in which moose are scattered everywhere. They are increasing wherever their ancient foe, the Indian, is dying off, and where white hunters do not pursue too persistently. In this entire region, from the Ottawa in the east to the Kenai Peninsula in the far west, moose are retiring toward the north before the advance of civilization, and are everywhere occupying new country.

Wary and keen, and with great muscular strength and hardihood, the moose is pitting his acute senses against the encroaching rifleman in the struggle for survival, and it is fair to believe that this superb member of the deer family will continue to be an inhabitant of the forest long after most other members of the group have disappeared.

The moose of Maine and the Maritime Provinces occupy a relatively small area, surrounded on all sides by settlements, which prevent the animals from leaving the country when civilization encroaches. In this district their habits have been greatly modified. They do not show the same fear of the sound of rifle, of the smell of fire, or even of the scent of human footsteps, as in the wilder portions of the country. In consequence of this change of habit, it is difficult for a hunter, whose experience is limited to Maine or the Maritime Provinces, to appreciate how very shy and wary a moose can be.

In the upper Ottawa country, when they first began to be hunted by sportsmen, the writer remembers landing from his canoe on the bank of a small stream, and walking around a marsh a few acres in extent to look at the moose tracks. Fresh signs, made that morning, were everywhere in evidence, and it had apparently been a favorite resort all summer. Snow fell that night and remained continuously on the ground for two weeks, when the writer again passed by this swamp and found that during the interval it had not been visited by a single moose. The moccasin tracks had been scented, and the moose had left the neighborhood. A moose with a nose as sensitive as this would find existence unendurable in New Brunswick or Maine.

I have already referred to the relative size of the antlers of the moose from different localities, and called attention to the inferiority of the heads from the extreme east. Large heads have, however, come from this section, and even now one hears of several heads being taken annually in New Brunswick running to five feet and a little over in spread. The test of the value of a moose head is the width of its antlers between the extreme points. The antlers of a young individual show but few points, but these are long and the webbing on the main blade is narrow. The brow antlers usually show two points. As the moose grows larger the palmation becomes wider, and the points more numerous but shorter, until in a very old specimen the upper part of the antler is merely scalloped along the edge, and the web is of great breadth. In the older and finer specimens the brow antlers are more complex, and show three points instead of two.

A similar change takes place in the bell. This pendulous gland is long and narrow in the young hull, but as he ages it shortens and widens, becoming eventually a sort of dewlap under the throat.

One of the best heads from Maine that I can recall, was in the possession of the late Albert Bierstadt, a member of the Boone and Crockett Club. The extreme spread of these antlers was 64-1/4 inches. This bull was killed in New Brunswick, near the Maine line, some twenty years ago; another famous Maine head was presented to President Cleveland during his first term. Photographs of both of these heads appear herewith. Many very handsome heads have been taken in the Ottawa district, sometimes running well over five feet. It is safe to assume that a little short of six feet is the extreme width of an eastern head.

The moose of the Rocky Mountains are relatively smaller than the eastern moose, and their antlers are seldom of imposing proportions.

As we go north into British Columbia, through the headwaters of the Peace and Liard rivers, the animal becomes very large in size, perhaps larger than anywhere else in the world as far as his body is concerned, and it is highly probable that somewhere in this neighborhood the range of the giant Alaska moose begins. The species, however, does not show great antler development in this locality, but for some reason the antlers achieve their maximum development in the Kenai Peninsula.

In the Kenai Peninsula and the country around Cook Inlet, Alaska, with an unknown distribution to south and east, we find the distinct species recently described as Alces gigas. The animal itself has great bulk, but perhaps not more so than the animals of the Cassiar Mountains, to which it is closely related. The antlers of these Alaska moose are simply huge, running, on the average, very much larger and more complex than even picked heads from the east. These antlers, in addition to their size, have a certain peculiarity in the position of the brow antlers, the plane of which is more often turned nearly at right angles to the plane of the palmation of the main beam than in the eastern moose. In a high percentage of the larger heads there is on one or both antlers an additional and secondary palmation. In the arrangement and development of the brow antlers, and in the complexity produced by this doubling of the beam, a startling resemblance is shown to the extinct _Cervalces_, a moose-like deer of the American Pleistocene, possibly ancestral to the genus Alces. If this resemblance indicates any close relationship, we have in the Alaska moose a survivor of the archaic type from which the true moose and Scandinavian elk have somewhat degenerated. The photographs of the Alaska moose shown herewith have this double palmation.

Several heads from the Kenai Peninsula ranging over six feet are authentic; a photograph of the largest moose head in the world is published herewith. This head is in the possession of the Field Columbian Museum at Chicago, and measures 78-1/2 inches spread. The animal that bore it stood about seven feet at shoulders, but this height is not infrequently equaled by eastern moose. The weight of the dried skull and antlers was ninety-three pounds, the palmation being in places 2-1/8 inches thick.

There are several large heads in the possession of American taxidermists, which, if properly authenticated, would prove of interest. No head, however, is of much value as a record unless its history is well known, and unless it has been in the hands of responsible persons. The measurements of antler spread can be considered authentic only when the skull is intact. If the skull is split an almost imperceptible paring of the skull bones at the joint would suffice to drop the antlers either laterally out of their proper plane, or else pitch the main beam backward. By either of these devices a couple of inches can be gained on each side, making a difference of several inches in the aggregate. But the possession of an unbroken skull is by no means a guarantee of the exact size of the head when killed.

Since large antlers, and especially so-called "record heads," of any species of deer command a price among those who desire to pose as sportsmen, and have not the strength or skill to hunt themselves, it has become a regular business for dealers to buy up unusual heads. The temptation to tamper with such a head and increase its size is very great, and heads passing through the hands of such dealers must be discarded as of little scientific value. A favorite device is to take a green head, force the antlers apart with a board and a wedge every few days during the winter. By spring the skull and antlers are dry and the plank can be removed. The spread of antlers has meantime gained several inches since the death of the animal that bore them. Such a device is almost beyond detection.

It is an exceedingly difficult matter to formulate a code of hunting ethics, still harder to give them legal force; but public opinion should condemn the kind of sportsmanship which puts a price on antlers. As trophies of the chase, hard won through the endurance and skill of the hunter, they are legitimate records of achievement. The higher the trophy ranks in size and symmetry, the greater should be its value as an evidence of patient and persistent chase. To slay a full grown bull moose or wapiti in fair hunt is in these days an achievement, for there is no royal road to success with the rifle, nor do the Happy Hunting Grounds longer exist on this continent; but to kill them by proxy, or buy the mounted heads for decorative purposes in a dining room, in feeble imitation of the trophies of the baronial banquet hall, is not only vulgar taste, but is helping along the extermination of these ancient types. An animal like the moose or the wapiti represents a line of unbroken descent of vast antiquity, and the destruction of the finest members of the race to decorate a hallway cannot be too strongly condemned.

The writer desires to express his thanks for photographs and information used in this article to Dr. J.A. Allen, of the American Museum of Natural History, New York City; Dr. Daniel Giraud Elliot, of the Field Columbian Museum, Chicago; and to Mr. Andrew J. Stone, the explorer.

Madison Grant.

The Creating of Game Refuges

It was my pleasant task, during the past summer, to visit a portion of the Forest Reserves of the United States for the purpose of studying tracts which might be set aside as Game Refuges. To this end I was commissioned by the Division of Biological Survey of the United States Department of Agriculture as "Game Preserve Expert," a new title and a new function.

The general idea of the proposed plan for the creation of Game Refuges is that the President shall be empowered to designate certain tracts, wherein there may be no hunting at all, to be set aside as refuges and breeding grounds, and the Biological Survey is accumulating information to be of service in selecting such areas, when the time for creating them shall arrive. The Forest Reserves of the United States are under the care of the Department of the Interior, and not under the Agricultural Department, where one would naturally expect them to be. Their transfer to the Department of Agriculture has been agitated more than once, and is still a result much to be desired. Although acting in this mission as a representative of the Biological Survey under the latter Department, I bore a circular letter from the Secretary of the Interior, requesting the aid of the superintendents and supervisors of the Forest Reserves. Through them I could always rely upon the services of a competent ranger, who acted as guide.

Arriving in California in March, I was somewhat more than six months engaged in the work; in that time visiting seven reserves in California and one in the State of Washington, involving a cruise of 1,220 miles in the saddle and on foot, within the boundaries of the forest, besides 500 miles by wagon and stage. Since the addition of an extra member to the party is ever an added risk of impaired harmony, and since the practice of any art involving skill is always a pleasure, I employed no packer during the entire time of my absence, but did this work myself, assisted on the off-side by Mr. Thurston, who accompanied me, and who helped in every way within his power. May I take this opportunity to thank him for aid of many sorts, and on all occasions, and for unflagging interest in the problem which we had before us. California has long since ceased to be a country where the use of the pack train is a customary means of travel. It is now an old and long settled region where the frontier lies neither to the east nor to the west, but has escaped to the vicinity of timber line, nearly two miles straight up in the air. Comparatively few people outside of the Sierra Club, that admirable open-air organization of "the Coast," have occasion to visit it, and such trips as they make are of brief duration.

Since it is not desirable to visit the high Sierras before the first of July, three full months were at my disposal for the study of the reserves of southern California, a section of great interest, and of the utmost importance to the State. In southern California one hears frequent mention of the Pass of Tehachapi; it is the line of demarcation between the great valley of central California, drained by the San Joaquin River on the north, and of southern California proper, which lies to the south. These two regions are of very different nature. In the San Joaquin Valley lie the great wheat fields of California. South of the Pass of Tehachapi, people are dependent upon irrigation. Here, too, lie wheat fields and also rich vineyards, and the precious orchards of oranges and lemons; further south the equally valuable walnut and almond groves.

The seven Forest Reserves of southern California may be regarded as one almost continuous tract embracing about 4,000,000 acres, lying on either side of the crest of the Coast Range; they are economically of enormous importance to California, but not on account of their timber. In many cases they are forest reserves without trees; for example, the little Trabuco Canyon Reserve, which has but a handful of Coulter pines, and on the northern slope a few scattered spruce. The western slope of the foothills of the San Jacinto, San Bernardino, San Gabriel, Zaca Lake and Pine Mountain, and Santa Ynez reserves, are clad only in chaparral, yet the preservation of these hillsides from fire is of vital importance to the people, since the mantle of vegetation protects, to a certain degree, the sources of the streams from which the supply of water is derived. In this country they believe that water is life; thus harking back to the teaching of the Father of Philosophy, to Thales of Miletus, who lived six hundred years before Christ: "The principle of all things is water, all comes from water, and to water all returns." Such trees as there are here possess unusual interest; approaching the crest of the mountains one finds a scattered growth of pines--the Coulter, ponderosa, Jeffrey's, the glorious sugar pine, the _Pinus contorta_, and _Pinus flexilis_, the single leaf or nut pine, and, in scattered tracts, the queer little knob-cone pine. Red and white firs are found, the incense cedar, the Douglas spruce, the big cone spruce, and a number of deciduous trees, mainly oaks of several varieties, with sycamore along the lower creeks, and the alder tree, strikingly like the alder bush of our eastern streams and pastures, but of Gargantuan proportions, grown out of all recognition. Scattered representatives of other species are found--the maple, cherry, dogwood, two varieties of sumac, the yerba del pasmo (or bastard cedar), madro駉 s, walnut, mesquite, mountain mahogany, cottonwood, willow, ash, many varieties of bushes, also the yucca, mescal, cactus, etc. I have given but a bald enumeration of these; the forming of an acquaintance with so many new trees, shrubs, and flowering herbs is of great interest, and increasingly so from day to day, as one comes to live with them in the different reserves. The pleasure to be derived is cumulative--each acquisition of knowledge adding to the satisfaction of that which comes after--it is of a sort, however, to be experienced in the presence of the thing itself; any description at a distance must necessarily be shadowy and unreal, only the dry bones of something which one sees there, a thing of beauty and instinct with life.

The characteristic feature of these southern forests is their open nature; so far as the roughness of the mountains will permit, one may go anywhere in the saddle without being hindered by underbrush. Outside of their limits, however, and on many hillsides within the reserves, the chaparral offers an impenetrable barrier; in some of them this growth has captured the greater portion of their surface. The forests themselves are often very beautiful; growing, as they do, openly, there is constant sunlight during many months of the year, so that all the ground is warm and vibrant with energy. As a natural consequence, great individuality is shown in the tree forms, as different as possible from the gloom and severe uniformity of the Oregon and Washington forests. The former are dry, light, and cheerful; the latter, moist, dark, silent, and somewhat forbidding. The northern forests of the Coast have their attractive features, to be sure; they are fecund, solemn, and majestic, but the prevailing note is not cheerfulness, as here in the south.

In a paper of the present proportions it is impossible to give, except in outline, a report of the summer's work. I began at San Juan Capistrano, one of the old mission towns with a beautiful ruin, lying near the sea on the west of the Trabuco Canyon Reserve. My first cruise was through a chaparral country on the slope overlooking the Pacific. I learned here of few deer and of relentless warfare against such as remain. After that, from Elsinore, strange echo of that sea-girt castle in Shakespeare's Denmark, I cruised so as to have as well an understanding of the eastern slope of this, the smallest of the Coast reserves. From Trabuco Peak we could study the physical geography of the northern half of its area. I saw here what I did not again come across in California--a small flock of the band-tailed pigeon, a bird as large as the mountain quail, very handsome, indeed, and one that now should be protected by law. These, as well as the mountain quail, swallow whole the acorns, which this season lay beneath the live oak trees in lavish abundance; long thin acorns, quite different from ours. In the San Jacinto Reserve I made a cruise through the southern half; much of this section is clothed in scrub oak, with scattered deer throughout. In the northern and more mountainous portions, on the contrary, one finds himself in the open forest, the summer range of the deer. At the time of our visit these were at a lower altitude, in the chaparral and among the scrub oaks of the foothills.

Going thence by rail north to Santa Barbara, I inspected the narrow strip of the Santa Ynez Reserve, and the eastern and western sections of the Zaca Lake and Pine Mountain Reserve. These are under the control of different forest supervisors; they are both largely composed of chaparral country, with scattered "pineries" on the mountains. The hunting here is regulated, to a certain degree, by the problem of feed and water for the stock used by the hunters in gaining access to the ground. Many enter these tracts from the south, as well as from the region adjacent to Santa Barbara, and the deer have a somewhat harassed and chivied existence, although, owing to the impenetrable nature of the chaparral outside of the pineries, there is a natural limit to the power of the sportsman to accomplish their entire extermination. The present control of hunters by the forest rangers is only tentative; naturally we hope to have in an ever-increasing degree more scientific management both of the deer and of those who illegally kill them. The sentiment of the community is enlightened, and would strengthen the hands of the Government in enforcing the law. At present a ranger can do little more than maintain, so far as he can, his authority by threats--threats which he has not the power to enforce.

In the San Gabriel and San Bernardino Reserves one finds himself at last in a forest country, with mountains which command respect, a section full of superb feed for the deer, feed of many sorts, for the deer have an attractive and varied bill of fare. Whole hillsides are found of scrub oak, their chief stand-by, and of wild lilac or "deer brush," the latter familiar to all readers of Muir as the Cleanothus, in those long periods of Miltonic sweep and dignity in which he summons the clans of the California herbs and shrubs; an enumeration as stately as the Homeric catalogue of the ships, and, to such as lack technical knowledge of botany, imposing respect rather by sonorous appeal to the ear than by visual suggestion to the memory. That herbs should be marshalled in so impressive an array fills one with admiration and with somewhat of awe for these representatives of the vegetable kingdom. As Muir pronounces their full-sounding titles, one feels that each is a noble in this distinguished company. No one unprotected by a botany should have the temerity to enter, amid these lists, alone.

We visited this country in the season of flowers. Whole hillsides bore their delicate, spirea-like, cream-colored blossoms--when seen at a distance, like a hovering breath, as unsubstantial as dew, or as the well-named bloom on a plum or black Hamburg grape. The superb yucca flaunted its glorious white standards, borne proudly aloft like those of the Roman legions, each twelve or fifteen feet in height, supporting myriads of white bells. The Mexicans call this the "Quixote"--a noble and fitting tribute to the knight of La Mancha. The tender center of the plant, loved as food equally by man and beast, is protected by many bristling bayonets, an ever-vigilant guard. At an altitude of seven thousand or eight thousand feet, one passed through acres of buckthorn, honey-fragrant, this also a favorite of the deer, now visited by every bee and butterfly of the mountain side. It is to be noted that as one ascends the mountains the butterflies increase in numbers as well as the flowers which they so closely resemble, save only the latter's stationary estate.

One sees in its perfection of color the "Indian paint brush," with its red of purest dye, and adjoining it solid fields of blue lupine--the colors of Harvard and Yale, side by side, challenging birds and all creatures of the air to a decision as to which of them bears itself the more bravely. Here is a chestnut tree; but look not overhead for its sheltering branches. This is a country of surprises, and if the alder tree towers on high, the dwarf chestnut or chinkapin here delegates to the mountains the pains of struggling toward the heavens, and, contented with its lowly estate, freely offers to the various "small deer" of the forest its horde of sweet, three-cornered nuts.

Under the pines one catches a distant gleam of the snow plant, an exquisite sharp note of color, of true Roman shade, such as Rossetti loved to introduce into his pictures, shrill like the vibrant wood of the flute. When a ray of the sun happens to strike this it gleams like a flaming fiery sword, symbol of that which marked the entrance to Paradise. One can circumvent this guard here, and when he is in these hills he is not far removed from a country well worth protecting by all possible ingenuity, a paradise open to all such as love pure air and wholesome strong exercise.

Much of the San Gabriel Reserve is rugged and well protected by nature to be the home of the deer. San Bernardino, on the contrary, is the most accessible of the southern reserves, with abundant feed for the horses of those who visit it, well watered, and full of noble trees. So open is the forest that in the hunting season much of it must be abandoned by the deer, who are perfectly cognizant of their danger, and, with somewhat of aid from man, are quite capable of taking care of themselves.

After visiting these southern reserves, I outfitted at Redstone Park, above Visalia, in the San Joaquin Valley, and cruised through the Sequoia National Park, among the big trees, at that time patrolled by colored soldiers under the able command of Captain Young, an officer who possesses the distinction of being the only negro graduate of West Point, I believe, now holding a commission in the United States Army. The impression produced by the giant Sequoias is one of increasing effect as the time among them is extended. In their province the world has nothing to offer more majestic and more satisfying than these trees; one must live among them to come fully beneath their charm.

Since the National Parks and military reservations are already game refuges, it was of importance that I should see the Mt. Whitney Military Reservation, and for this purpose I crossed the Sierra Reserve, through broad tracts suitable for Game Refuges, thus acquiring familiarity with a large and most interesting section of forest country. From the top of Mt. Whitney, the highest bit of land in the United States, exclusive of Alaska, one looks down two miles in altitude to Owen's Lake almost directly beneath. I picked up, on the plateau of the summit, a bit of obsidian Indian chipping, refutation in itself of the frequently repeated statement that Indians do not climb high peaks. A month was spent with great profit in and about the Sierra Reserve, and one might go there many summers, ever learning something new.

Having seen these southern reserves, and desiring to bring home with me an impression of the northern woods, sharpened by immediate contrast, I next visited that one which is the most to the northwest of them all, the Olympic

Reserve in Washington. Here, at the head of the Elwha Valley, near Mt. Olympus, we lived among the glaciers. The forest between the headwaters and the sea affords a superb contrast to California; here are found fog and moisture, and super-abounding heavy vegetation. In the thick shade grow giant ferns of tropic luxuriance. The rhododendron thrives, its black glossy leaves a symbol of richly nourished power. The devil's club flaunts aloft its bright berries, and poisonously wounds whomsoever has the misfortune even to touch its great prickly leaves, nearly as big as an elephant's ear; if there be a malignant old rogue of the vegetable kingdom, this is he, sharing with the wait-a-bit thorn of Africa an evil eminence. Many new plants meet the eye, a wealth of berries-- the Oregon grape, the salmon berry, red or yellow, as big as the yolk of an egg, the salal berry, any quantity of blueberries, huckleberries, both red and blue, sarvis berries, bear berries, mountain ash berries (also loved of bears), thimble berries, high bush cranberries, gooseberries--large and insipid--currants, wild cherries, choke cherries; many of these friends of old, others seen here for the first time, dainty picking in the autumn for deer, bears, foxes, squirrels and many birds. What particularly appealed to me was a wild apple, no larger than the eye of a hawk, but quite able to survive in a fierce contest for life, and with a pleasant, clean, sharp taste, very tonic to the palate, and with diminutive rosy cheeks as tempting as a stout Baldwin--a fine, courageous little product of the wild life, symbol of the energetic quality of the Olympic air. I, for one, am a firm believer in the axiom that a climate which will give the right "tang" to an apple will also produce determined and energetic men; this whole region, spite of its fogs, has a glorious future before it. Superb firs towered hundreds of feet above our heads, and archaic-looking cedars, a thousand years old, thrust their sturdy shoulders firmly against the storms and the winds. But the valleys, the trees and the glaciers, were only the _mise-en-sc鑞e_ of that which constituted primarily the reason of my visiting this peninsula. Here is the only wild herd of elk of any considerable size outside of the Yellowstone National Park, a most beautiful elk now separated from the Rocky Mountain species. Besides this herd there are only a few survivors of the once innumerable herds of the Pacific Coast, one little bunch in California, and a few scattered individuals in the mountains of Oregon and Washington. It is excessively hard to form any correct estimate of how many remain; probably there are at least a thousand, possibly several times that number. At all events, there is a scattered herd large enough to insure the existence of the species if they might now be protected. Unfortunately the sentiment of the community in the vicinity of the Olympics is just about what it was in Colorado in the seventies and in the early eighties--almost complete apathy, so far as taking effective precaution is concerned, to prevent the killing of these animals in violation of the law. I saw one superb herd south of the headwaters of the Elwha, and was informed that in the winter a large number come lower down into the valley of that river; here and elsewhere the finest specimens are slaughtered by head-hunters for the market, and by anyone, in fact, who may covet their hides or meat or their "tusks," now unfortunately very valuable.

Presumably, in so killing them, picked specimens are selected. Of course the finest bulls may not thus be systematically eliminated without causing the general deterioration of the herd. Nature's method of progress is by the survival of the fittest. Man reverses this so soon as cupidity makes him the foe of wild animals. The country here is an excessively hard one to get about in with stock, owing to its very rugged nature and to the scarcity of feed, so that there is slight danger of the extermination of these elk by sportsmen during the open season. In the winter, however, the hunters have them at their mercy. I was assured by one very level-headed man that, in the winter of 1902-3, two men killed seventeen elk from the Elwha herd. Since the individuals who killed the elk are well known and are practically unmolested, the immunity which they enjoy tempts others to similar violation of the law. More recently still, during this last winter, the game warden of Washington reports the finding of the carcasses of nineteen elk, killed for their tusks.

This country, with its splendid glaciers and mountains covered with snow, presents quite the most beautiful scenery to be found within the limits of the United States, exclusive of Alaska, and, before many years, is destined to become a place of general resort for travelers. For this to be accomplished, all that is needed is greater facility of travel. It would be a thousand pities if we should tolerate the extermination of the elk, which would afford delight to every one who visited the Olympics, if only the herd might be preserved. One can hardly blame the hunters for taking advantage of the laxity of public sentiment. The State has it within its power easily to protect these animals by the employment of two or three game detectives of the right sort--keen, energetic men. These would soon break up the illicit traffic and bring the offenders to justice. The people of the whole Pacific seaboard, who are justly proud of their region, and of every trait peculiarly its own, would bitterly lament the final disappearance of elk from this whole countryside, yet the fact remains that hardly a voice there, outside of the organization of the "Elks," is raised to protest against these flagrant acts of vandalism which are taking place beneath their very eyes.

This visit to the northern forest was full of varied and commanding interest, but the chief occupation of my summer, when all is said, was with California.

Deer are practically the only game to be considered in these southern California reserves. There are mountain sheep to the east, in the mountains of the Mojave and Colorado deserts, but they are almost unmolested by the hunters of the seaboard country, and, except in rare instances, are no longer found in the reserves. Occasionally odd ones are seen, venturesome, determined individuals, on their travels, in the energy of youthful maturity, tempted by curiosity, but these soon realize that they are not secure where so many humans abound, and scurry back to their desert fastnesses. As refuges are created and breeding grounds established, sheep will return, and, it is hoped, make their permanent home in the reserves. There are still enough of them in scattered places for this purpose. I was told of one method of hunting in the desert hills, sometimes resorted to by Indians and white men of the baser sort, that seems hateful and unsportsmanlike. The springs at which they drink are long distances apart. In some instances the alleged sportsmen camp by these and watch them without intermission for three days and nights, at the end of which period, when the sheep are exhausted by thirst, the hunter has them at his mercy. This has nearly as much to commend it to the self-respecting sportsman as the practice of imitating the cry of the female moose to lure the bull to mad recklessness and his undoing, a challenge hard for a courageous animal to resist, a treacherous snare set before his feet. It would seem as if a right-minded man would hesitate to take so base an advantage as by either of these two methods of hunting.

Antelope are nearly exterminated in southern California, and there is but a single little bunch of elk--those in the San Joaquin Valley, sole survivors of the vast herds which ranged throughout those lowlands when Fremont came to the country in 1845. These elk are smaller than those of the mountains, and bear a striking resemblance to the Scotch red deer, so familiar to us in Landseer's pictures. For years they have been protected by the generosity and wisdom of one man, now no longer young, an altogether public-spirited and generous act. I was taken by the manager of this ranch to see these elk as they came at night to feed in the alfalfa fields, and again in the morning we followed their trail into the foothills and had a capital view of seven superb bulls in their wild estate, as pretty a sight as one might see in California. Who can feel ought save commiseration for a man who, standing on London bridge, could say, "Earth has not anything to show more fair"?

Twice during the summer was I told of the presence in the mountains, by men who thought they had seen them, of the mythical ibex. My informant, in each instance a ranger, assured me that he had had a good look at the animal, and was sure that it was not a mountain ram. The back-curving horns he said were "as long as his forearm," one added instance of the fact that a fish in the brook is worth two on the string--if a good story be at stake! What my informant had seen, of course, was a ewe, or young mountain ram before he had arrived at the age when the horns begin to form their characteristic spiral. As for the great size of the horns, the animal was running away, and every hunter is aware of the enormous proportions which the antlers attain of an escaping elk or deer. How they suddenly shrink when the beast is shot is another story.

Incidentally, the refuges of southern California will include the breeding places of the trout in the upper reaches of the streams, and will afford protection to grouse, quail, and other birds, but primarily their purpose is to prevent the extermination of big game. In California this has gone as far as it is safe to go if we are to save the remnant. Even the California grizzly has been killed off so relentlessly that it was a question, when I was there, whether a single pair survived which might possibly in that State preserve the species. The ranger who knew the most about this was of the opinion that two or three were still left alive. He had seen their tracks within a year.[11] There are, I have been assured, others in Oregon.

[Footnote 11: I have been informed since the above was written that he saw the tracks of a single grizzly after I was there, toward the end of July.]

If I had my way, the first act in creating a game refuge should be to insure the survival of the few that remain. These bears are pitifully wary as compared with their former bold and domineering attitude; they would gladly keep out of harm's way if only they might be allowed to do so. It is time, it seems to me, to call a truce to man's hostility to them, once a foe not to be despised. Now they are so completely conquered that man owes it to himself not too relentlessly to pursue a vanquished enemy. When we think of the enormous period of time, involving millions of years, required to develop a creature of such gigantic strength as the California grizzly, so splendidly equipped to win his living and to maintain his unquestioned supremacy--the Sequoia of the animal kingdom of America--and when we contemplate this creature as the very embodiment of vitality in the wild life, we shall not wantonly permit him to be exterminated, and thus deprive those who are to come after us of seeing him alive, and of seeing him where his presence adds a fine note of distinction to the landscape, a fitting adjunct to the glacier-formed ravines of the Sierras.

The domestic sheep, which were once the prey of the bears, no longer range in these forests, and so far as the depredation of bears among cattle is concerned, it is of so trifling a nature as practically not to exist. It would seem that a nation of so vast wealth as ours could afford to indulge in an occasional extravagance, such as keeping alive these few remaining bears; of maintaining them at the public expense simply for the gratification of curiosity, of a quite legitimate curiosity on the part of those who love the wild life, and every last vanishing trait that remains of its old, keen energy. So far as danger to man is involved by their presence, the experience in the Yellowstone National Park is that there is no such danger; when allowed to do so, they draw their rations as meekly as a converted Apache; if they err at all, it is on the side of exaggerated and rather pitiful humility.

It is mainly with the deer, however, that we are concerned. It is out of the question for any thinking man who takes the slightest interest in these creatures to stand passively by and permit them to be exterminated. To prevent such a catastrophe proper measures must be taken. The hunting community increases with as great rapidity as that with which game decreases. Where one man hunted twenty-five years ago, a score hunt for big game to-day. Unfortunately it has become the fashion. It is a diversion involving no danger and, for those that understand it, but slight hardship. If people are to continue to have this source of amusement, some well matured and concerted plan must be devised to insure the continuance of game. Never in the past history of the world has man held at his command the same potential control of wild beasts as now, the same power to concentrate against them the forces of science. Man's supremacy has advanced by leaps and bounds, while the animal's power to escape remains unchanged; all the conditions for their survival constantly become more difficult. Man has, in its perfection, the rapid-firing rifle, which, with the use of smokeless powder, gives him an enormous increase of effectiveness in its flat trajectory. This is quite as great an element of its destructiveness as its more deadly power and capacity for quick shooting, since it eliminates the necessity for accurately gauging distance, one of the hardest things for the amateur hunter to learn. If man so desires, he can command the aid of dogs. By their power of scent he has wild animals at his mercy, and unless he deliberately regulates the slaughter which he will permit, their entire extermination would be a matter of only a few years. Only at the end of the last year we were told of the celebration in the Tyrol of the killing, by the Emperor of Austria, of his two thousandth chamois. Eight years ago this same record was achieved by another Austrian, a Grand Duke. This was in both instances, as I understand, by the means of fair and square stalking, quite different from the methods of the more degenerate battue. At a single shooting exhibition of this latter sort by the Crown Prince of Germany at his estate in Schleswig, on one day in December last, were killed two hundred and ten fallow deer, three hundred and forty-one red deer, and on the day following, eighty-seven large wild boar, one hundred and twenty-six small ones, eighty-six fallow deer, and two hundred and one red deer. Any man, private citizen as well as emperor or prince, has it within his power, if he be possessed of the blood craze, to kill scores and hundreds of every kind of game. By the facilities of rapid travel the hunter, with the least possible sacrifice of time, is transported with whatever of luxury a Pullman car can confer (luxury to him who likes it) to the haunts and almost within the very sanctuaries of game. Where formerly an expedition of months was required, now in a few days' time he is carried to the most out-of-the-way places, to the barrens, the forests, the peaks, the mountain glades--almost to the muskeg and the tundra.

How far the rage for hunting has captured the community in this country of the western seaboard it is surprising to learn. In the year 1902 there were issued for the seven forest reserves south of the Pass of Tehachapi, a tract three-quarters the size of Massachusetts, four thousand permits to hunt. Inasmuch as one permit may admit more than a single person to the privileges of hunting, it was estimated that at least five thousand people bearing rifles entered the reserves. This besides the enormous horde of the peaceably disposed who also seek diversion here, and who naturally disturb the deer to a certain extent. The supervisor of two reserves--the San Gabriel and San Bernardino--embracing a tract less than half the size of Connecticut, assured me that in 1902 sixty thousand persons entered within their borders; in the summer of 1903 this number was estimated at no less than ten thousand in excess of the previous year. In these two reserves the number of permits for rifles and revolvers issued between June 1 and December 31, increased from 1,900 in the year 1902, to 3,483 in 1903, and as, in some cases, these were issued for two or more persons, the supervisor estimates that at least 4,500 rifles were carried last summer into these two reserves. He was of the opinion that two-thirds of these were borne by hunters, the remainder as protection against bears and other ferocious wild beasts, which exist only in imagination.[12]

[Footnote 12: "Relative to the figures for game permits, and the reason for the larger number issued for 1903 over 1902, I cannot myself altogether explain the large increase. One reason, however, was that our rainfall for the winter of 1902-3 was very large compared with that of the five previous winters. As a result grass and feed were plentiful, and attracted many more travelers and hunters, who figured that game would be much more plentiful owing to the abundance of feed. I believe that this was the principal reason why so many obtained permits. The abundant rain made camping more pleasant, as it started up springs which had been dry for several years. I believe that this very thing, however, also tended to protect the game as it permitted them to scatter more than for several years before, as water was more abundant. With all the increase in guns and hunters I do not think that any more deer were killed than during the summer of 1902." (Letter from Forest Supervisor, Mr. Everett B. Thomas, Los Angeles, Feb. 13, 1904.) It is to be noted that in the southern California reserves, on the ground of precaution against forest fires, no shotguns may be carried into the reserves. As a result quail have greatly increased in numbers.]

It is to be borne in mind that all through this California country there exists a race of hunters--active, determined men, who passionately love this diversion. The people there have not been so long graduated as we of the Atlantic Coast from the conditions of the frontier. The ozone of a new country stirs more quickly the predatory instinct, never quite dead in any virile race. The rifle slips easily from its scabbard, and there in plain sight before them are the forest-clad mountains, a mile above their heads, in the cool and vital air, ever beckoning the hunter to be up and away. These people feel in their blood the call of the wild. With a very considerable proportion of the people upon farms, and still more in villages and small towns, the Fall hunt is the commanding interest of the year. This is the one athletic contest into which they enter heart and soul; it is foot-ball and yachting and polo and horse racing combined. For a young man to go into the forest after deer and to come back empty-handed, is to lose prestige to a certain extent among his fellows. Oftentimes, when a beginner returns in this way unsuccessful, he is so unmercifully chaffed by his companions that he mentally records a vow not to be beaten a second time, and, when he finds himself again in the forest for his annual hunt, with the enthusiasm of youth, he would almost rather die than be defeated.

How hard the conditions are for the hunter no one would believe who has not himself seen the country. In many places the hills are covered with an almost impenetrable chaparral of scrub oak, buckthorn, greasewood, manzanita, and deer-brush, in which the wary deer have taken refuge. In and through these, guided sometimes by the tracks of the deer, or encouraged by the presence of such tracks even if he cannot follow them, up steep mountains, exposed to the heat of the sun, in dust, over rocks, and without water, toils the hunter, who accounts himself lucky if, by tramping scores of miles through this sort of impediment, he succeeds, after days of toil, in killing his deer. Perhaps he has been without fresh meat for a week or a fortnight, and often on short commons; is it to be wondered at that when a shot offers he avails himself of the opportunity even if it be a doe that he fires at? How can the deer withstand such concentration of fury?

Dr. Bartlett, Forest Supervisor of the Trabuco and San Jacinto Reserves, assured me that the number of licenses to hunt in those two reserves issued annually exceeded, in his opinion, the entire number of deer within their boundaries.

Everyone now is ready to admit that the extermination of the herd of buffalo in the seventies was permitted by a crude, short-sighted policy on our part as a nation, and should we of the early twentieth century allow the remaining deer, elk, mountain sheep, and antelope, the last of the great bears, and the innumerable small creatures of the wild, to be crowded off the face of the earth, we should be depriving our children and our children's children of a satisfaction and of a source of interest which they would keenly regret. It would be well if we bore in mind that we stand in a sort of fiduciary relation to the people who are to come after us, so far as the wild portion of our land is concerned, those few remote tracts still untarnished by man's craze to convert everything in the world, or beneath the surface of the earth, into dollars for his own immediate profit. He has the same short-sighted policy in his hunting. He is content to gratify the impulse of the hour without thought of those who are to spend their lives here when we have led our brief careers and have gone to a well merited oblivion, to reap our reward--

Heads without names, no more remembered.

Let us look this matter squarely in the face. We are the inheritors of these domains. It is one of the most precious assets of posterity. Here, year by year, in steadily increasing proportion, as wisdom more prevails, will men take comfort; and as the comprehension of nature's charms penetrates their minds will they find content. One chief satisfaction that every American feels from the mere fact of his nationality is the full assurance in his heart that any measure founded on sound reason and prompted by generous impulse will receive, if not immediate acceptance, at all events eventual recognition. In the end justice will prevail. Thus, in this matter before us, it will naturally take a few years for Congress to realize that a genuine demand exists for the creation of these refuges in every State, East as well as West, but the interest in wild creatures, and the desire for their protection, if not a clamorous demand, is one almost universally felt. All men, except a meager few of the dwarfed and strictly city-bred, partake of this, and it is so much a sign of the times that no Sunday edition is complete without its column devoted to wild creatures, their traits, their habits, or their eccentricities. One could hardly name, outside of money-making and politics, an interest which all men more generally share.

Every lad is a born naturalist, and the true wisdom, as all sensible people know, is to carry unfatigued through life the boy's power of enjoyment, his freshness of perception, his alertness and zest. Where the child's capacity for close observation survives into manhood, supplemented by man's power of sustained attention, we have the typical temperament of the lover of the woods, the mountains, and the wild--of the naturalist in the sense that Thoreau was a naturalist, and many another whose memory is cherished.

It is not impossible for a man to be deeply learned and still to lack the power of awakening enthusiasm in others; as a matter of fact, to be so heavily freighted with information that he forgets to nourish his own finer faculties, his intuition, his sympathy, and his insight. One must have lived for a time in the California mountains to realize how great is the service to the men of his own and to succeeding generations of him who more than any one else has illuminated the study of the Sierras and of all our forest-clad mountains, our glacier-formed hills, valleys and glades. Not by any means do all lovers of nature, however faithful their purpose, come to its study with the endowment of John Muir. In him we see the trained faculties of the close and accurate observer, joined to the temperament of the poet--the capacity to think, to see and to feel--and by the power of sustained and strong emotion to make us the sharers of his joy. The beauty and the majesty of the forest to him confer the same exaltation of mind, the same intellectual transport, which the trained musician feels when listening to the celestial harmonies of a great orchestra. In proportion as one conceives, or can imagine, the fineness of the musical endowment of a Bach or Beethoven, and in proportion as he can realize in his own mind the infinity of training and preparation which has contributed to the development of such a master musician--in such proportion may he comprehend and appreciate the unusual qualities and achievements of a man like Muir. He will realize to some degree--indistinctly to be sure, "seeing men as trees walking"--the infinity of nice and accurate observation, the discriminating choice of illustration, the infallible tact and unvarying sureness with which he holds our interest, and the dominant poetic insight into the nature of things, which are spread before the reader in lavish abundance, in Muir's two books, "The Mountains of California" and "Our National Parks." No other books, in this province, by living author offer to the reader so rich a feast. Recognizing the fine endowments of Thoreau, and how greatly all are his debtors, still we of this generation are lucky in having one greater than he among us, if wisdom of life and joyousness be the criterion of a sound and of a sane philosophy. The time will come when this will be generally recognized. The verdict of posterity is the right one, and the love of mankind is given throughout the centuries to the men of insight, who possess the rare mental endowment of sustained pleasure. Call it perpetual youth, or joyousness, or what you like, the fact remains that the power of sustained enthusiasm, lightness of heart and gaiety, with the faculty of communicating to others that state of mind, is not one of the commonest endowments of the human brain. It is one that confers great happiness to others, and one to whose possessor we are under great obligation. Compare the career of Thoreau, lonely, sad, and wedded to death--on the one hand, with that of Muir, on the other--a lover of his kind, healthful, inspiring to gaiety, superabounding in vitality. Naturalists of this type of mind, and so faithful in perfecting the talents entrusted to them, do not often appear in any age.

In the designations of refuges for deer, various questions are to be considered, such as abundance of food, proximity to water, suitable shelter, an exposure to their liking, for they may be permitted to have whims in a matter of this sort, just as fully as Indians or the residents of the city, when they deign to honor the country by their presence. The deer feel that they are entitled to a certain remote absence from molestation; moderate hunting will not entirely discourage them--a dash of excitement might prove rather entertaining to a young buck with a little recklessness in his temperament--but unless a deer be clad in bullet-proof boiler iron, there are ranges in the reserves of southern California where he would never dare to show his face during the open season--regular rifle ranges. Where very severely hunted, like the road agent, they "take to the brush," that is, hide in the chaparral. This is almost impenetrable. It is very largely composed of scrub oak, buckthorn, or greasewood, with a scattered growth of wild lilac, wild cherry, etc. So far as the deer make this their permanent home, there is no fear of their extermination. They may be hunted effectively only with the most extreme caution. Not one person in a thousand ever attains to the level of a still-hunter whose accomplishment guarantees him success under such conditions. There are men of this sort, but these are artists in their pursuit, whose attainments, like those of the professional generally, are beyond comparison with those of the ordinary amateur. To hunt successfully in the chaparral, requires a special genius. One must have exhaustless patience, tact trained by a lifetime of this sort of work, perseverance incapable of discouragement, the silence of an Indian, and in this phrase--when we are dealing with the skill of one who can make progress without sound through the tangles of the dry and stiff California chaparral--is involved an exercise of skill comparable only to the fineness of touch of a Joachim or a St. Gaudens. This sort of hunter marks one end of the scale of perfection; near the other and more familiar extreme is found the individual of whom this story is told. He was an Englishman and had just returned from a trip into the jungle of India after big game, where he was accompanied by a guide, most expert in his profession. One of the sportsman's friends asked this man how his employer shot while on the trip. His reply was a model of tact and concise statement: "He shot divinely, but God was very merciful to the animals."

He who reads this brief account may naturally ask: What were the practical results of your Western trip? Have you any ideas which may be of value in the solution of this problem of Game Refuges? My primary conception of the duties of a Game Expert, sent out by a Bureau of a United States Department, was to approach this entire subject without preconceived theories, with an open and unbiased mind; to see as many of the various reserves as possible, under the guidance of the best men to be had, and, increasing in this manner my knowledge by every available means, to reserve the period of general consideration and of specific recommendation until the whole preliminary reconnoissance should be accomplished. The thing of prime importance is that the game expert should see the reserves, and see them thoroughly. In a measure of such scope what we desire is a well thought-out plan, based on knowledge of the actual conditions, knowledge acquired in the field for the future use of him who has acquired it. No report can transfer to the mind of another an impression thus derived.

I had been but a short time engaged in this campaign of education before it seemed wise to abandon the limitations imposed by traveling in wagons; these held one to the valleys and to the dusty ways of men. After that emancipation I lived in the haunts of the deer, traveling with a pack train, and cruising in about the same altitude affected by that most thoroughbred of all the conifers, the sugar pine. Trust the genius of that tree, the pine, of all those that grow on any of the mountains of North America, of finest power, beauty, individuality, and distinction, to select the most attractive altitude for its home, the daintiest air, the air fullest of strong vitality and determination, whether man or deer is to participate in the virtues of the favored zone. Many a time I went far beyond the region of the sugar pine, and not infrequently cruised beneath its lower limits.

What that tree loves is a zone of about four thousand feet in width extending from three to seven thousand feet above the level of the sea. The upper reaches of this belt are where the deer range during the open season of the summer when they must be afforded protection. These were traversed with care, and seen with as much thoroughness as possible. More of the reserves might easily have been visited in other States, had I been content to do this in a sketchy and cursory manner, but my idea was to derive the greatest possible amount of instruction for a definite specific purpose, and it seemed to me for the accomplishment of this end to be essential that one should spend a sufficiently long time in each forest to receive a strong impression of its own peculiar and distinctive nature, to get an idea into one's head, which would stick, of its individuality, and, if I may say so, of its personal features and idiosyncrasies. Not until more than three months had been spent in the faithful execution of this plan was the problem studied from any other view than that refuges were to be created of considerable size, and that their lines of demarcation would naturally be formed by something easily grasped by the eye, either rivers or the crests of mountain ranges.

After the lapse of that time, looking at this from every point of view, it became my opinion that the ideal solution was the creation of many small refuges rather than the establishment of a few large ones. To be effective, the size of these ranges should not be less than ten miles square; if slightly larger, so much the better. Should, therefore, these be of about four townships each, the best results would be obtained. The bill for the creation of Game Refuges after it had passed the Senate, and as amended by the Committee on Public Lands of the House of Representatives, in the spring of 1903, read:

"The President of the United States is hereby authorized to designate such areas in the public Forest Reserves, _not exceeding one in each State or Territory_, as should, in his opinion, be set aside for the protection of game animals, birds, and fish, and be recognized as a breeding place therefor."

If this bill were to become law in its present form, the object for which it was created would be largely defeated. One may easily overlook the fact that an area corresponding to that of California would, on the Atlantic Coast, extend from Newport, R. I., to Charleston, S. C. It embraces communities and interests in many respects as widely separated as those of New England and the Atlantic Southern States. Were one Game Refuge only to be created in the State of California, unless it included practically the whole of the reserves south of Tehachapi, protection would not be afforded to the different species of large a constantly increasing population, and an ever-increasing interest in big-game hunting. The designation of one Game Refuge in the Sierra Reserve would practically not reduce the slaughter of deer in this whole vast region of southern California. Were the single Game Refuge, which might under the law be designated, to be placed in southern California, even although it embraced the entire area of the seven southern reserves, it would not aid to any great extent in preventing the extinction of game in the region of the Sierra Reserve, of the Stanislaus Reserve, or of the great reserves which are doubtless soon to be created in the northern half of the State. A bill so conceived would not fulfill the purpose of its creation.

There are just as cogent reasons of a positive nature why many small refuges are preferable to a few large ones. It is said that in the vicinity of George Vanderbilt's game preserves at Biltmore, North Carolina, deer, when started by dogs even fifteen or twenty miles away, will seek shelter within the limits of that protected forest, knowing perfectly well that once within its bounds they will not be disturbed. The same may be observed in the vicinity of the Yellowstone National Park; the bears, for instance, a canny folk, and shrewd to read the signs of the times, seem to be well aware that they are not to be disturbed near the hotels, and they show themselves at such places without fear; at the same time that outside the Park (and when the early snow is on the ground their tracks are often observed going both out and in) these same beasts are very shy indeed. The hunter soon discovers that it is with the greatest difficulty that one ever sees them at all outside of the bounds of the Park. Bears, as well as deer, adapt themselves to the exigencies of the situation; the grizzly, since the white man stole from him and the Indian the whole face of the earth, has become a night-ranging instead of a diurnal creature. The deer, we may safely rest assured, makes quite as close a study of humans as man does of the deer. It is a question of life and death with them that they should understand him and his methods. Both the deer and the hunters would profit by the widest possible distribution of these protected areas. Each section of the State is entitled to the benefit to be derived from their presence in its vicinity. Moreover, and I believe that this is a consideration of no slight moment, the creation of many small refuges, not too close together, would obviate one great difficulty which threatens to wreck the entire scheme. There have appeared signs of opposition in certain quarters to the creation in the various reserves of game refuges by Federal power on the ground that this would be to surrender to the Government at Washington authority which should be solely exercised by the State. In a certain sense it is the old issue of State rights. Where this feeling exists it is adhered to with extraordinary tenacity, and it is as catching as the measles; just so soon as one State takes this stand, another is liable to raise the same issue. They are jealous of any power except their own which would close from hunting to their citizens considerable portions of the forest reserves within the confines of the State. Their claim is that by an abuse of such delegated power, a President of the United States might, if so inclined, shut out the citizens from hunting at all in the forest reserves of their own State.

This argument is not an easy one to wave aside. Should, however, the size of the individual refuges be limited to four townships each, and the minimum distance between such refuges be defined, one grave objection to these refuges would be overcome, and the citizens of the various States would cooperate with Federal authority to accomplish that which the sentiment at home in many instances is not at present sufficiently enlightened to demand, and which by reason of party differences the State legislatures are powerless to effect.

Having elaborated in one's mind the idea that a Game Refuge, in order to be a success, should be about ten or twelve miles square, the question arises, how near are these to be placed to one another? If they are established at the beginning, not less than twenty or twenty-five miles from each other, it seems to me that the exigencies of the situation would be met. It is not our purpose, in creating them, seriously to interfere with the privileges of hunters adjoining the forests where they are established. On the contrary, all that is wished is to preserve the present number of the deer, or to allow them slightly to increase. The system of game refuges of the size indicated, would, I believe, accomplish this end. In all probability, at the beginning of the open season, the deer would be distributed with a considerable degree of uniformity throughout the reserve, outside of the game refuges as well as within. They would go, of course, where the food and conditions suited them. As the hunting season opened, and the game, in a double sense, become more lively, the deer would naturally seek shelter where they could find it. Since this, with them, would be a question literally of vital interest, their education would progress rapidly, particularly that of the wary old bucks, experienced in danger which they had survived in the past simply because their bump of caution was well developed, these would soon realize that they were safe within the bounds of a certain tract--that there the sound of the rifle was never heard, that there far less frequently they ran across the hateful scent of their enemies, and for some mysterious reason were left to their own devices. When once this idea has found firm lodgment in the head of an astute deer, the very first thing that he will do will be to get into an asylum of this sort, and to stay there; if he has any business to transact beyond its boundaries, exactly as an Indian would do in similar circumstances, he will delegate the same to a young buck who is on his promotion, and has his reputation to make, and who possesses the untarnished courage of ignorance and youth. It seems to me that this system of small refuges would have the merit of fairness both to the hunters and to the deer, and it is respectfully submitted to the legislators of the United States. This may seem one of the simplest of solutions, and hardly worth a summer's cruise to discover. It may prove that this is not the first occasion when the simplest solution is the best. Because a thing is simple it is not always the case, however, that it finds the most ready acceptance. If, in my humble capacity of public service, I am the indirect means of this being accomplished, I shall feel that my summer's work was not altogether in vain.

Alden Sampson.

Temiskaming Moose

The accompanying photographs of moose were taken about the middle of July, 1902, on the Montreal river, which flows from the Ontario side into Lake Temiskaming.

A number of snap shots were obtained during the three days' stay in this vicinity, but the others were at longer range and the animals appear very small in the negative.

As is well known, during the hot summer months the moose are often to be found feeding on the lily pads or cooling themselves in the water, being driven from the bush where there are heat, mosquitoes and flies.

Not having been shot at nor hunted, all the moose at this time seemed rather easy to approach. Two of these pictures are of one bull, and the other two of one cow, the two animals taken on different occasions. I got three snaps of each before they were too far away. When first sighted, each was standing nibbling at the lily pads, and the final spurt in the canoe was made in each case while the animal stood with head clear under the water, feeding at the bottom. The distance of each of the first photographs taken was from 45 to 55 feet.

Paul J. Dashiell.

Two Trophies from India

In the early part of March, 1898, my friend, Mr. E. Townsend Irvin, and I arrived at the bungalow of Mr. Younghusband, who was Commissioner of the Province of Raipur, in Central India. Mr. Younghusband very kindly gave us a letter to his neighbor, the Rajah of Kahrigur, who furnished us with shikaris, beaters, bullock carts, two ponies and an elephant. We had varied success the first three weeks, killing a bear, several nilghai, wild boar and deer.

One afternoon our beaters stationed themselves on three sides of a rocky hill and my friend and I were placed at the open end some two hundred yards apart. The beaters had hardly begun to beat their tom toms and yell, when a roar came from the brow of the hill, and presently a large tiger came out from some bushes at the foot. He came cantering along in a clumsy fashion over an open space, affording us an excellent shot, and when he was broadside on we both fired, breaking his back. He could not move his hind legs, but stood up on his front paws. Approaching closer, we shot him in a vital spot.

The natives consider the death of a tiger cause for general rejoicing, and forming a triumphal procession amid a turmoil such as only Indian beaters can make, they carried the dead tiger to camp.

One morning word was brought to our camp, at a place called Bernara, that a tiger had killed a buffalo, some seven miles away. The natives had built a bamboo platform, called _machan_, in a tree by the kill, and we stationed ourselves on this in the late afternoon. Contrary to custom, the tiger did not come back to his kill until after the sun had set. The night was cloudy and very dark, and although several times we distinctly heard the tiger eating the buffalo, we could not see it. At about midnight we were extremely stiff, and not hearing any sound, we returned to our temporary camp; but on the advice of an old shikari I returned with him to the machan to wait until daylight. Being tired, I fell asleep, but an hour before dawn the Hindu woke me, as the clouds had cleared away and the moon was shining brightly. I heard a munching sound, and could dimly discern a yellow form by the buffalo, and taking a long aim I fired both barrels of my rifle. I heard nothing except the scuttling off of the hyenas and jackals that had been attracted by the dead buffalo, so I slept again until daylight, when, to my surprise, I saw a dead leopard by the buffalo. He had come to the kill after the tiger had finished his meal.

John H. Prentice.

Big-Game Refuges

Since the inception of the Boone and Crockett Club its plans and purposes have changed not a little. Originally organized for social purposes, for the encouragement of big-game hunting, and the procuring of the most effective weapons with which to secure the game, it has, little by little, come to be devoted to the broader object of benefiting this and succeeding generations by preserving a stock of large game. It is still made up of enthusiastic riflemen, and their love of the chase has not abated. But, since the Club's formation, an astonishing change has come over natural conditions in the United States--a change which, fifteen or twenty years ago, could not have been foreseen. The extraordinary development of the whole Western country, with the inevitable contraction of the range of all big game, and the absolute reduction in the numbers of the game consequent on its destruction by skin hunters, head hunters and tooth hunters, has obliged the Boone and Crockett Club, in absolute self-defense, and in the hope that its efforts may save some of the species threatened with extinction, to turn its attention more and more to game protection.

The Club was established in 1888. The buffalo had already been swept away. Since that date two species of elk have practically disappeared from the land, one being still represented by a few individuals which for some years have been preserved from destruction by a California cattle company; the other, found only in the Southwest, in territory now included within the Black Mesa forest reservation, may be, perhaps, without a single living representative. Over a vast extent of the territory which the antelope once inhabited, it has ceased to exist; and so speedy and so wholesale has been its disappearance that most of the Western States, slow as they always are to interfere with the privileges of their citizens to kill and destroy at will, have passed laws either wholly protecting it or, at least, limiting the number to be killed in a season to one, two or three. In 1888 no one could have conceived that the diminution of the native large game of America would be what it has proved to be within the past fifteen years.

That the game stock may re-establish itself in certain localities, the Club has advocated the establishment in the various forest reserves of game refuges, where absolutely no hunting shall be permitted.

Through the influence of William Hallett Phillips, a deceased member of the

Club, a few lines inserted in an act passed by Congress March 3, 1891, permitted the establishment of forest reserves, and Hon. John W. Noble, then Secretary of the Interior, at once recommended the application of the law to a number of forest tracts, which were forthwith set aside by Presidential proclamation. Since then, more and more forest reserves have been created, and, thanks to the wisdom and courage of the Chief Magistrates of the Nation within the past twelve years, we now have more than sixty millions of acres of such reservations. These consist largely of rough, timbered mountain lands, unfit for cultivation or settlement. They are of enormous value to the arid West, as affording an unfailing water supply to much of that region, and in a less degree they are valuable as timber reserves, from which hereafter may be harvested crops which will greatly benefit the country adjacent to them.

In the first volume of the Boone and Crockett Club Books, it was said: "In these reservations is to be found to-day every species of large game known to the United States, and the proper protection of the reservations means the perpetuating in full supply of all these indigenous mammals. If this care is provided, no species of American large game need ever become absolutely extinct; and intelligent effort for game protection may well be directed toward securing, through national legislation, the policing of forest preserves by timber and game wardens."--American Big Game Hunting, p. 330.

When these lines were written, Congressional action in this direction was hoped for at an early day; but, except in the case of the Yellowstone National Park, such action has not been taken. Meantime, hunting in these forest reserves has gone on. In some of them game has been almost exterminated. Two little bunches of buffalo which then had their range within the reserves have been swept out of existence.

It is obvious that effectively to protect the big game at large there must be localities where hunting shall be absolutely forbidden. That any species of big game will rapidly increase if absolutely protected is perfectly well known; and in the Yellowstone Park we have ever before us an object lesson, which shows precisely what effective protection of game can do.

It is little more than twenty years since the first efforts were made to prevent the killing of game within that National Reservation, and only about ten years since Congress provided an effective method for preventing such killing. He must be dull indeed who does not realize what that game refuge has done for a great territory, and of how much actual money value its protection has been to the adjoining States of Montana and Idaho, and especially of Wyoming. The visit of President Roosevelt to the National Park last spring made these conditions plain to the whole nation. At that time every newspaper in the land gave long accounts of what the President saw and did there, and told of the hordes of game that he viewed and counted. He saw nothing that he had not before known of, nothing that was not well known to all the members of the Boone and Crockett Club; but it was largely through the President's visit, and the accounts of what he saw in the Yellowstone Park, that the public has come to know what rigid protection can do and has done for our great game.

Since such a refuge can bring about such results, it is high time that we had more of these refuges, in order that like results may follow in different sections of the West, and for different species of wild game; as well for the benefit of other localities and their residents, as for that wider public which will hereafter visit them in ever increasing numbers.

A bill introduced at the last session of Congress authorized the President, when in his judgment it should seem desirable, to set aside portions of forest reserves as game refuges, where no hunting should be allowed. The bill passed the Senate, but failed in the House, largely through lack of time, yet some opposition was manifested to it by members of Congress from the States in which the forest reserves are located, who seemed to feel that such a law would in some way abridge the rights and privileges of their constituents. This is a narrow view, and one not justified by the experience of persons dwelling in the vicinity of the Yellowstone National Park.

If such members of Congress will consider, for example, the effect on the State of Wyoming, of the protection of the Yellowstone Park, it seems impossible to believe that they will oppose the measure. Each non-resident sportsman going into Wyoming to hunt the game--much of which spends the summer in the Yellowstone Park, and each autumn overflows into the adjacent territory--pays to the State the sum of forty dollars, and is obliged by law to hire a guide, for whose license he must pay ten dollars additional; besides that, he hires guides, saddle and pack animals, pays railroad and stage fare, and purchases provisions to last him for his hunt. In other words, at a modest calculation, each man who spends from two weeks to a month hunting in

Wyoming pays to the State and its citizens not less than one hundred and fifty dollars. Statistics as to the number of hunters who visit Wyoming are not accessible; but if we assume that they are only two hundred in number, this means an actual contribution to the State of thirty thousand dollars in cash. Besides this, the protection of the game in such a refuge insures a never-failing supply of meat to the settlers living in the adjacent country, and offers them work for themselves and their horses at a time when, ranch work for the season being over, they have no paying occupation.

The value of a few skins taken by local hunters is very inconsiderable when compared with such a substantial inflow of actual cash to the State and the residents of the territory neighboring to such a refuge. Moreover, it must be remembered that, failing to put in operation some plan of this kind, which shall absolutely protect the game and enable it to re-establish itself, the supply of meat and skins, now naturally enough regarded as their own peculiar possession by the settlers living where such a refuge might be established, will inevitably grow less and less as time goes on; and, as it grows less, the contributions to State and local resources from the non-resident tax will also grow less. Thirty years ago the buffalo skinner declared that the millions of buffalo could never be exterminated; yet the buffalo disappeared, and after them one species of big game after another vanished over much of the country. The future can be judged only by the past. Thirty years ago there were elk all over the plains, from the Missouri River westward to the Rocky Mountains; now there are no elk on the plains, and, except in winter, when driven down from their summer range by the snows, they are found only in the timbered mountains. What has been so thoroughly accomplished will be sure to continue; and, unless the suggested refuges shall be established, there will soon be no game to protect--a real loss to the country.

It has long been customary for Western men of a certain type to say that Eastern sportsmen are trying to protect the game in order that they themselves may kill it, the implication being that they wish to take it away from those living near it, and who presumably have the greatest right to it. Talk of this kind has no foundation in fact, as is shown by the laws passed by the Western States, which often demand heavy license fees from non-residents, and hedge about their hunting with other restrictions. Many Eastern sportsmen desire to preserve the game, not especially that they themselves may kill it, but that it shall be preserved; if they desire to kill this game they must and do comply with the laws established by the different States, and pay the license fees.

A fundamental reason for the protection of game, and so for the establishment of such game refuges, was given by President Roosevelt in a speech made to the Club in the winter of 1903, when he expressed the opinion that it was the duty of the Government to establish these refuges and preserves for the benefit of the poor man, the man in moderate circumstances. The very rich, who are able to buy land, may establish and care for preserves of their own, but this is beyond the means of the man of moderate means; and, unless the State and Federal Governments establish such reservations, a time is at hand when the poor man will have no place to go where he can find game to hunt. The establishment of such refuges is for the benefit of the whole public-- not for any class--and is therefore a thoroughly democratic proposition.

There is no question as to the right of Congress to enact laws governing the killing of game on the public domain, or within a forest reserve where this domain lies within the boundaries of a Territory. Moreover, it has been determined by the courts and otherwise that within a State the Federal Government has, on a forest reserve, all the rights of an individual proprietor, "supplemented with the power to make and enforce its own laws for the assertion of those rights, and for the disposal and full and complete management, control and protection of its lands."

In January, 1902, the Hon. John F. Lacey, of Iowa, a member of this Club, whose efforts in behalf of game protection are generally recognized, and whose name is attached to the well-known Lacey Law, received from Attorney-General Knox an opinion indicating that there is reasonable ground for the view that the Government may legislate for the protection of game on the forest reserves, whether these forest reserves lie within the Territories or within the States. From this opinion the following paragraphs are taken:

"While Congress certainly may by law prohibit and punish the entry upon or use of any part of those forest reserves for the purpose of the killing, capture or pursuit of game, this would not be sufficient. There are many persons now on those reserves by authority of law, and people are expressly authorized to go there, and it would be necessary to go further and to prohibit the killing, capture or pursuit of game, even though the entry upon the reserve is not for that purpose. But, the right to forbid intrusion for the purpose of killing, _per se_, and without reference to any trespass on the property, is another. The first may be forbidden as a trespass and for the protection of the property; but when a person is lawfully there and not a trespasser or intruder, the question is different.

"But I am decidedly of opinion that Congress may forbid and punish the killing of game on these reserves, no matter that the slayer is lawfully there and is not a trespasser. If Congress may prohibit the use of these reserves for any purpose, it may for another; and while Congress permits persons to be there upon and use them for various purposes, it may fix limits to such use and occupation, and prescribe the purpose and objects for which they shall not be used, as for the killing, capture or pursuit of specified kinds of game. Generally, any private owner may forbid, upon his own land, any act that he chooses, although the act may be lawful in itself; and certainly Congress, invested also with legislative power, may do the same thing, just as it may prohibit the sale of intoxicating liquors, though such sale is otherwise lawful.

"After considerable attention to the whole subject, I have no hesitation in expressing my opinion that Congress has ample power to forbid and punish any and all kinds of trespass, upon or injury to, the forest reserves, including the trespass of entering upon or using them for the killing, capture or pursuit of game.

"The exercise of these powers would not conflict with any State authority. Most of the States have laws forbidding the killing, capture or pursuit of different kinds of game during specified portions of the year. This makes such killing, etc., lawful at other times, but only lawful because not made unlawful. And it is lawful only when the State has power to make it lawful, by either implication or direct enactment. But, except in those cases already referred to, such as eminent domain, service of process, etc., no State has power to authorize or make lawful a trespass upon private property. So that, though Congress should prohibit such killing, etc., upon its own lands, at all seasons of the year, this would not conflict with any State authority or control. That the preservation of game is part of the public policy of those States, and for the benefit of their own people, is shown by their own legislation, and they cannot complain if Congress upon its own lands goes even further in that direction than the State, so long as the open season of the State law is not interfered with in any place where such law is paramount.

"It has always been the policy of the Government to invite and induce the purchase and settlement of its public lands; and as the existence of game thereon and in their localities adds to the desirability of the lands, and is a well-known inducement to their purchase, it may well be considered whether, for this purpose alone, and without reference to the protection of the lands from trespass, Congress may not, on its own lands, prohibit the killing of such game."

In this opinion the Attorney-General further calls attention to the difficulties of enforcing the State law, and suggests that it might be well to give marshals and their deputies, and the superintendents, supervisors, rangers, and other persons charged with the protection of these forest reserves, power on the public lands, in certain cases approaching "hot pursuit," to arrest without warrant. All who are familiar with the conditions in the more sparsely settled States will recognize the importance of some such provision. A matter of equal importance, though as yet not generally recognized, is that of providing funds for the expenses of forest officers making arrests. It is often the fact that no justice of the peace resides within fifty or a hundred miles of the place where the violation of the law occurs. The ranger making the arrest is obliged to transport his prisoner for this distance, and to provide him with transportation, food and lodging during the journey and during the time that he may be obliged to wait before bringing the prisoner arrested before a proper court. This may often amount to more than the penalty, even if the officer making the arrest secures a conviction; but, on the other hand, the individual arrested may not be able to pay his fine, and may have to go to jail. In this case the officer making the arrest is out of pocket just so much. Under such circumstances, it is evident that few officers can afford to take the risk of losing this time and money.

In most States of the Union there exist considerable tracts of land, mountainous, or at least barren and unfit for cultivation. Legislation should be had in each State establishing public parks which might well enough be stocked with game, which should there be absolutely protected. Some efforts in this direction have been made, notably Massachusetts, New York, Pennsylvania and Minnesota. In many of the New England States there are tracts absolutely barren, unoccupied and often bordered by abandoned farms, which could be purchased by the State for a very modest compensation; and it is well worth the while of the Boone and Crockett Club to endeavor by all means in its power to secure the establishment in the various States of parks which might be breeding centers for game, great and small, on the same plan as the proposed refuges hoped for within the forest reservations. Michigan, Wisconsin, Minnesota, and practically all the States to the west of these, possess such areas of unoccupied land, which might wisely be acquired by the State and devoted to such excellent purposes. In Montana there is a long stretch of the Missouri River, with a narrow, shifting bottom, bordered on either side by miles of bad-lands, which would serve as such a State park. Settlers on this stretch of river are few in number, for the bottoms are not wide enough to harbor many homes, and, being constantly cut out by the changes of the river's course, are so unstable as to be of little value as farming lands. On the other hand, the new bottoms constantly formed are soon thickly covered by willow brush, while the extensive bad-lands on either side the stream furnish an admirable refuge for deer, antelope, mountain sheep and bear, with which the country is already stocked, and were in old times a great haunt for elk, which might easily be reintroduced there.

There is a tendency in this country to avoid trouble, and to do those things which can be done most easily. From this it results that efforts are constantly being made to introduce into regions from which game has been exterminated various species of foreign game, which can be had, more or less domesticated, from the preserves of Europe. Thus red deer have been introduced in the Adirondack region, and it has been suggested that chamois might be brought from Europe and turned loose in certain localities in the United States, and there increase and furnish shooting. To many men it seems less trouble to contribute money for such a purpose as this than to buckle down and manufacture public sentiment in behalf of the protection of native game. This is a great mistake. From observations made in certain familiar localities, we know definitely that, provided there is a breeding stock, our native game, with absolute protection, will re-establish itself in an astonishingly short period of time. It would be far better for us to concentrate our efforts to renew the supply of our native game rather than to collect subscriptions to bring to America foreign game, which may or may not do well here, and may or may not furnish sport if it shall do well.

Forest Reserves of North America

In the United States something over 100,000 square miles of the public domain has been set aside and reserved from settlement for economic purposes. This vast area includes reservations of four different kinds: First, National Forest Reserves, aggregating some 63,000,000 acres, for the conservation of the water supply of the arid and semi-arid West; second, National Parks, of which there are seventeen, for the purpose of preserving untouched places of natural grandeur and interest; third, State Parks, for places of recreation and for conserving the water supply; and fourth, military wood and timber reservations, to provide Government fuel or other timber. Most military wood reserves were originally established in connection with old forts.

The forest reservations, as they are by far the largest, are also much the most important of these reserved areas.

Perhaps three-quarters of the population of the United States do not know that over nearly one-half of the national territory within the United States the rainfall is so slight or so unevenly distributed that agriculture cannot be carried on except by means of irrigation. This irrigation consists of taking water out of the streams and conducting it by means of ditches which have a very gentle slope over the land which it is proposed to irrigate. From the original ditch, smaller ditches are taken out, running nearly parallel with each other, and from these laterals other ditches, still smaller, and the seepage from all these moistens a considerable area on which crops may be grown. This, very roughly, is irrigation, a subject of incalculable interest to the dwellers in the dry West.

It is obvious that irrigation cannot be practiced without water, and that every ditch which takes water from a stream lessens the volume of that stream below where the ditch is taken out. It is conceivable that so many ditches might be taken out of the stream, and so much of the water lost by evaporation and seepage into the soil irrigated, that a stream which, uninterfered with, was bank full and even flowing throughout the summer, might, under such changed condition, become absolutely dry on the lower reaches of its course. And this, in fact, is what has happened with some streams in the West. Where this is the case, the farmers who live on the lower stretches of the stream, being without water to put on their land, can raise no crops. Nothing, therefore, is more important to the agriculturists of the West than to preserve full and as nearly equal as possible at all seasons the water supply in their streams.

This water is supplied by the annual rain or snow fall; but in the West chiefly by snow. It falls deep on the high mountains, and, protected there by the pine forests, accumulates all through the winter, and in spring slowly melts. The deep layer of half-rotted pine needles, branches, decayed wood and other vegetable matter which forms the forest floor, receives this melting snow and holds much of it for a time, while the surplus runs off over the surface of the ground, and by a thousand tiny rivulets at last reaches some main stream which carries it toward the sea. In the deep forest, however, the melting of this snow is very gradual, and the water is given forth slowly and gradually to the stream, and does not cause great floods. Moreover, the large portion of it which is held by the humus, or forest floor, drains off still more gradually and keeps the springs and sources of the brook full all through the summer.

Without protection from the warm spring sun, the snows of the winter might melt in a week and cause tremendous torrents, the whole of the melted snowfall rushing down the stream in a very short time. Without the humus, or forest floor, to act as a soaked sponge which gradually drains itself, the springs and sources of the brooks would go dry in early summer, and the streams further down toward the cultivated plains would be low and without sufficient water to irrigate all the farms along its course.

It was for the purpose of protecting the farmers of the West by insuring the careful protection of the water supply of all streams that Congress wisely passed the law providing for the establishing of the forest reserves. It is for the benefit of these farmers and of those others who shall establish themselves along these streams that the Presidents of the United States for the last twelve or fourteen years have been establishing forest reserves and have had expert foresters studying different sections of the western country to learn where the water was most needed and where it could best be had.

It is gratifying to think that, while at first the establishment of these forest reserves was very unpopular in certain sections of the West, where their object was not in the least understood, they have--now that the people have come to see what they mean--received universal approval. It sometimes takes the public a long time to understand a matter, but their common sense is sure at last to bring them to the right side of any question.

The list of reservations here given is brought down to December, 1903, and is furnished by the U.S. Forester--a member of the Club.

Government Forest Reserves in the United States and Alaska ALASKA. Area in Acres

Afognak Forest and Fish Culture Reserve 403,640 The Alexander Archipelago Forest Reserve 4,506,240

Total 4,909,880

ARIZONA.

The Black Mesa Forest Reserve 1,658,880 The Prescott Forest Reserve 423,680 Grand Canyon Forest Reserve 1,851,520 The San Francisco Mountains Forest Reserve 1,975,310 The Santa Rita Forest Reserve 387,300 The Santa Catalina Forest Reserve 155,520 The Mount Graham Forest Reserve 118,600 The Chiricahua Forest Reserve 169,600

Total 6,740,410

CALIFORNIA. Acres.

The Lake Tahoe Forest Reserve 136,335 The Stanislaus Forest Reserve 691,200 Sierra Forest Reserve 4,096,000 The Santa Barbara Forest Reserve 1,838,323 San Bernardino Forest Reserve 737,280 Timber Land Reserve San Gabriel 555,520 The San Jacinto Forest Reserve 668,160 Trabuco Canyon Forest Reserve 109,920 --------- Total 8,832,738

COLORADO.

Battle Mesa Forest Reserve 853,000 Timber Land Reserve, Pike's Peak 184,320 Timber Land Reserve, Plum Creek 179,200 The South Platte Forest Reserve 683,520 The White River Forest Reserve 1,129,920 The San Isabel Forest Reserve 77,980 --------- Total 3,107,940

IDAHO.

The Bitter Root Forest Reserve (see note) 3,456,000 The Priest River Forest Reserve (see note) 541,160 The Pocatello Forest Reserve 49,920 --------- Total 4,047,080

MONTANA.

The Yellowstone Forest Reserve (see note) 1,311,600 The Bitter Root Forest Reserve (see note) 691,200 The Gallatin Forest Reserve 40,320 The Lewis and Clark Forest Reserve 4,670,720 The Madison Forest Reserve 736,000 The Little Belt Mountains Forest Reserve 501,000 The Highwood Mountains Reserve 45,080 --------- Total 7,995,920

NEBRASKA. Acres.

The Niobrara Forest Reserve 123,779 The Dismal River Forest Reserve 85,123 --------- Total 208,902

NEW MEXICO.

The Gila River Forest Reserve 2,327,040 The Pecos River Forest Reserve 430,880 The Lincoln Forest Reserve 500,000 --------- Total 3,257,920

OKLAHOMA TERRITORY.

Wichita Forest Reserve 57,120

OREGON.

Timber Land Reserve, Bull Run 142,080 Cascade Range Forest Reserve 4,424,440 Ashland Forest Reserve 18,560 --------- Total 4,585,080

SOUTH DAKOTA.

The Black Hills Forest Reserve (see note) 1,165,240

UTAH.

The Fish Lake Forest Reserve 67,840 The Uintah Forest Reserve 875,520

The Payson Forest Reserve 111,600 The Logan Forest Reserve 182,080 The Manti Forest Reserve 584,640 The Aquarius Forest Reserve 639,000 --------- Total 2,460,680

WASHINGTON.

The Priest River Forest Reserve (see note) 103,960 The Mount Rainier Forest Reserve 2,027,520 The Olympic Forest Reserve 1,466,880 The Washington Forest Reserve 3,426,400 --------- Total 7,024,760

WYOMING. Acres.

The Yellowstone Forest Reserve (see note) 7,017,600 The Black Hills Forest Reserve (see note) 46,440 The Big Horn Forest Reserve 1,216,960 The Medicine Bow Forest Reserve 420,584 ---------- Total 8,701,584 ---------- Grand Total 63,095,254

NOTE.

Total of Bitter Root, in Idaho and Montana 4,147,200 Total of Priest River, in Idaho and Washington 645,120 Total of Black Hills, in S. Dakota and Wyoming 1,211,680 Total of Yellowstone, in Wyoming and Montana 8,329,200

United States Military Wood and Timber Reservations Kansas-- Acres. Fort Leavenworth 939

Montana-- Fort Missoula 1,677

Nebraska-- Fort Robinson 10,240

New Mexico-- Fort Wingate 19,200

New York-- Wooded Area of West Point Mil. Res., about 1,800

Oklahoma-- Fort Sill 26,880

South Dakota-- Fort Meade 5,280

Wyoming-- Fort D.A. Russell 2,541 ------ Total 68,557

National Parks in the United States Montana and Wyoming-- Acres. Yellowstone National Park 2,142,720

Arkansas-- Hot Springs Reserve and National Park 912

District of Columbia-- The National Zoological Park 170 Rock Creek Park 1,606

Georgia and Tennessee-- Chickamauga & Chattanooga Nat. Mil. Parks 6,195

Maryland-- Antietam Battlefield and Nat. Mil. Park 43

California-- Sequoia National Park 160,000 General Grant National Park 2,560 Yosemite National Park 967,680

Arizona-- The Casa Grande Ruin (Exec. Order) 480

Tennessee-- Shiloh National Military Park 3,000

Pennsylvania-- Gettysburg National Military Park 877

Mississippi-- Vicksburg National Military Park 1,233

Washington-- The Mount Rainier National Park 207,360

Oregon-- Crater Lake 159,360

Indian Territory-- Sulphur Reservation and National Park 629

South Dakota-- Wind Cave ....

---------- Total 3,654,825

Forest Reserves of North America

State Parks, State Forest Reserves and Preserves, State Forest Stations, and State Forest Tracts in the United States

CALIFORNIA. Acres.

Yosemite Valley State Park 36,000 The Big Basin Redwood Park, about 2,300 Santa Monica Forest Station 20 Chico Forest Station 29 Mt. Hamilton Tract 2,500

KANSAS.

Ogallah Forestry Station 160 Dodge Forestry Station 160

MASSACHUSETTS.

Blue Hills Reservation 4,858 Beaver Brook Reservation 53 Middlesex Fells Reservation 3,028 Stony Brook Reservation 464 Hemlock Gorge Reservation 23 Hart's Hill Reservation 23 Wachusett Mountain Reservation 1,380 Greylock Reservation 3,724 Goodwill Park 70 Rocky Narrows 21 Mount Anne Park 50 Monument Mountain Reservation 260

MICHIGAN.

Mackinac Island State Park 103 Michigan Forest Reserve 57,000

MINNESOTA.

Minnehaha Falls State Park, or Minnesota State Park 51 Itasca State Park 20,000 St. Croix State Park, or the Interstate Park at the Dalles of the St. Croix 500

NEW YORK. Acres.

The State Reservation at Niagara, or Niagara Falls Park. (Area of Queen Victoria Niagara Falls Park in Canada--730 Acres) 107 Adirondack Forest Preserve 1,163,414 Catskill Forest Preserve 82,330 The St. Lawrence Reservation, or International Park 181

PENNSYLVANIA.

Twenty Reserves scattered 211,776 The Hopkins Reserve 62,000 Pike County Reservation 23,000 McElhattan Reservation 8,000

WASHINGTON.

Sanitarium Lake Reservation 193

WISCONSIN.

The Interstate Park of the Dalles of the St. Croix 600

WYOMING.

The Big Horn Springs Reservation 640

Total 1,685,023

Canadian National Parks and Timber Reserves The Dominion of Canada has established a large number of public parks and forests reserves, of which a list has been very kindly furnished by the Dominion Secretary of the Interior, as follows:

BRITISH COLUMBIA. Acres.

Long Lake Timber Reserve 76,800 Yoho Park (a part of Rocky Mt. Park of Can) .... Glacier Forest Park 18,720

NORTHWEST TERRITORY. Acres.

Rocky Mountain Park of Canada 2,880,000 Foot Hills Timber Reserve 2,350,000 Waterton Lakes Forest Park 34,000 Cooking Lakes Timber Reserve 109,000 Moose Mountain Timber Reserve 103,000 Beaver Hills Timber Reserve 170,000

MANITOBA.

Turtle Mountain Timber Reserve 75,000 Spruce Woods Timber Reserve 190,000 Riding Mountain Timber Reserve 1,215,000 Duck Mountain Timber Reserve 840,000 Lake Manitoba West Timber Reserve 159,460

ONTARIO.

Algonquin Park 1,109,383 Eastern Reserve 80,000 Sibley Reserve 45,000 Temagami Reserve 3,774,000 Rondeau Park .... Missisaga Reserve 1,920,000

QUEBEC.

Laurentides National Park 1,619,840 ----------- Total 16,769,203

Besides these, there are two or three other reservations in Quebec and New Brunswick and Manitoba that have not as yet been finally reserved, but which are in contemplation. Many of the timber reserves are still to be cut over under license. On the other hand, many of them find their chief function as game preserves, as do also to still greater extent the national parks. A large number of these parks and timber reserves are clothed with beautiful and valuable forests, as yet untouched by the ax.

APPENDIX

In order to be in a position to make intelligent recommendations, in case legislation authorizing the setting aside of game refuges should be had, the Boone and Crockett Club, in the year 1901, made some inquiry into the game conditions on certain of the forest reservations and as to the suitability as game refuges of these reserves.

Among the reports was one on the Black Mesa Forest Reserve. Mr. Nelson is a trained naturalist and hunter of wide experience, and possesses the highest qualifications for investigating such a subject. He is, besides, very familiar with the reservation reported on. His report is printed here as giving precisely the information needed by any one who may have occasion to deal with a forest reserve from this viewpoint, and it may well serve as a model for others who may have occasion to report on the reserves. The report was made to the Executive Committee of the Boone and Crockett Club through the editor of this volume, and was printed in Forest and Stream about two years ago. It follows:

Forest Reserves as Game Preserves

THE BLACK MESA FOREST RESERVE OF ARIZONA AND ITS AVAILABILITY AS A GAME PRESERVE.

The Black Mesa Forest Reserve lies in central-eastern Arizona, and contains 1,658,880 acres, is about 180 miles long in a northwesterly and southeasterly direction and a direct continuation southeasterly from the San Francisco Mountain Forest Reserve. On the north it contains a part of the Mogollon Mesa, which is covered with a magnificent open forest of Arizona yellow pine (_Pinus ponderosa_) in which there is an abundance of bunch grass and here and there are beautiful grassy parks. To the southeast the reserve covers a large part of the White Mountains, one of the largest areas of generally high elevation in Arizona. The yellow pine forest, similar in character to that on the Mogollon Mesa, is found over a large part of the reserve between 7,000 and 8,500 feet altitude, and its general character is shown in the accompanying view.

The Black Mesa Reserve is irregular in outline. The large compact areas at each end are joined by a long, narrow strip, very irregular in outline and less than a township broad at various points. It lies along the southern border of the Great Colorado Plateau, and covers the southern and western borders of the basin of the Little Colorado River. Taken as a whole, this reserve includes some of the wildest and most attractive mountain scenery in the West.

Owing to the wide separation of the two main areas of the reserve, and certain differences in physical character, they will be described separately, beginning with the northwestern and middle areas, which are similar in character.

THE NORTHWESTERN SECTION OP THE BLACK MESA RESERVE.

With the exception of an area in the extreme western part, which drains into the Rio Verde, practically all of this portion of the reserve lies along the upper border of the basin of the Little Colorado. It is a continuation of the general easy slope which begins about 5,000 feet on the river and extends back so gradually at first that it is frequently almost imperceptible, but by degrees becomes more rolling and steeper until the summit is reached at an altitude of from 6,000 to 9,000 feet. The reserve occupies the upper portion of this slope, which has more the form of a mountainous plateau country, scored by deep and rugged canyons, than of a typical mountain range. From the summit of this elevated divide, with the exception of the district draining into the Rio Verde, the southern and western slope drops away abruptly several thousand feet into Tonto Creek Basin. The top of the huge escarpment thus formed faces south and west, and is known as the rim of Tonto Basin, or, locally, "The Rim." From the summit of this gigantic rocky declivity is obtained an inspiring view of the south, where range after range of mountains lie spread out to the distant horizon.

The rolling plateau country sloping toward the Little Colorado is heavily scored with deep box canyons often hundreds of feet deep and frequently inaccessible for long distances. Most of the permanent surface water is found in these canyons, and the general drainage is through them down to the lower plains bordering the river. The greater part of this portion of the reserve is covered with yellow pine forests, below which is a belt, varying greatly in width, of pinyons, cedars and junipers, interspersed with a more or less abundant growth of gramma grass. This belt of scrubby conifers contains many open grassy areas, and nearer the river gives way to continuous broad grassy plains. Nowhere in this district, either among the yellow pines or in the lower country, is there much surface water, and a large share of the best watering places are occupied by sheep owners.

The wild and rugged slopes of Tonto Basin, with their southerly exposure, have a more arid character than the area just described. On these slopes yellow pines soon give way to pinyons, cedars and junipers, and many scrubby oaks and various species of hardy bushes. The watering places are scarce until the bottom of the basin is approached. Tonto Basin and its slopes are also occupied by numerous sheep herds, especially in winter.

There are several small settlements of farmers, sheep and cattle growers within the limits of the narrow strip connecting the larger parts of the reserve, notably Show Low, Pinetop and Linden. The wagon road from Holbrook, on the Santa Fe Pacific Railroad, to the military post at Camp Apache, on the

White Mountain Indian Reservation, passes through this strip by way of Show Low. The old trails through Sunset Pass to Camp Verde and across "The Rim" into Tonto Basin traverse the northern part of the reserve, and are used by stockmen and others at short intervals, except in midwinter.

The climate of this section of the reserve is rather arid in summer, the rainfall being much more uncertain than in the more elevated areas about the San Francisco Mountains to the northwest and the White Mountains to the southeast. The summers are usually hot and dry, the temperature being modified, however, by the altitude. Rains sometimes occur during July and August, but are more common in the autumn, when they are often followed by abundant snowfall. During some seasons snow falls to a depth of three or more feet on a level in the yellow pine forests, and remains until spring. During other seasons, however, the snowfall is insignificant, and much of the ground remains bare during the winter, especially on southern exposures. As a matter of course, the lower slope of the pinyon belt and the grassy plains of the Little Colorado, both of which lie outside of the reserve, have less and less snow, according to the altitude, and it never remains for any very considerable time. On the southern exposure, facing Tonto Basin, the snow is still less permanent. The winter in the yellow pine belt extends from November to April.

LARGE GAME IN THE NORTHERN PART OF THE BLACK MESA RESERVE.

Black-tailed deer, antelope, black and silver tipped bears and mountain lions are the larger game animals which frequent the yellow pine forests in summer. Wild turkeys are also common.

The black-tailed deer are still common and generally distributed. In winter the heavy snow drives them to a lower range in the pinyon belt toward the Little Colorado and also down the slope of Tonto Basin, both of these areas lying outside the reserve. The Arizona white-tailed deer is resident throughout the year in comparatively small numbers on the brushy slopes of Tonto Basin, and sometimes strays up in summer into the border of the pine forest. Antelope were once plentiful on the plains of the Little Colorado, and in summer ranged through the open yellow pine forest now included in the reserve. They still occur, in very limited numbers, in this forest during the summer, and at the first snowfall descend to the lower border of the pinyon belt and adjacent grassy plains. Both species of bears occur throughout the pine forests in summer, often following sheep herds. As winter approaches and the sheep are moved out of the higher ranges, many of the bears go over "The Rim" to the slopes of Tonto Basin, where they find acorns, juniper berries and other food, until cold weather causes them to hibernate. The mountain lions are always most numerous on the rugged slopes of Tonto Basin, especially during winter, when sheep and game have left the elevated forest.

From the foregoing notes it is apparent that the northwestern and middle portions of the Black Mesa Reserve are without proper winter range for game within its limits, and that the conditions are otherwise unfavorable for their use as game preserves.

THE SOUTHEASTERN SECTION OF THE BLACK MESA RESERVE.

The southeastern portion of the reserve remains to be considered. The map shows this to be a rectangular area, about thirty by fifty miles in extent, lying between the White Mountain Indian Reservation and the western border of New Mexico, and covering the adjacent parts of Apache and Graham counties. It includes the eastern part of the White Mountains, which culminate in Ord and Thomas peaks, rising respectively to 10,266 feet and to 11,496 feet, on the White Mountain Indian Reservation, just off the western border of the Forest Reserve. This section of the reserve is strikingly more varied in physical conditions than the northern portion, as will be shown by the following description:

The northwestern part of this section, next to the peaks just mentioned, is an elevated mountainous plateau country forming the watershed between the extreme headwaters of the Little Colorado on the north and the Black and San Francisco rivers, tributaries of the Gila, on the south. The divide between the heads of these streams is so low that in the midst of the undulating country, where they rise, it is often difficult to determine at first sight to which drainage some of the small tributaries belong. This district is largely of volcanic formation, and beds of lava cover large tracts, usually overlaid with soil, on which the forest flourishes.

The entire northern side of this section is bordered by the sloping grassy plains of the Little Colorado, which at their upper border have an elevation of

6,500 to 7,500 feet, and are covered here and there with pinyons, cedars and junipers, especially along the sides of the canyons and similar slopes. At the upper border of this belt the general slope becomes abruptly mountainous, and rises to 8,000 or 8,500 feet to a broad bench-like summit, from which extends back the elevated plateau country already mentioned. This outer slope of the plateau is covered with a fine belt of yellow pine forests, similar in character to that found in the northern part of the reserve. Owing to the more abrupt character of the northerly slope of this belt, and its greater humidity, the forest is more varied by firs and aspens, especially along the canyons, than is the case further north. Here and there along the upper tributaries of the Little Colorado, small valleys open out, which are frequently wooded and contain beautiful mountain parks.

The summit of the elevated plateau country about the headwaters of the Little Colorado and Black rivers (which is known locally as the "Big Mesa"), is an extended area of rolling grassy plain, entirely surrounded by forests and varied irregularly by wooded ridges and points of timber. This open plain extends in a long sweep from a point a few miles south of Springerville westward for about fifteen miles along the top of the divide to the bases of Ord and Thomas peaks. These elevated plains are separated from those of the Little Colorado to the north by the belt of forests already described as covering the abrupt northern wall of the plateau. On the other sides of the "Big Mesa" an unbroken forest extends away over the undulating mountainous country as far as the eye can reach. The northerly slopes of the higher elevations in this section are covered with spruce forest.

The most varied and beautiful part of the entire Black Mesa Reserve lies in the country extending southeasterly from Ord and Thomas peaks and immediately south of the "Big Mesa." This is the extreme upper part of the basin of Black River, which is formed by numerous little streams rising from springs and wet meadows at an elevation of from 8,500 to 9,500 feet. The little meadows form attractive grassy openings in the forest, covered in summer with a multitude of wild flowers and surrounded by the varied foliage of different trees and shrubs. The little streams flow down gently sloping courses, which gradually deepen to form shallow side canyons leading into the main river. Black River is a clear, sparkling trout stream at the bottom of a deep, rugged box canyon, cut through a lava bed and forming a series of wildly picturesque views. The sides of Black River Canyon and its small tributaries are well forested. On the cool northerly slope the forest is made up of a heavy growth of pines, firs, aspens and alder bushes, which give way on the southerly slope, where the full force of the sun is felt, to a thin growth of pines, grass and a little underbrush.

At the head of Black River, between 8,000 and 9,000 feet, there are many nearly level or gently sloping areas, sometimes of considerable extent. These are covered with open yellow pine forests, with many white-barked aspens scattered here and there, and an abundance of grasses and low bushes. This was once a favorite summer country for elk, and I have seen there many bushes and small saplings which had been twisted and barked by bull elk while rubbing the velvet from their horns.

Immediately south and east of Black River lies the Prieto Plateau, a well wooded mountain mass rising steeply from Black River Canyon to a broad summit about 9,000 feet in altitude. The northerly slopes of this plateau, facing the river, are heavily forested with pines, firs, aspens and brushy undergrowth, and are good elk country. The summit is cold and damp, with areas of spruce thickets and attractive wet meadows scattered here and there. Beyond the summit of the plateau, to the south and east, the country descends abruptly several thousand feet, in a series of rocky declivities and sharp spur-like ridges, to the canyon of Blue River, a tributary of the San Francisco River. This slope, near the summit, is overgrown with firs, aspens and pines, which give way as the descent is made, to pinyons, cedar and scrubby oak trees and a more or less abundant growth of chaparral. Small streams and springs are found in the larger canyons on this slope, while far below, at an altitude of about 5,000 feet, lies Blue River.

The country at the extreme head of Blue River forms a great mountain amphitheater, with one side so near the upper course of Black River that one can traverse the distance between the basins of the two streams in a short ride. The descent into the drainage of Blue River is very abrupt, and is known locally as the "breaks" of Blue River. The scenery of these breaks nearly, if not quite, equals that on "The Rim" of Tonto Basin in its wild magnificence. The vegetation on the breaks shows at a glance the milder character of the climate, as compared with that of the more elevated area about the head of Black River. In the midst of the shrubbery growth on the breaks there is a fine growth of nutritious grasses, which forms excellent winter forage.

The entire southern part of the reserve lying beyond the Prieto Plateau is an excessively broken mountainous country, with abrupt changes in altitude from the hot canyons, where cottonwoods flourish, to the high ridges, where pines and firs abound.

The northeastern part of the section of the reserve under consideration is cut off from the rest by the valley of Nutrioso Creek, a tributary of the Little Colorado, and by the headwaters of the San Francisco River. It is a limited district, mainly occupied by Escudilla Mountain, rising to 10,691 feet, and its foothills. Escudilla Mountain slopes abruptly to a long truncated summit, and is heavily forested from base to summit by pines, aspens and spruces. On the south the foothills merge into the generally mountainous area. On the north, at an altitude of about 8,000 feet, they merge into the plains of the Little Colorado, varied by grassy prairies and irregular belts of pinyon timber.

The upper parts of the Little Colorado and Black Rivers, above 7,500 feet, are clear and cold, and well stocked with a native species of small brook trout.

Owing to the generally elevated character of the southeastern section of the Black Mesa Reserve, containing three mountain peaks rising above 10,000 feet, the annual precipitation is decidedly greater than elsewhere on the reserve. The summer rains are irregular in character, being abundant in some seasons and very scanty in others; but there is always enough rainfall about the extreme head of Black River to make grass, although there is always much hot, dry weather between May and October. The fall and winter storms are more certain than those of summer, and the parts of the reserve lying above 8,000 feet are usually buried in snow before spring--frequently with several feet of snow on a level. The amount of snow increases steadily with increase of altitude. Some of the winter storms are severe, and on one occasion, while living at an altitude of 7,500 feet, I witnessed a storm during which snow fell continuously for nearly two days. The weather was perfectly calm at the time, and after the first day the pine trees became so loaded that an almost continual succession of reports were heard from the breaking of large branches. At the close of the storm there was a measured depth of 26 inches of snow on a level at an altitude of 7,500 feet. A thousand feet lower, on the plains of the Little Colorado, a few miles to the north, only a foot of snow fell, while at higher altitudes the amount was much greater than that measured.

The summer temperatures are never excessive in this section, and the winters are mild, although at times reaching from 15 to 20 degrees below zero. Above 7,500 feet, except on sheltered south slopes, snow ordinarily remains on the ground from four to five months in sufficient quantity to practically close this area from winter grazing. Cattle, and the antelope which once frequented the "Big Mesa" in considerable numbers, appeared to have premonitions of the coming of the first snow in fall. On one occasion, while stopping at a ranch on the plains of the Little Colorado, just below the border of the Big Mesa country, in November, I was surprised to see hundreds of cattle in an almost endless line coming down from the Mesa, intermingled with occasional bands of antelope. They were following one of the main trails leading from the mountain out on the plains of the Little Colorado. Although the sun was shining at the time, there was a slight haziness in the atmosphere, and the ranchmen assured me that this movement of the stock always foretold the approach of a snowstorm. The following morning the plains around the ranch where I was stopping were covered with six inches of snow, while over a foot of snow covered the mountains. Bands of half-wild horses ranging on the Big Mesa show more indifference to snow, as they can dig down to the grass; but the depth of snow sometimes increases so rapidly that the horses become "yarded," and their owners have much difficulty in extricating them.

The southerly slopes leading down from the divide to the lower altitudes along the Black River and the breaks of the Blue, are sheltered from the cold northerly winds of the Little Colorado Valley, while the greater natural warmth of the situation aids in preventing any serious accumulation of snow. As a result, this entire portion of the reserve forms an ideal winter game range, with an abundance of grass and edible bushes. The varied character of the country about the head of Black River makes it an equally favorable summer range for game, and that this conjunction of summer and winter ranges is appreciated by the game animals is shown by the fact that this district is probably the best game country in all Arizona.

LARGE GAME IN THE SOUTHEASTERN PART OF TUB BLACK MESA RESERVE.

The large game found in this section of the reserve includes the elk, black-tailed deer, Arizona white-tailed deer, black and silver-tipped bears, mountain lions and wildcats, timber wolves and coyotes.

Elk were formerly found over most of the pine and fir forested parts of this section of the reserve, but were already becoming rather scarce in 1885, and, although they were still found there in 1897, it is now a question whether any survive or not. If they still survive, they are restricted to a limited area about the head of Black River from Ord Peak to the Prieto Plateau. Black-tailed deer are still common, and their summer range extends more or less generally over all of the forested part of this section above 7,500 feet. In winter only a few stray individuals remain within the reserve on the Little Colorado side, but a number range out into the pinyon country on the plains of the Little Colorado. The country about the head of Black River is a favorite summer range of this deer, but in winter they gradually retreat before the heavy snowfalls to the sheltered canyons along Black River and the breaks of the Blue. In September and October the old males keep by themselves in parties of from four to ten and range through the glades of the yellow pine forest.

The Arizona white-tailed deer is not found on the part of the reserve drained by the Little Colorado River, but is abundant in the basin of Blue River, and ranges in summer up into the lower part of the yellow pine forest along Black River. They retreat before the early snows to the breaks of the Blue, where they are very numerous. During hunting trips into their haunts in October and November, I have several times seen herds of these deer numbering from thirty to forty, both before and after the first snowfall. Antelope formerly ranged up in summer from the plains of the Little Colorado over the grassy Big Mesa country and through the surrounding open pine forest, retreating to the plains in the autumn, but they are now nearly or quite exterminated in that section. Bears of both species wander irregularly over most of the reserve in summer, but are most numerous on the breaks of the Blue and about the head of Black River. In autumn, previous to their hibernation, they descend along the canyon of the Black River and among the breaks of the Blue, where acorns and other food is abundant.

Mountain lions also wander over all parts of the reserve, but are common only in the rough country along the Blue. Wildcats are rather common and widely distributed, but are far more numerous on the Black and the Blue rivers. Timber wolves were once rather common, but are now nearly extinct, owing to their persecution by owners of sheep and cattle. Coyotes occur in this district occasionally in summer. Wild turkeys are found more or less generally throughout this section of the reserve, retreating in winter to the warmer country along the breaks of the Blue and the canyon of Black River, where they sometimes gather in very large flocks.

NOTES ON SETTLEMENTS, ROADS AND OTHER MATTERS.

The greater part of this section of the Black Mesa Reserve is unsettled, but the northeastern corner, along Nutrioso Creek and the head of San Francisco River, is traversed by a wagon road leading to Springerville. Within the limits of the reservation on this road are two small farming villages of Nutrie and Alpine. The owners of the small farms along the valleys of these streams also raise a limited number of cattle and horses on the surrounding hills. A few claims are also held at scattered points along the extreme northern edge of the reserve between Springerville and Nutrioso. Between 1883 and 1895 several herds of cattle were grazed on the head of Black River, and ranged in winter down on the breaks of the Blue and the canyons of Black River; but I understand that these ranges have since been abandoned by the cattle men. For some years the sheep men have grazed their flocks in summer over the Big Mesa country and through the surrounding open forest. In addition to the damage done by the grazing of the sheep, the carelessness of the herders in starting forest fires has resulted in some destruction to the timber. Fortunately, the permanent settlers on this section of the reserve are located in the northeastern corner, which is the least suitable portion of the tract for game. In addition to the wagon road from Springerville to Nutrioso another road has been made from Springerville south across the Big Mesa to the head of Black River. Trails run from Nutrioso and Springerville to the head of Blue River and down it to the copper mining town of Clifton, but are little used. At various times scattered settlers have located along the Blue, and cultivated small garden patches. The first of these settlers were killed by the Apaches, and I am unable to say whether these farms are now occupied or not. In any case, the conditions along the tipper Blue are entirely unsuited for successful farming.

Perhaps the most serious menace to the successful preservation of game on this tract is its proximity to the White Mountain Indian Reservation. This reservation not only takes in some of the finest game country immediately bordering the timber reserve, including Ord and Thomas peaks, but is often visited by hunting parties of Indians.

During spring and early summer, all of the yellow pine and fir country in this section is subjected to a plague of tabano flies, which are about the size of large horse-flies. These flies swarm in great numbers and attack stock and game so viciously that, as a consequence, the animals are frequently much reduced in flesh. The Apaches take advantage of this plague to set fire to the forest and lie in wait for the game, which has taken shelter in the smoke to rid itself from the flies. In this way the Indians kill large numbers of breeding deer, and at the same time destroy considerable areas of forest. While on a visit to this district in the summer of 1899 Mr. Pinchot saw the smoke of five forest fires at different places in the mountains, which had been set by hunting parties of Indians for the purpose. The only method by which not only the game but the forest along the western side of this reserve can be successfully protected will be to have the western border of the forest reserve extended to take in a belt eight to twelve miles wide of the Indian reservation. This would include Ord and Thomas peaks, and would serve efficiently to protect the country about the headwaters of the rivers from these destructive inroads.

The northern border of this section of the reserve is about one hundred miles by wagon road from the nearest point on the Santa Fe Pacific Railroad. Seven miles from its northern border is the town of Springerville, with a few hundred inhabitants in its vicinity engaged in farming, cattle and sheep growing. From Springerville north extends the plains of the Little Colorado to St. Johns, the county seat of Apache county, containing a few hundred people. To the south and east of the reserve there are no towns for some distance, except a few small settlements along the course of the San Francisco River in New Mexico, which are far removed from the part of the reserve which is most suitable for game. The fact that deer continue abundant in the district about the head of Black River, although hunted at all seasons for many years, and the continuance there of elk for so long, under the same conditions, is good evidence of the favorable conditions existing in that section for game.

E.W. Nelson.

Made in the USA
Columbia, SC
27 March 2022

58214105R00137